AF555928

azaad

'Ghulam Nabi Azad's autobiography is not just the story of an exceptional political journey but also an archive of landmark moments in Indian politics witnessed from close quarters. His conduct and interventions in Parliament from the treasury as well as Opposition benches will serve as a guiding light for all Parliamentarians. This book does justice in covering the breadth of his political experience.'

—Harivansh
Deputy Chairman, Rajya Sabha

'The autobiography of Ghulam Nabi Azad ji is a captivating account of his long journey in Indian politics. With honesty and candour, Azad ji shares his experiences and challenges, offering a unique perspective on the complexities of leadership and governance. A must-read for anyone interested in contemporary history, politics and personal stories of resilience and determination.'

—Piyush Goyal
Minister of Commerce and Industry, Consumer Affairs, Food and Public Distribution, and Textiles; and Leader of House in Rajya Sabha

'The book is a riveting read of a political career spanning close to five decades during which Jammu and Kashmir, and India at large, weathered many storms and political upheavals. A must read for those looking for a nonpartisan delineation of events from a man who truly stayed a voice of reason in public life.'

—Bhupender Yadav
Union Cabinet Minister for Environment, Forest and Climate Change, and Labour and Employment; and Member of Parliament, Rajya Sabha

'Ghulam Nabi Azad is one of those rare grassroots politicians, seeped in the culture of politics yet familiar with its muddied waters. His proximity to successive Congress prime ministers and his outreach to leaders across the political spectrum made him the pointsman who got things done. The story of his political journey, including his run of electoral successes for the Congress, is a tour de force.'

—Kapil Sibal
Senior Lawyer, Former Union Minister and Member of the Rajya Sabha

'Wazwan is a multi-course meal in Kashmiri cuisine. The autobiography of this senior parliamentarian and my neighbour for more than a decade in South Avenue in Delhi is as varied as Wazwan.'

—Derek O'Brien
Parliamentary Leader, Rajya Sabha, All India Trinamool Congress

'I am a bosom friend of Ghulam Nabi Azad Ji, but know very little of him like many others. My close association with him, though only for a decade, is much thicker for such is his sweet character irrespective of the various dignified positions he has adorned. His autobiography has increased the curiosity. I am eagerly waiting for untold interesting episodes of his life flowing from his pen.'

—Tiruchi Siva
Parliamentary Leader, Rajya Sabha, DMK

azaad

AN AUTOBIOGRAPHY

GHULAM NABI AZAD

RUPA

Published by
Rupa Publications India Pvt. Ltd 2023
7/16, Ansari Road, Daryaganj
New Delhi 110002

Sales Centres:
Prayagraj Bangalore Chennai
Hyderabad Jaipur Kathmandu
Calcutta Mumbai

P-ISBN: 978-93-5520-571-1
E-ISBN: 978-93-5520-573-5

First impression 2023

10 9 8 7 6 5 4 3 2 1

Printed in India

CONTENTS

INTRODUCTION

If you don't have time to read,
you don't have the time (or the tools) to write. Simple as that.

—Stephen King

I am somewhat in agreement with the observation of the international bestselling author Stephen King. I did not think that I had either the aptitude or the tools to pen the story of my life. I was so busy throughout my political career that I did not find time to read as much as I wanted to. Further, I did not keep notes, nor did I maintain a diary. In the past years, I did try once in a while to scribble my thoughts. I would begin and then discontinue. The exercise continued in fits and starts until I finally ended the agony by giving up. Writing, I believed, was for scholars and researchers and for those who were gifted with the talent to write stories.

Whenever I managed to catch up with friends and well-wishers from across the country and spend some quality time with them, we would discuss the country's politics. I would share with them my experiences and set right the erroneous perceptions they had about people and events. In more recent months, my friends began to egg me on to share my experiences in the form of a book. They said that readers would not only be interested in what I had to say but also had a right to know, since they are stakeholders in our democratic system.

They also pointed out that I was privy and party to significant material and events, and they deserved to be shared. I had worked with the stalwarts of our political system, from Indira Gandhi, Sanjay Gandhi and Rajiv Gandhi to P.V. Narasimha Rao, Sitaram Kesri and Manmohan Singh. I also had the opportunity of working with the present leadership of the Congress party, Sonia Gandhi and Rahul Gandhi. My friends suggested that I was, thus, in a position to compare the functioning of the old leadership with the current leadership of the party, particularly the Gandhi family, with whom I have had a chance to work through *three* generations.

I feel proud that during Sanjay's time, I worked as the president of the Indian Youth Congress's (IYC's) Jammu and Kashmir (J&K) unit and as general secretary of the same in the most difficult times for the Congress party. Working with him was challenging and a great experience. He was intelligent and undoubtedly the most dynamic youth leader of his time. After Sanjay's death, I not only worked with Indira ji as president of the IYC from 1980 to 1982 but was also a deputy minister in her government from 1982 to 1984 (till her death). During Rajiv's and Rao's tenures as prime ministers (PMs) and party presidents, I was the general secretary in charge of several states and a Union minister holding a number of portfolios from time to time. I continued to hold important responsibilities during the presidentship of Kesri, Sonia ji and Rahul. In short, I was always in the thick of things.

As a parliamentary affairs minister with three PMs, I got the golden opportunity to have an interface with parliamentarians cutting across political parties and personally got to know senior leaders of other parties, including Atal Bihari Vajpayee, Lal Krishna Advani, Madhu Dandavate, Murli Manohar Joshi, Indrajit Gupta, George Fernandes, Jyotirmoy Basu, Chandra Shekhar, Somnath Chatterjee, Basudeb Acharia, Gulam Mehmood Banatwalla, Ram Jethmalani, Chitta Basu, Geeta Mukherjee, Jaswant Singh, Frank Anthony, Chandrajit Yadav, Ram Niwas Mirdha, Pratibha Devisingh Patil, Ebrahim Sulaiman Sait, Sheikh Shahabuddin, Rasheed Masood, Ram Vilas Paswan, Nitish Kumar, Bhairon Singh Shekhawat, S.B. Chavan, Sharad Yadav, Sharad Pawar, Balram Jakhar, Shivraj Patil and many others. Although some of them were far senior to me both in terms of age and experience, I shared a cordial relationship with them.

But there were some leaders who, despite me being good to them, tried to belittle me. Though I have written about them in the later chapters of the book, I would like to relate one instance here, about which little is known to the public. My home state of J&K was under central rule from January 1990 (after Farooq Abdullah quit as chief minister [CM] in protest against Jagmohan Malhotra's appointment as governor) right until October 1996. I was looking after our party's affairs in J&K from 1991 to 1996 besides being a Union minister. Ghulam Rasool Kar from Kashmir was the state Pradesh Congress Committee (PCC) chief and Pandit Mangat Ram Sharma from the Jammu region was his general secretary. Both were thick as thieves. Kar was also close to Mufti Mohammad Sayeed. The party general secretary was Madhav Singh Solanki. Then there was Rajesh Pilot, who showed a great deal of interest in matters pertaining to J&K.

I had problems with all five of these people, and the reasons for that were different in each case. I recall that as the external affairs minister (EAM) under PM Rao, Solanki had made some controversial remarks, and Parliament had been in turmoil. The Opposition had claimed that when Solanki visited Davos in 1992 to attend the World Economic Forum, he had allegedly met the Swiss foreign minister and told him that inquiries conducted into the Bofors issue had failed to produce any result and the request for mutual assistance was based on political considerations.

As I was the parliamentary affairs minister, I was asked by Rao to meet Solanki and secure his resignation. It was typical of Rao—he never did the dirty work himself but would deploy someone else for the purpose. So, I went to Solanki and conveyed the PM's desire. Solanki was a gentleman, quite courteous. He wrote down his resignation then and there and handed it over to me. Thereafter, Rao asked me to make the announcement of Solanki's resignation on the floor of the House, which I did. Since then, Solanki nursed a grudge against me, perhaps believing that I had somehow conspired in his ouster. Rao probably must have told him something.

As for Pilot, while he had every authority to intervene in the affairs of J&K as a minister of State (MoS) for internal security—a position that I had convinced Rao to give him—I did not like his interference in the J&K party unit's functioning. He knew of my displeasure.

My problems with Kar and Mangat Ram stemmed out of another matter. In those days, Leh was in the grip of a massive agitation in favour of a Union Territory (UT) status. Both Kar and Mangat Ram were vehemently opposed to the demand because they feared their loss of control once Leh came under direct central rule. But the Union government could not brush aside the agitation, and I was asked by Rao to open a dialogue with the leaders of the agitation. I told them that while granting UT status to Leh was not possible, an autonomous status could be favourably considered, which would give the local administration more power and bring in central government funds. The leaders agreed to the proposal after a series of meetings held over a period of a few weeks. The government, thereafter, announced an autonomous status to both Leh and Kargil. Initially, the people of Kargil were not enthusiastic about the solution, but after a few years, once they saw the central funds flowing in Leh's direction, they too accepted it. Anyhow, both Kar and Mangat Ram held me responsible for clipping their wings, while my purpose as the Union minister was to bring normalcy in the strategically important Ladakh.

In 1996, assembly elections were due in J&K. Thus, a meeting of the party's central election committee was summoned by the party president Rao at his residence. When I walked into the room, I was surprised to find Mufti present. He was not even formally in the Congress then, let alone being a member of the central election committee. Kar and Mangat Ram too were there, and so was Pilot, even though none of them were members of the election committee, while I was member of both the Congress Working Committee (CWC) and the central election committee. But I did not say anything.

We all had a panel of names suggested by the J&K PCC. I suggested five names initially, mostly from Jammu. But Mufti, Pilot, Kar and Mangat Ram, who had ganged up against me, did not approve. I moved on with other names. But the response was the same. I then kept the file on the table and said that since people who were not even in the central election committee wished to decide on the distribution of tickets, I would be pulling out of the exercise.

Rao intervened, saying that these leaders had met him a day before and told him that only Mufti could lead the party to victory against the Jammu & Kashmir National Conference (NC). He added that the foursome had assured him that under Mufti's leadership, the

Congress could win 50–55 seats, way above the halfway mark of 44. Rao told me that if I could guarantee such a performance with the names I had in mind, I could go ahead. I told him bluntly that on my own, I could promise not more than 15–20 seats, but even with the combined effort of all the others, the figure would not cross 25 seats. I added that the foursome was free to go ahead and do whatever they wished. I would interfere neither in the ticket distribution nor in the election campaign. I said that I would even withdraw the five names I had forwarded earlier. The meeting ended on that acrimonious note. The four sat with the general secretary in charge and distributed tickets according to their choice.

Mufti returned to Jammu and Kashmir (J&K) and, to his shock, discovered that he could not even find enough candidates to contest the elections. This was not surprising since he had been out of touch with the party rank and file. He then gave tickets to his daughter Mehbooba, his wife, his brother-in-law and one another relative. The five men I had recommended also got tickets. If I recall correctly, only two candidates, including Mehbooba, won from Kashmir, while four of the five names I had given won the elections in Jammu region. It was a huge setback for Mufti, who then quit the Congress (which he had joined after that meeting of the election committee) and formed the J&K Peoples Democratic Party (PDP).

Notwithstanding such unsavoury incidents, I did have the occasion to develop close bonds with several leaders of all political parties when I was the leader of Opposition (LoP) in the Rajya Sabha from 2014 to 2021. In this role, I got an opportunity to work closely with the likes of the affable M. Venkaiah Naidu, the meticulous and erudite Arun Jaitley, the charming and forceful orator Sushma Swaraj, the most experienced and knowledgeable (and presently one of the senior-most legislators in the country) Sharad Pawar, the articulate Sitaram Yechury, Ram Gopal Yadav, Sharad Yadav, Satish Chandra Mishra, Tiruchi Siva, Derek O'Brien, Sukhendu Sekhar Roy, D. Raja, Sanjay Singh, Manoj Kumar Jha and many others.

As LoP, I had to maintain cordial relations with not only like-minded parties but also with the representatives of the government for smooth functioning of Parliament. Besides Arun Jaitley, I had a good rapport with Bhupender Yadav, Piyush Goyal, Ananth Kumar, Mukhtar Abbas Naqvi, Pralhad Joshi and V. Muraleedharan among others. Similarly, I got full cooperation from Congress Members of Parliament (MPs). I am beholden to all the MPs, including deputy leader Anand Sharma, whom I had known for the last four decades since the time we worked in the Youth Congress. He proved to be a great asset not only in performing his duties as deputy leader but also by raising issues of national and international significance in Parliament. My whips who assisted me in mobilizing my party MPs were great assets and we all worked as a team.

My period as LoP in the Rajya Sabha also provided me an opportunity to listen and understand from PM Narendra Modi, both inside the House and particularly during his interaction with the leaders of Opposition parties. As LoP, I tried my best to raise issues of social, political and economic importance, and confronted the PM and his colleagues every time on the floor of the House, but he never reacted to the harsh words I used against his government's performance. I found him to be a great listener with a capacity to tolerate criticism.

In many ways, my political journey also reflects the journey of the country's politics from the mid-1970s to the present. There have been many ups and downs and various changes—not always for the good of democracy—in the quality of our elected representatives, in the political language we use, in our priorities as public representatives and in our social and political conduct. My friends insisted that all these issues deserved to be brought before the public.

Even so, I would perhaps not have taken the plunge had my family not backed me. The support that I received from my wife Shameem Dev in my new avatar as an author especially touched me. Under the impression that I would have to pay money to get the autobiography published, she offered to sell off her jewellery to raise the funds. My son Saddam and daughter Sofiya provided the encouragement I needed to go ahead with this new venture. But they also used the opportunity to taunt me; they reminded me that I was always missing during their school functions, such as Parents' Day, when other children would be accompanied by both their parents. Given my busy schedule due to party politics, I could never make it to those events.

My party colleague and Lok Sabha MP Manish Tewari, who is like a younger brother to me, played a big role too. He once called to inform me that he had spoken with a prominent publisher, who would get in touch with me to take the matter forward. That clinched the issue and I took up the publisher's offer to write.

I am thankful to Rupa Publications for giving me the opportunity to write the book. Managing director Kapish Mehra, senior commissioning editor Yamini Chowdhury and members of the Rupa family who were involved with the project have my gratitude. I also thank Rajesh Singh for his help.

I was reminded of a quote that I had come across by the French-Cuban-American writer Anaïs Nin: 'We write to taste life twice, in the moment and in retrospect.' I have tasted life as a politician for close to five decades. Perhaps the time has come for me to taste it once more, in retrospect. Despite the misgivings, I finally took the plunge to tell my story.

Politics in the Age of Decline

It is my firm belief that my experiences could be useful to the present generation of politicians, especially those belonging to the Congress party, who believe that people like me have enjoyed the fruits of power and are now trying to undermine that very tree that gave us fruits. They do not know about the huge sacrifices that I made, that I gave my youth and neglected my parents, wife and children. I worked even at the cost of my health to ensure that the Congress tree, planted in 1885, did not wither, and sacrifices made by great freedom fighters right from 1857 till 1947 didn't go to waste. They are unaware of many other sacrifices I made to nurture the party with my blood and sweat.

During the freedom struggle, politics revolved around attaining freedom for the country. Leaders made immense sacrifices. As stakeholders in the independence movement, they went to jail, ignored their families and even gave up their lives. Once we got freedom, the policymakers were busy in consolidating gains, creating institutions and infrastructure that would ensure the continuance of our new-found democracy. A Constitution came into being, which promised justice and equal rights to all citizens irrespective of region, caste, creed and religion.

But unfortunately, issues relating to caste, region, religion did come up, and so did criminalization of politics. All these, coupled with money and muscle-power, began to play a major role in politics, thus pulling out the talented and honest from the political race and space. Baahubalis emerged, and they made our politics hostage to their whims and fancies. The sad development was a betrayal of every single ideal that our forefathers in the freedom struggle had held high.

Our forefathers would also be deeply saddened by the manner in which the virus of communalism has crept into our politics. Every party is guilty of exploiting and using it to their advantage; the only difference is that some use it less and some more. But the modus operandi remains the same, as a result of which people who believe in casteless society, secularism and socialism are becoming gradually marginalized. Politics, today, is not about policies and programmes but about religious sentiments. I, too, faced temptations to indulge in these vices, but I kept away from them.

I belong to that old breed that believes that politics is a medium of public service and not of promoting one self or vested interests. My primary purpose is to work hard to strengthen the organization and, through the organization, work for the poor and the downtrodden. Positions came to me as by-products of that hard work.

This becomes even more relevant, given that today many people come into politics to make money, safeguard their ill-gotten wealth or conduct nefarious and criminal activities by taking shelter under one political party or the other. Unfortunately, politics today has become largely the preserve of the financially well-off. Those with little money but the talent and desire to do good get marginalized because they are not financially empowered.

I remember an instance when I contested the Lok Sabha election in 1996 from Yavatmal, Maharashtra, unsuccessfully. For this election, my first choice was naturally my earlier constituency of Washim in Maharashtra. But Rao told me that he had already promised

Sudhakarrao Naik, former CM, the seat. I was in a fix. Eventually, it was decided that I would contest from the neighbouring Yavatmal constituency. Like Washim, it too had a sizeable number of minority voters as well as Banjara voters. I filed my nomination papers. The MP readily vacated the seat for me in lieu of an assembly ticket.

Naik's supporters began to spread the talk that he had to be made victorious since he would be inducted into the Union Cabinet on victory. On the other hand, they spread the rumour that if 'Azad wins, then as sitting Union minister, he would again return to the ministry, and Naik would lose out on the Cabinet berth. Hence, Azad was to be defeated'. This remark had an adverse impact on us both, since the minority voters in his constituency did not support him and the Banjara voters of my constituency did not back me. Ironically, not only did both of us lose but our party, too, lost power at the Centre.

So far, so good. But then they also began saying that since there was no chance of two MPs from contiguous constituencies becoming ministers, I had little prospects of becoming a minister. This turned the tide against me in my new constituency, since many voters, especially of the Banjara community, thought it would be a waste of their vote if they backed me as I would not become a minister. So, they turned against me.

Soon, yet another dimension emerged: money power. One day before polling had to take place, a group of people belonging to a particular community, which had a significant vote bank of 50,000–60,000 in a particular area of my constituency, approached me at midnight and asked me to give them a considerable sum of money, assuring that they could then fetch me votes that would swing the result in my favour. Being a Union minister (with the charge of civil aviation, tourism and parliamentary affairs), I could have raised the amount—personally, I didn't have that kind of money—but I declined. Had I got 15,000 more votes, I would have won. But I preferred to lose rather than pay money to buy votes.

But I have no regrets since I had taken a principled stand. I have never indulged in such tactics. I had spent just a couple of thousand rupees in the first Lok Sabha election in 1979 that I had contested and won. Today, sadly, Lok Sabha candidates are said to spend from ₹20 crore to ₹50 crore in a constituency election! When one spends that kind of money, he or she is going to find ways to recover that amount once they are elected. Naturally, this breeds large-scale corruption. Such elections are not my cup of tea. There are many other leaders who prefer to give up legislative politics rather than get into a political venture where the play of money is dominant.

I have also, from the start, been opposed to the practice of leaders getting their family members into politics and securing for them important positions in government. I believe that it is the worst form of nepotism. Unfortunately, today, no political organization, including the Congress party, is free from this malaise. While I could naturally not prevent others from promoting 'family politics', I have, at a personal level, stuck to my commitment throughout my political career.

My father, besides being a businessman, was also a politician, active at the tehsil level. Once I decided to enter the political arena after completing my post-graduation, I had a long discussion with my father and suggested that he should withdraw from political activities; I did not want people to point fingers at us and accuse us of using politics to benefit family interests. My father appreciated my stand and pulled himself out of politics.

I have mentioned in the book about the written directives that I had issued to my officials when I was a Union minister and the CM of J&K that they should not entertain any requests from my family members and that such moves, if any, by my family should be immediately brought to my notice. Of course, my family never misused my position, nor did any of my family members visit my office when I was a Union minister or CM. Knowing my inclination, they kept themselves scrupulously away, and I owe a debt of gratitude to them.

It has become common practice for senior leaders to recommend the names of their family members to fill up seats in Parliament or Assembly or corporations and boards that have been vacated by them for whatever reasons. This is not just nepotism; it also demonstrates that these leaders don't trust their party workers who deserve to be given those seats. There were at least four occasions when seats in the Assembly or Parliament were offered to my family members, but I politely but firmly declined the offer.

The first instance was in the run-up to the 1989 Lok Sabha elections. Rajiv had asked me and other general secretaries of the All India Congress Committee (AICC) to not contest the Lok Sabha elections because he wanted us to concentrate on campaigning across the country; he said that I could be a Rajya Sabha member and my wife Shameem could contest the Lok Sabha election from Washim. While I had immediately agreed to his first suggestion, I declined the second proposal. Many of my supporters including Members of the Legislative Assembly (MLAs) and other elected representatives from Washim literally pitched a tent on Rajaji Marg, where I resided, demanding that I or my wife be given a Lok Sabha ticket.

Shameem was equally known to the voters in Washim, having toured and nurtured the constituency with me and also on my behalf when I was too occupied with my ministerial work to visit. Although I had rejected the offer to get her into politics, Rajiv continued to press on and raised the matter again when the names of candidates were being finalized. I told him that if he gave the ticket to my wife, then I would not enter Parliament through the Rajya Sabha. Sensing my resolve, he gave up and asked me to name a fit candidate. I suggested the name of a sitting MLA, who was a non-Muslim and a Maratha, Anantrao Vitthalrao Deshmukh. He got the ticket. My wife campaigned for him, while I campaigned in the rest of the country for the party. Deshmukh emerged victorious.

The second chance came in 2002–03 in J&K when Mufti was the CM. It had been decided that the heads of 50 per cent of government boards and corporations would be from the PDP and the remaining half from the Congress party—we were in a coalition then. One day, Mufti told me that he had decided to make Shameem the chairperson of the women's commission from the PDP's quota. I was overwhelmed by his thoughtfulness but declined the offer. I told him of my resolve of not having more than one member of my family in politics.

The third occasion was in 2005. I was an MP and a Union minister in the Manmohan Singh government. I still had three-and-a-half years for my Rajya Sabha tenure to end. Since I would be vacating the Rajya Sabha seat, having become the CM of J&K, party chief Sonia ji asked my opinion on a suitable candidate to complete my remaining term. Earlier, some of my well-wishers had asked me to suggest the name of my wife or son, adding that the party would surely accept it. But I was against it, and so I told Sonia ji that she could name anybody except any of my family members. She was surprised; the ticket went to a Scheduled Tribe (ST) leader whose name I had recommended.

The fourth chance came three years later, in 2008, after I had to quit as CM, post the withdrawal of support from the PDP. I had contested the assembly elections that were held thereafter, and won. But within a month, I had vacated the seat and come to the Centre as a Rajya Sabha member and become a Union minister. Again, there was a demand that I name a family member to the vacated assembly seat, and again, I firmly refused.

Looking back, when I see families flourish with more than one member in politics, I wonder if I made a mistake. Maybe it was; some from my family who were in business made conscious efforts to keep away from government departments even when they had reasons to approach them for legitimate work, such as clearances, etc. This adversely impacted their business. On the other hand, businesses of other people who were brought into politics prospered because they made full use of their political status to further their interests. However, it's a 'mistake' that I don't regret making. I had taken the resolve, fully aware of the consequences it would have.

I must also mention that I have earned every term that I had in the Rajya Sabha, particularly three times from J&K, because of the support I received from members of other parties also. Although my party did not have enough votes that could see me through, I won in 1996, 2009 and again in 2014. In fact, the elections in 1996 were rather dramatic, with both comic and tragic elements. From 1990 to 1996, three members from the Congress party were Rajya Sabha members from Maharashtra—S.B. Chavan, N.K.P. Salve and me. Salve was close to Sharad Pawar and Chavan was a personal friend of Rao. I was 'non-aligned'—although I got along well with Rao, I was never his camp-follower, and subsequent events mentioned in the book will serve to demonstrate my contention.

For the 1996 Rajya Sabha polls, the party could get only two candidates elected due to a paucity of votes in the Assembly. Rao, who was the party president besides being the PM, decided on Chavan's and my candidature through the Rajya Sabha route and dropped Salve. After the names were finalized, I made plans to go to Maharashtra to file my nomination. My luggage was taken to the airport by my staff, and I decided to call on Rao to formally thank him before proceeding to the airport. It was around four in the evening when I reached PM's residence; my flight was scheduled to take off at 6.00 p.m. When I entered the waiting room, I found Salve seated there, looking morose. He was in his late seventies and looked fragile. On seeing me, he got up with some effort, hugged me and began to cry profusely. Taken aback with embarrassment, I disengaged myself, calmed him down and asked him what the matter was.

Salve said that while he was happy to know that I had got the Rajya Sabha ticket, he was feeling greatly let down that Chavan, had been chosen for the second seat instead of him. He resumed his wailing, saying in between sobs that Rao should have at least had some consideration for his age. Chavan, being a Maratha, could get elected on a Lok Sabha ticket too, he said, while he, a Christian and a minority, would find it difficult to win. But Rao had succumbed to the friendship he shared with Chavan and cut him (Salve) out, the veteran Congressman lamented.

I was moved by Salve's tears. He was twice my age, and I felt that I had to do something to placate him. I assured him that he would get a Rajya Sabha ticket. How, he wondered aloud. I added that I would surrender my ticket in his favour. He was surprised and asked what I would do then. 'Fight the Lok Sabha from old constituency of Washim,' I replied, adding that I had age on my side and would take the risk. That dried his tears. He again hugged me, thanking me copiously for my 'sacrifice'. Just then, a peon arrived and informed that the PM had asked me to come in. When I told Salve to accompany me, the peon said that only I had been called in. I told him that Salve was with me, and we both went in; I held his hands to lend him support.

Rao was enormously surprised to see Salve. Having cut off him, he naturally had no inclination to confront the senior leader, and so had not given him an appointment. Salve had reached PM's residence without any appointment. I told Rao that my ticket should be given to Salve and that I would contest the Lok Sabha election. In conversations with me, Rao always chose his words with care and never resorted to frivolous language. On that occasion though, he was so taken aback by my offer that he blurted, 'Have you gone mad? You want to sacrifice your political career for this man! People like him and me have reached the retirement age. Besides, he is well-off; his legal practice is flourishing and his son too is a top lawyer.' I stood my ground, and an exasperated Rao said, 'As you wish…'

Outside, Salve insisted that I accompany him to Maharashtra and be with him when he filed his nomination papers. He was scared of the hostile reception he would get there once the information filtered that he had been given the ticket after my name, which had been approved and announced for the seat, was withdrawn. I had, over the years, built a large following in Maharashtra. Reluctantly, I agreed. At the Bombay (now Mumbai) airport, there was a big crowd waiting for me. They were not aware of the change in candidature, and when I announced that I would contest the Lok Sabha election and Salve would be the nominee for the Rajya Sabha seat, there was a wail of disappointment. I calmed the crowd and later accompanied Salve when he filed his nomination papers the next morning.

Rao later told me that he had decided on my name for the Rajya Sabha seat precisely because he had promised the seat from which I was Lok Sabha Member earlier to Sudhakar Naik. 'But you ruined everything by handing over the Rajya Sabha seat to Salve,' he added.

The sum and substance of all this was that from May 1996 till October that year, I was not an MP. In October, Farooq Abdullah became the CM of J&K. Many of his MLAs and senior leaders became ministers, and four Rajya Sabha seats from J&K got vacated. Farooq came to Delhi and offered the Congress three seats, which we could contest under the NC banner. Since Farooq had made all his senior party leaders ministers in the state government, and the state was in turmoil with elections being held after a long gap of seven years, he wanted senior leaders to represent the state in Parliament. That is why he suggested the names of three former Union ministers.

One was for Syed Mir Qasim—he refused, pointing out that being bed-ridden, he could not handle the responsibility. The other was for Karan Singh—he accepted. The third was for me—I agreed on the condition that I would contest only on a Congress ticket. Farooq agreed, saying that he could transfer 22 surplus votes to me but that I would have to manage the balance eight needed to sail through. I pulled 46 votes! Members of other parties voted for me since the Congress had only three-four members; it was a demonstration of the goodwill I enjoyed cutting across party lines. Karan Singh also won, but on the NC ticket.

Yet another point that I wish to make through the book is that politics can be conducted in a decent manner, without resorting to personal attacks on opponents. Policies, ideology and programmes of political rivals should be challenged whenever needed, both inside Parliament and in the midst of the people. But that does not mean we call our opponents vile names. It is a Lakshman Rekha that I never crossed. Those who do so perhaps believe that they are creating a strong and positive impression on the voters. They are only fooling themselves. Voters are actually put off by such language. Developments in just the last few years will bear me out. Those who used foul language against their political rivals have been marginalized.

I never once stooped to bad-mouthing my political opponents. I opposed their policies and political philosophies in Parliament and outside, yet maintained cordial and personal relations with them. The first Cabinet of Jawaharlal Nehru had right-wing leader Syama Prasad Mookerjee. The two were poles apart in their political thinking, and yet Nehru included him in his ministry. While such an inclusion may be unthinkable in present times, we can at least be civil in our conduct. Abuses do not further the image of those who hurl it, nor does such behaviour elevate the stature of our political system, Parliament or democracy.

In thousands of speeches that I may have given across the country, right from my Youth Congress days till date, I never took the names of the candidates contesting against my party candidates, be it for Parliament, Assembly, local bodies or Zila Parishad elections. This is how politics should be done. Had I abused my opponents, I would have lost my prestige and image and would not have gained anything worthwhile.

The book largely centres on my involvement in various issues of the party and the government. I have tried to be truthful to myself and to the readers. Possibly, what I have said here may hurt some people, but I could not have been dishonest in my opinions and analyses.

However, readers should excuse me for not elaborating on certain matters, important as they have been in our political history. This is because I was not personally involved with them, and thus, have no insight to share with the readers. One example is the separatist movement that had engulfed Punjab in the early 1980s. I had little to do with the deliberations that Indira ji had had to resolve the crisis, though I have recounted some personal experiences in connection with the subject. Then there have been issues that were strictly personal to the people involved, like the confrontation between Indira ji and Sanjay's widow, Maneka Gandhi. I have not expanded on it because I believe that some personal matters are best left to the families concerned.

Benjamin Franklin said, 'Either write something worth reading or do something worth writing.' I cannot claim to have done something remarkable that is worth writing about. I am certainly not in the league of stalwarts such as Nehru, Sardar Patel, Maulana Azad or Indira ji. But I have tried to write something that is worth reading. I hope that readers not just enjoy the narration but also take back some lessons from my experience.

1

THE BOY FROM LITTLE KASHMIR

I consider myself blessed many times over. One, that I was born in a free India—a country that has people from different religions, castes and communities coexisting harmoniously; a nation that throbs vibrantly as a democracy, in both letter and spirit, though lately there have been a few aberrations. Two, that I was born in J&K, the jewel in India's crown. And, three, that I was born in Jammu's Bhadarwah—that same enchanting tehsil famous as Little Kashmir, for it matches Kashmir in beauty: the tall pine and cedar trees, the dense forests, the snowfall, the imposing snow-clad mountains, the fruit orchards and the lush green meadows. You could be forgiven for believing that you are in Kashmir. Words can never be enough to describe its scenic splendour; one has to see it to experience its dazzle.

Situated in Doda district—the biggest in area until some years ago (when as the CM, I divided it into three districts) and constituting a major part of the Chenab Valley—Bhadarwah finds mention in one of our ancient texts that narrates the story of Vasuki, the serpent king around Lord Shiva's neck. It says that a unique place such as Bhadarwah cannot be found anywhere else, not even in Paatal Lok or Brahma Lok! There are as many as four Vasuki Nag temples in Bhadarwah region, but the one located in the town is especially mesmerizing; the idol of Vasuki is made of black stone and stands at a tilted angle without support. There is also the Gupt Ganga Temple on the banks of the Neru, dedicated to Lord Shiva, with a Shiva Linga installed. The ancient temple draws large crowds of devotees throughout the year.

It was in 1841 that Bhadarwah became part of J&K. Thereafter, when Maharaja Pratap Singh was crowned the king of the region, he gifted it to his younger brother, Raja Amar Singh. It comprised Bhadarwah proper (now a sub-district), Bhalessa (now a sub-division) and the sprawling areas left of the Chenab, right from Thathri to Khellani.

Maharaja Pratap Singh, also affectionately called Sri Pratap Singh, was the third Dogra ruler of J&K. His 40-year-long reign (from 1885 to 1925) is considered a golden period for the region. He was a visionary and a just ruler, though he was hobbled by the British in his efforts to rule. British historian Walter Lawrence said, 'He has done much to change the position of his subjects. His kindness to all classes in Kashmir has won the affection of his people.'[1]

By the time Sri Pratap Singh's rule ended, the Kashmir Valley had been connected to the outside world by two major road networks—the Jhelum Valley Cart Road, the region's first major road initiative connecting Kohala with Baramulla, and the Banihal Cart Road that connected Jammu and Srinagar, and was thrown open to the public in 1922. These and other projects of road connectivity led to a spurt of transportation methods. Buses and trucks became a regular mode of commutation. The Maharaja was also keen to get rail connectivity to Srinagar, but the project could not be executed because the costs were too high. Nonetheless, in 1890, Jammu was linked to Sialkot (now in Pakistan) by rail, thus facilitating its connectivity to the rest of India.

The Maharaja also paid a great deal of attention to enhancing educational facilities across the region, and the succeeding generations that lived in J&K benefited from that far-sighted decision. I was one of them, having studied at Sri Pratap College, Srinagar, established in 1905. A college in his name also came up in Jammu in 1907, which was subsequently renamed the Prince of Wales College; it is now called Government Gandhi Memorial Science College. I am lucky to have done my graduation from that college. The Maharaja was also way ahead of his time in realizing the need to equip the youth with technical training. The Amar Singh Technical Institute (known

[1]'Maharaja Who Transformed Kashmir', *Daily Excelsior*, 17 July 2016, https://bit.ly/3MGjhCZ. Accessed on 18 May 2022.

as Amar Singh College today) was set up in Srinagar in 1913, and the Sri Pratap Technical School was established in Jammu in 1924.

The ruler's remarkable achievements did not end with education. He established a silk factory in Srinagar, which, during its time, became the largest of its kind in the world. He also took steps to establish local self-governance models.

The Maharaja gave great attention to healthcare too. Modern hospitals were established in both Srinagar and Jammu. During those days, smallpox was the scourge of the population, taking a toll of thousands of precious lives. The ruler ordered a mass vaccination drive in 1894 to tackle the disease.

The Maharaja was succeeded by his nephew, Hari Singh, who eventually signed the Instrument of Accession in October 1947, thus bringing the princely state into the Indian Union.

A few years after the Instrument of Accession was signed, I was born on 7 March 1949 in Soti village in the Bhalessa block of Bhadarwah tehsil. By then, the town had already acquired an importance of its own. Although it was part of Doda district, it was home to the district and sessions court, and boasted of the district's only degree college.

The Batt Household

My father, Rahamatullah Batt, had a business as a forest contractor. Our family was quite well-off from the village point of view; we had a retinue of domestic helps. We owned large tracts of land and small orchards of various fruits such as apples, plums, peaches, pears, grapes, cherry, apricot, etc. In those days, we were the only family in entire district to own orchards in Bhalessa. The apple trees—particularly the large, red, juicy and tasty Amri variety of apples, which retained their taste and odour even a year after being stored without preservatives—had been planted by my great-grandfather. This variety of apples was a specialty. The trees had massive trunks, large enough to support 20 apple trees that comprise the ordinary variety of today. Over time, the Amri trees have almost disappeared, though apple producers and marketers still claim to be selling the Amri variety to lure customers with the brand name!

My father was enamoured by fine horses for personal use, which were useful to cover and reach areas of the tehsil in the absence of motorable roads. He was tall (almost 6 feet 3 inches in height) and was quite a figure straddled on a horse. As a student, I had a key role to play in the training of a newly acquired young horse. I was lean as a boy, so I was made to mount an uninitiated horse to make it familiar with a rider. But there was always the chance of the horse disagreeing and toppling me to the ground. To reduce the chances of grievous injury, nearby fields would be ploughed and the soft soil brought up, and it was there that the horse and I would have our trysts. I had quite a few falls but, in the process, also became a decent horseman.

While my father was into business, he was also the tehsil president of the National Conference (NC) and would mostly get elected unopposed in the village panchayat.[2] Besides doing his business, my father was also involved in political work for the party, going from village to village, recruiting members and interacting with villagers. Occasionally, I too joined him and would come to know of the types of conversations, problems and issues discussed between him and the villagers.

I also learnt the techniques of membership drive from my father, an experience that would come in handy when I launched myself into a full-fledged political career. People who worked for my father in the forests—there were close to 500–600 of them—would come home to settle their dues, and I would give them the party membership for two annas (one-eighth of a rupee) each and issue receipts. I would even take membership forms to school and conduct an enrolment drive there. In addition, when I visited shops for home purchases, I would hand out the forms and recruit members. In those days, there was no question of any fake membership that Congressmen of today indulge in—one of the reasons why I couldn't reconcile to this practice during my entire political career in the party.

My father had only one elder brother and the rest were sisters. My uncle Ghulam Rasool Bhatt, whom I called Bade Abbaji (elder papa), was into academics and was a bright student. He had completed

---

[2]The Indian National Congress came into existence only in 1965 in the state.

his master's in maths from Lahore University and immediately got a government job as a teacher. Subsequently, he was the headmaster of the government teacher's training school in Bhadarwah. In 1955, he went to London for further studies. During his absence, his wife, who was also my mother's first cousin, died during labour in 1956. We lived in a joint family, and my father informed my uncle of the death of his wife through a letter, which he received many days after her death. There was no question of his immediate return, since the journey from London to India, mostly by ship, would take weeks. More so, there was the question of expenses.

On his return from London, he was appointed the principal of the higher secondary school in RS Pura in Jammu. He would go on to occupy various important positions in the state's education department, rising right to the top. He was also the president of the State Teachers' Association and vice president of the All-India Teachers' Association. In many ways, my own academic life would be linked to Bade Abbaji's career progression.

In those days, there were two seats reserved for teachers in the State Legislative Council—one from Jammu and the other from Kashmir division. Bade Abbaji, as the principal of the higher secondary school and also the president of the State Teachers' Association, decided that the association should fight both the Jammu and Kashmir seats against the ruling party's official candidates. Thus, he decided to contest from the Jammu province, and one of his friends, Dina Nath Kaul 'Nadim' (whom I would call uncle), who was a Kashmiri Pandit, literary figure and educationist, was asked to contest from the Kashmir division.

Initially, the ruling party, the NC, headed by the mighty prime minister (PM) of J&K, Bakshi Ghulam Mohammad, thought it would be impossible for them to win the elections against the ruling party candidates. This was more so since unlike the ruling party candidates, Bade Abbaji was contesting from Jammu region against the official candidate Prof. Shanti Gupta, and Dina Nath uncle was contesting from Kashmir region against a Muslim ruling party candidate. This must have been one of the rarest occasions when a Hindu contested from a region in Kashmir with an overwhelming Muslim majority while a Muslim contested from a Hindu-dominated region of Jammu.

But within days, the entire teachers' association of Jammu, Kashmir and Ladakh threw their weight behind the two candidates, not bothering about region, religion, caste and government pressure. This posed a big challenge for Bakshi and his government, but the general belief was still that the two candidates would lose. To the surprise of both the government and the public at large, both Bade Abbaji and Dina Nath uncle won with huge margins; Prof. Gupta even lost her deposit against Bade Abbaji.

Bade Abbaji remained a Member of the Legislative Council (MLC) from 1957 to 1962, and in 1962, when he contested again, he got elected unopposed. He got many works sanctioned for his area, the most prominent being the Thathri Kilohtran Road connecting Bhalessa with Doda, Bhadarwah and Kishtwar.

In less than two years of Bade Abbaji becoming an MLC, there was a change of guard, and Bakshi was replaced by Ghulam Mohammad Sadiq, who had great regard for my uncle. He persuaded Bade Abbaji to resign as an MLC and return to the education department to inculcate the spirit of hard work, honesty and integrity amongst the teachers and students. My uncle could not refuse him, since Sadiq sahab himself was an embodiment of secularism, socialism and a symbol of honesty and integrity.

Both Bade Abbaji and Dina Nath uncle were educationists and literary personalities. Dina Nath uncle was an Urdu poet. Bade Abbaji had appended 'Azad' to his name that went with his writings because he believed in a free mind that was not shackled by dogmas and fundamentalist beliefs. Since mine was a joint family, I lived with him while he was in service, and soon people began to refer to me as Azad too while I was in college. Thus, my family surname, Batt, was replaced by Azad for good.

From my student days till date, I have been greatly influenced by the honesty, integrity, fearlessness and hard work of Bade Abbaji. While being in service as an educationist (except for the period when he was an MLC for seven years) and a government employee till his retirement as the head of the state education department, he never hesitated to speak at public forums against the non-performance of the government. But the government never took offence at his speeches, nor did it take any action against him. This was perhaps in recognition of his honesty, integrity and selfless service to the state. Which is why, after his retirement, he was appointed as a member of the state's anti-corruption commission.

Thus, from my childhood, I was witness to the value of money and education, though I cannot claim to have either in abundance! But at least I retained the spirit from Bade Abbaji of being Azad, a quality that often landed me in trouble in my later political years but also gave me immense satisfaction.

Surviving and Thriving in School

Like most children, I was naughty to some extent and was more attached to my grandmother, who, like most doting grandparents, exaggerated my qualities. I indulged in my hobby of gardening and photography; I learned the former from my grandmother. Whenever she would go to our kitchen garden to sow vegetable seeds and plant flowers side by side, I would always accompany her and enquire about every seed she would sow. Then, after some months, the saplings would appear, leading to their transplantation and subsequent collection of seeds in autumn, all of which I took a keen interest in.

When I was five or six years of age, the decision to enrol me in school was taken. The problem was that I had developed a morbid fear of school, thanks to my elder brother, who would often tease me that I would be given a sound beating by the teachers once I began attending school. The high school was at a distance of about 2 km from our residence. The day I was to go to school, I was given special treatment—my favourite dishes were served to me, I was dusted up for the occasion and given new clothes to wear.

Unimpressed by the show, I flatly refused to go. I was seated on a low wooden stool, called a *peedha,* while being feted. I declined to get up, and many futile efforts were made to disengage me from the wooden plank. Finally, a burly manservant was summoned into service. He effortlessly lifted me up, even as I clung on to the stool, and hoisted me on his shoulders. Thereafter, he began the march to the school on foot, while I continued to howl loudly in protest, tears streaming down my face.

In those days, Bade Abbaji was the district inspector of schools (today, the post is known as district education officer). Everyone, thus, knew who I was, but that did not mean I was privileged in any way. After depositing me in the class, the manservant went out and waited at the gate. The teacher, an elderly man from a nearby village who wore a huge turban and looked smart and handsome even at that age, was nearing retirement. Today, inexperienced teachers are asked to take the lower classes. In those days, the experienced ones were entrusted with the task of teaching lower classes because it requires experience and special skills to handle smaller children.

I was still crying. The teacher placed me on his table while he sat across me on the chair and began to console me. He opened a book of pictures of birds, animals and fruits, and deliberately pointed to those that I was acquainted with—cows, goats, hens, horses, apples, etc. He did not show me animals like the giraffe or the elephant. I would not have known them since I had never seen them. There was no TV, only a huge radio that helped us keep abreast of the happenings around the world by tuning in to BBC Urdu service. We also listened to Hindi film songs, especially on Radio Ceylon.

I promptly gave the right responses to the kind teacher's questions. He praised me effusively for my replies, much to my delight. After an hour or two, my first day in class came to an end. I arrived home in high spirits and triumphantly told my brother, who was in the same school but in a higher class, how wrong he had been. I also gloated that while he was seated in a chair, I had the honour of sitting higher, on a table right across the teacher! The family heaved a sigh of relief over my change of heart. That's how my fear of school evaporated. I became the class monitor when I was in Class 6 and again in Class 8. I enjoyed the responsibility and went about the job sounding busy as a bee and puffed up with self-importance.

But something less pleasurable also happened that left a lasting impact on my life. Being tall for my age, I generally hung out with students of higher classes and even played cricket with them. On one such occasion, I was hit by a cricket ball on the nose and began to bleed profusely. It took some time for me to reach the hospital, as it was at a distance. For the next 18 days, I could not attend school—such was the loss of blood and nose damage. The bleeding problem remained with me for decades. Once, while on an official visit to Himachal Pradesh during my tenure as the Union deputy minister for information and broadcasting (I&B), I began to bleed heavily from the nose and had to be shifted to Delhi by helicopter and admitted in the All India Institute of Medical Sciences (AIIMS) for two to three days.

Since that school incident, I developed a dislike for cricket—and for sports in general and, at times, took it to great extent. In 2012, British PM David Cameron had invited health ministers of 20–25 countries for a conference on health-related issues and policies and their implementation. The PM had sent out invitations under his signature to all the federal health ministers, and I, too, had received one; perhaps it was first time that the PM of a foreign country had written directly to health ministers of other countries. I was representing my country as the Union health minister and was in London from 30 July to 2 August 2012.

The event coincided with the Summer Olympics, which the city was hosting. An invitation to attend the same was extended to us during the lunch at the PM's residence, with Cameron saying that he had specially timed the meeting of health ministers so they could watch the Olympics. Each minister was given five VIP passes for the games, promising a ringside view. I skipped the games and distributed my passes to the Indian Mission officials there. They were amazed and, needless to add, greatly elated, though they must have privately wondered at my insanity to let such a chance pass.

Pursuit of Higher Education

I studied in the village until Class 10 in Government High School, Kilhotran. Thereafter, I enrolled in the degree college in Bhadarwah, one of the state's oldest, where my uncle was the principal. I studied for a year in the pre-university class. Here, I also enrolled in the National Cadet Corps (NCC), a vibrant organization in my college campus, especially since my uncle was a big votary of its activities as it imbibed in students discipline, character, brotherhood, the spirit of adventure and ideals of selfless service and loyalty to the country. I learnt to shoot, among other activities. A week-long camp for .303 rifle-shooting practices was held at Jai Valley, a popular tourist destination some 30 km from Bhadarwah town. Managing the recoil of the .303 gun after it fired was a challenge. I was taught to place the butt of the rifle firmly on the shoulder to avoid injuries. With practice, I became quite a marksman.

In those days, the trousers given to us for the NCC classes were huge and baggy. Cine star Rajesh Khanna was the rage of the nation, and he wore tight trousers. Driven by an impulse to emulate our favourite hero, we got our baggy trousers altered by a tailor to suit the fashion of the day. Our instructor, Tasduq Malik, an imposing figure of 6 feet 2 inches with a large, well-trimmed moustache and three stars on each of his broad shoulders, was furious. But since all of us students were one on that, he could hardly punish each one of us. We got away, feeling at least a little bit like Rajesh Khanna!

When my uncle became the deputy director of education for Kashmir division, I also shifted to Kashmir and joined Amar Singh College in Srinagar. But since it was an arts (non-medical) college then and I was a medical student, it took me about a month to shift to Sri Pratap College, Srinagar. It was (then) the biggest and the oldest college of higher education in Kashmir.

In college, at the initiative of my closest friend Basharat Ahmed, some of us joined hands to form an anti-copying front. Our zeal got us into trouble, on several occasions, with students who had been getting through the classes by wrongful means. One other popular activity that we were engaged in was to watch Urdu mushairas, symposiums, seminars, skits, etc. The mushaira was an all-India event in which several known Urdu poets from across the country—Ali Sardar Jafri, Kaifi Azmi, Kunwar Mohinder Singh Bedi, Bekal Utsahi and Jagan Nath Azad—were invited to recite their ghazals and poetry to an appreciative audience. All these functions were organized by the State Cultural Academy in Tagore Hall. My friend and I had formed a cultural committee called Bazm-e-Adab to promote cultural and other social-related activities.

A year later, after serving as deputy director of education (Kashmir division), when my uncle returned to Jammu as the principal of a teachers' training college, I too came to Jammu and took admission in Government Gandhi Memorial Science College. The graduation courses lasted four years in those days. A year into the course, my uncle then became director of education of the entire state. The director in those days had enormous power, including appointing and transferring teachers; there was no separate director for higher or lower education and youth, etc. The J&K government would shift to Jammu during winter and to Srinagar during summer. During this move, called the Durbar Move, being a family member of a government officer, I had the permission to study six months in Kashmir and six months in Jammu. Thus, I studied in both colleges of Jammu and Kashmir simultaneously till graduation.

After I completed my graduation, I did my post graduation (MSc in zoology) from Kashmir University. It was an old and established university with nearly every subject, whereas the university in Jammu was new and did not have many of the science subjects, such as botany and zoology. Once my uncle retired, I shifted from his official residence to a hostel in the Kashmir University campus. Unlike in the rest of the country, in J&K, only postgraduate students could study on the university campus. The campus housed the boys' hostel as well as the accommodation of the vice chancellor and faculty members. Overlooking the famous Dal Lake and teeming with apple trees, it was undoubtedly one of most beautiful campuses of the country in those days.

Mahatma and Me

In 1969, while I was still a student at Sri Pratap College, a major political and social event took place, which left a deep and everlasting impact on my political life to come. That year, Mahatma Gandhi's birth centenary celebrations were being held across the country. Kashmir was chosen to host the North India event by the national Gandhi Smarak Nidhi (GSN). It was supposed to be a week-long camp in the sprawling lawns of the youth hostel in Srinagar near Iqbal Park behind Tagore Hall.

The GSN had been established after Gandhi's assassination in 1948, and an ad hoc committee was constituted with the likes of Rajendra Prasad, Jawaharlal Nehru, Sardar Vallabhbhai Patel, Maulana Abul Kalam Azad and C. Rajagopalachari as its members. The stated objective of the trust was to promote Gandhi's teachings on social harmony, health, rural welfare, education, non-violence and truth. Until the beginning of the 1960s, its activities were centralized in Delhi. But during 1962–63, various state bodies of the GSN were constituted and registered with an aim to take the project forward. Thereafter, the work of the trust expanded rapidly across the country.

A month before the event, some Gandhians from the GSN arrived in Kashmir and went from college to college to persuade students to attend the camp organized as part of the celebrations. Shockingly, they could get just two students from all over Kashmir—my friend Basharat Ahmed and I. In a way, this was not surprising because the sentiment in Kashmir during those days was largely one of distrust towards the ruling dispensation. The students could be grouped in two categories: the pro-15 August ones and the pro-14 August ones. As the names suggest, the first ones celebrated India's Independence Day, while the second celebrated the creation of Pakistan. Basharat and I were the pro-August 15 ones and an absolute minority.

We had, of course, during our school days, heard and read about the contributions Gandhi had made to the cause of India's independence. But as students, we were not too deep into the subject, and were certainly not Gandhians in any sense. Being young, we were attracted by anything that was new and exciting, and so, it was out of a mix of curiosity and respect for the Father of the Nation that we enrolled for the camp.

The GSN's choice of Kashmir as the venue for its North Indian celebrations had left me wondering, given the far-from-conducive environment. I was to learn the reason later. During the days of Partition and immediately thereafter, large parts of North India, particularly Punjab, Jammu and Noakhali (now in Bangladesh), had been enveloped in communal bloodshed, with millions losing their lives, homes and hearths. While the violence rattled the nation's conscience, Kashmir, unlike the rest of the country, had remained an oasis of calm and peace, with the majority Muslim population living alongside the minority Hindus. Gandhi had been deeply impressed by this demonstration of brotherhood and praised the people of Kashmir. He had said that he saw a ray of hope in Kashmir. It was in remembrance of those words that the GSN had decided to hold the camp in Kashmir.

When Basharat and I walked into the venue for the camp, little did I know that it would be a defining moment in my life. Many changes would take place in me, and the first one—for that moment—was in the matter of attire. We came across a stall in the camp where a large stock of khadi kurtas and pyjamas was displayed. We were encouraged to wear them. The makers had apparently taken the 'one size fits all' phrase seriously. The dresses were so large that five men of my lean size could fit into one! We wore them during the camp's duration, slowly imbibing its spirit. But it was the other change that was more significant: I left the camp totally influenced by Gandhi's teachings of secularism, brotherhood, truth and non-violence, to mention a few.

The two qualities that impressed me the most about Gandhi was his emphasis on truth and non-violence. We all laud the virtues of truth but hardly practice it in our lives. Gandhi did not just speak the truth but also practised it in the absolute sense. History is full of kings, emperors, dictators and rulers who established and expanded their fiefdoms at sword-point. The concept of using non-violent methods to achieve just means simply did not exist until Gandhi came along with his brand of non-violence—making civil disobedience and peaceful protests mass movements to get rid of the British rule in India. I found it amazing that an emaciated-looking man with frugal habits and barely dressed in coarse clothes could bring an end to the reign of what was then the world's most powerful empire.

Over time, I read the works of several leading figures, including Nehru, Azad, Patel and others, but Gandhi has remained my ideal all through. I have tried to emulate his teachings in my day-to-day life in my own little ways. I do not remember intentionally lying or physically harming any person. One more thing that impressed me was that Gandhi never smoked or consumed alcohol. I, too, have followed this in my life till date.

The GSN had apparently been so impressed by my enthusiasm that it appointed me as its honorary secretary for J&K. The trust had a full-time salaried secretary, S.K. Bajaj from Delhi, but he was not a local and was based in the headquarters, which was in Jammu, and thus, had difficulty expanding the GSN's work in the Kashmir region. On the other hand, I was not only a local but also a student and had a connection with a large cross-section of the people across the state.

Soon after, I received large portraits, books and various other publicity materials on Gandhi from the Delhi head office of the GSN, with instructions that I should use them to propagate his ideals. I plunged into the act with vigour, organizing seminars, exhibitions and cultural programmes at various other places and roping in prominent public figures to make an appearance. I frequently invited the governors and various ministers of the government to those exhibitions and seminars. My invites to political figures cut across political lines. I brought in leaders such as Maulana Masoodi, a freedom fighter; Mirza Mohammad Afzal Beg; Abdul Ghani Lone, then Minister for Education and Health and Mufti Mohammad Sayeed, then Public Works Department minister and others. Gandhi, after all, was not limited to one political party but was the nation's pride. Through these initiatives, the GSN began to gain traction in the region. I thoroughly enjoyed the new role, more so because, by then, I had become an ardent follower of Gandhi.

Soon thereafter, the GSN received an invite from Sri Lanka-based Sarvodaya Shramadana Movement (SSM) to send its representatives to that country for a visit of 1,000 villages that had been adopted as Gandhian model villages. It was founded in 1958 by Gandhi Peace Prize awardee, Dr Ahangamage Tudor Ariyaratne, who had been deeply impressed by Acharya Vinoba Bhave's work in India and by Gandhi's approach to rural development. The SSM is a self-governance campaign that offers comprehensive development and conflict resolution solutions to villages.

The GSN chose me and Basharat for the trip. It was indeed an honour for us, since there were several senior Gandhians in the country who could have been selected. We set out for Colombo, but our first halt was in Wardha, at Acharya Bhave's ashram. Nirmala

Deshpande (Nirmala didi), who was the all-in-all of the ashram, took charge of us there. For the next two days, we enjoyed a frugal existence and moments of genuine mental calm. The staple diet during our stay included rice, vegetable, jaggery and bananas.

After the brief but memorable halt, we went to Rameswaram in Tamil Nadu by train, from where we boarded a small ship to Colombo. Nirmala didi came to see us off at Rameswaram. We had yet another short halt at the guest house of the famous Ramanathaswamy Temple at Rameswaram. The guesthouse was located on a sprawling campus outside the premises of the temple, and people had to use horse-driven carts to travel from one point to another within the temple precincts. We partook of the historic South Indian city's hospitality and basked in its rich and ancient cultural traditions that people from the world over came to witness.

Our experience of the tour of Gandhian model villages in Colombo was an eye-opener. We covered about 200 villages and stayed at a few of them overnight. The SSM model was simple enough. It acquired fallow land, some of which was donated, and then took charge of that land. Unemployed youth, both men and women of the region, were engaged in farming, which included conventional cultivation, dairy farming, honey extraction, etc. The youth were given accommodation in those villages. They managed their homes from the produce they grew and the sale of surplus. They even ran their own schools, in which teachers were paid from the surplus sale of their produce like rice, spices and pulses. In this manner, the Gandhian model villages functioned in a self-sufficient environment.

My regret is that in India, the country of Gandhi, while the land donated to Acharya Bhave was distributed to the poor, we failed to promote the concept of the Gandhian model villages on the lines Acharya Bhave had envisaged and the way Ariyaratne had implemented in Sri Lanka.

On my return after a few weeks, I organized a Gandhian camp in Leh in 1973. It took me four months to get the requisite permit to visit Leh. In those days, people from J&K and the rest of the country were not allowed to visit Leh without a permit from the state home department for security reasons. It was also my first trip to Leh and

Kargil, an arduous 20-hour journey by bus on a bumpy road on which the only visible vehicles were army trucks and private trucks carrying ration for civilians and army personnel.

In 1973, after I completed my MSc with a first class, I applied for research, the subject being 'Trachea of the Insect Vector'. But the study of insects was left unfinished because of certain political developments. Mufti was the president of J&K Pradesh Congress Committee (PCC), and I had known him while I studied in Kashmir University. I used to organize a number of cultural functions in the campus, and my favourite chief guests were Mufti sahab (then the Public Works Department minister) and Lone (then the education minister). I had interactions with them on political issues on a number of occasions and was a frequent visitor to their residences as student leader. Little did I know that my leadership and activism would soon be put to the ultimate test.

2

TO RAISINA VIA TIHAR

On 24 February 1975, the Indira Gandhi–Sheikh Abdullah Accord was signed in New Delhi. Diplomat G. Partharsarathy inked the agreement for the Government of India, while Mirza Afzal Beg put his signature on behalf of Sheikh sahab. Among other things, the agreement reiterated that J&K was a constituent of the Union of India and that it would be governed by Article 370 of the Constitution. It also made it clear that while the residuary powers of legislation would remain with the then state, Parliament would continue to have the power to make laws relating to the sovereignty and integrity of India.

The political fallout for the Congress in the state was that CM Syed Mir Qasim stepped down along with his entire Cabinet, and Sheikh Abdullah, representing the NC, was sworn in as CM. Since the NC did not have any MLAs, Sheikh sahab and Beg, who was the second in command (in the NC and the government), had to be elected within six months.

Two Congress MLAs were asked to resign, so that those NC leaders could be elected unopposed from the respective seats of the Congress leaders. Similarly, a couple of other leaders of the NC were elected as MLCs and made ministers. The sop the Congress got was that some of its MLAs were to be included in Sheikh sahab's Cabinet.

After a few months, Mir Qasim was appointed Union minister for food and civil supplies, and Mufti, Mir Qasim's choice, was appointed the new PCC president. The decision of appointing Mufti as PCC chief did not go down well with some other senior leaders and former ministers, and immediately after his appointment, there was a vertical split in the Congress party at the state level.

Senior leaders like Abdul Ghani Lone led the splintered group, which comprised a number of other former ministers such as Trilochan Dutt, the senior-most Cabinet minister; Mohammad Ayub Khan, former PCC chief and former minister and ministers Noor Mohammad, Gayasuddin and Abdul Aziz Zargar and many others. Though Qasim and Mufti had accepted the accord and Sheikh sahab taking over the reins of government, in their heart of hearts, they had not reconciled with it.

Sheikh sahab, on his part, had no love lost for Mufti and the others. This was also because even after handing over the power to Sheikh sahab, Mufti, as party president, would not miss a single opportunity to oppose the policies of Sheikh's government. He had to constantly fight on two fronts: one, with Sheikh sahab and his overwhelming popularity and two, with the leaders who had split from the Congress party. Hence, conditions were not conducive for Mufti to consolidate and assert his and his party's position.

Despite this, within six months of taking over as the PCC chief, Mufti decided to strengthen his position and started touring Jammu, Kashmir and Ladakh regions, while the group that had broken away confined itself to either Jammu or Srinagar. Thus, its members could not expand their activities beyond these cities where the NC and the Bharatiya Janata Party (BJP) were the main players in Srinagar and Jammu, respectively. It was by virtue of Mufti's hard work and determination that the Congress party was given a new lease of life, right from the block to the state level.

Mufti's efforts also generated some hilarious moments. He had once organized a one-day convention of Congress workers at the district headquarters in Anantnag. One Mr Raju, Congress general secretary in charge of South India, was invited as the chief guest. At that convention, Mufti and other Congress leaders spoke in Kashmiri against Sheikh sahab. Raju couldn't understand a word, but he was told that Sheikh sahab was being praised. But when Raju started speaking in English, the interpreter was told by Mufti to translate his speech totally contrary to what Raju was speaking.

After a few months, I was appointed the state president of the Indian Youth Congress (IYC). Before I took charge, there had been no presence of a structured youth wing of the party in J&K. I had no difficulty in coordinating with the parent organization headed by Mufti. During my entire period as the IYC chief, he ensured that I attended, along with him, all the functions organized by the parent organization. We had many political differences over the years, and he later parted ways with the Congress party. He also did not play fair with me when the PDP's support to my government was withdrawn while I was CM. However, I shall always remain indebted to him for his backing and affection during my tenure as the state IYC president.

Mufti loved to work and travel. This was a boon since we had to move across Jammu, Kashmir and Ladakh, building the Congress cadre almost from scratch. We travelled together along with other leaders from the parent organization, which included G.R. Kar, Ali Mohammad Naik, Peer Hissam-ud-din, Mir Lasjan and Moulvi Iftikar Ansari from Kashmir province as well as Girdhari Lal Dogra, Mian Bashir Ahmed, Mangat Ram Sharma, Motilal Begda, Bhagat Chajju Ram, Sardar Rangeel Singh, Mir Ghulam Mohammad Poonchi, Mohammad Din Banday, Thakur Randhir Singh, Chaudhary Mohammad Aslam and Mirza Abdul Rashid from Jammu province. There were also P. Namgyal and Kachu Ali Mohammad from Leh and Kargil, respectively. All leaders had a standing in their respective areas.

The extensive travelling gave me valuable experience and opportunity to organize the Youth Congress. I got to know Jammu, Kashmir and Ladakh, both geographically and politically. I also came to know their people and their problems intimately.

Barely four months after the Indira–Sheikh Accord, while we were busy with organization building in the state, Emergency was imposed across the country on 25 June 1975. Its impact in J&K was, however, non-existent. Sheikh sahab was the supreme leader and, being a minor player in the state government, the Congress was struggling to expand its influence against all odds. None of us had any time to mull over Emergency or the excesses, if any, that were allegedly taking place in Delhi and elsewhere in the country. One of the things I was busy with in J&K was grooming IYC leaders, who later rose high in the ranks and played significant roles in state politics.

As the state president of the IYC, I had the opportunity to get close to both Indira ji and Sanjay Gandhi. While Indira ji was the chairperson of the National Advisory Committee of the IYC, Sanjay was the leader of the IYC. Every three or four months, I would visit the national capital to participate in the national council meetings of the IYC (in those days, there used to be a national council like the CWC of the parent party), which would be attended by Sanjay. During my Delhi visits, I would seek appointments with both Indira ji and Sanjay, besides IYC president Ambika Soni, to get better acquainted with them and to also brief them about the situation in Kashmir. Both Indira ji and Sanjay took a keen interest in matters pertaining to my state. In addition to my individual meetings with Indira ji and Sanjay, I would always get an opportunity to meet them along with Mufti as and when he would seek appointments with them. It was during all those frequent meetings that I developed closeness with both. Kashmir had a special place in their hearts, since Indira ji's ancestors originally belonged to J&K. She was emotionally attached to Kashmir and would remember most of the state leaders and even some district leaders by name.

Sanjay, as I Knew Him

Since a great deal has already been written by various people on Emergency days, I will not dwell on the subject in detail. But being an IYC leader at that time and having known Sanjay well, I can say one thing with great certainty: He was unfairly demonized and wrongly projected by the media, which, unfortunately, sent a completely distorted image of the man to the people at large.

Sanjay had simple habits. He did not smoke or drink, nor did he have even tea or coffee. However, he liked Coca-Cola. He was always dressed in plain khadi kurta-pyjamas and wore Kolhapuri chappals. His old kurtas used to have *rafoo* (intricate repair thread work) at two or three places. All sorts of canard with no iota of truth were spread against him. The only woman he had an affair with was the one he married and remained a devoted husband until the end.

He was passionate about the nation's progress and his five-point programme—each one, teach one (education); tree plantation (environment); small family, happy family (population control); cleanliness and anti-dowry—could not be faulted. Today, global conferences attended by world leaders are held on health, hygiene, environment, education and population control, all of which Sanjay had emphasized four-and-a-half decades ago.

It is possible that some excesses might have happened during Emergency, but they were conveniently placed at Indira ji's and Sanjay's doorsteps, although they had nothing to do with them. One of the biggest falsehoods spread was that Sanjay was anti-Muslim and had, thus, targeted the community with his sterilization programme and the demolition of their homes in the Jama Masjid area in Delhi and elsewhere in the country. None of that was intended to target Muslims in particular. He had a large number of close Muslim friends, both inside and outside the party. Of course, he tried to clean some slums in Delhi, but the drive hit both Muslim and non-Muslim areas. It was part of the cleanliness campaign, not a matter of targeting any particular community.

In any case, I believe that the incidents of excesses had been hyped up and many of the accusations were proved false. When the Janata Party came to power in 1977, its minister for health and family welfare, Raj Narain, who harboured a pathetic dislike for Indira ji, announced that people who had been forced into sterilization could come forward to claim compensation. During the Janata Party's two-and-a-half years in government, I don't recall any person coming forward to claim compensation.

Sanjay had one shortcoming though. He was a reckless driver. I had told him several times to keep a driver, but he would scoff at the suggestion. He had a blue Matador and drove it like he was participating in a race. Terrified by his rashness, I would refuse to sit next to him in the front while he maneuvered the traffic. He would laugh and call me a coward and persuade some other person accompanying us to sit in the front. The poor fellow would comply, praying for his dear life all through the journey. I told Sanjay often that someday he would meet with a fatal accident. Sadly, my fears would come true some years later; a light aircraft that he was flying in June 1980 in Delhi's skies crashed to the ground, killing him on the spot.

Congress (I) Is Born

The negative projection of Sanjay, the IYC, Emergency and Indira ji's government in general had a bad impact on the public, as a result of which the party lost the 1977 Lok Sabha polls. Another major reason for the loss was that three stalwarts of the Congress party—Babu Jagjivan Ram (Babuji), H.N. Bahuguna and Nandini Satpathy—had resigned from the party along with many other senior leaders and grassroots workers from across the country. These leaders formed a new party, the Congress for Democracy (CFD), which joined the Janata Party alliance to contest elections. It was a huge setback for the Congress party in general and for Indira ji in particular, who too was defeated from her Lok Sabha constituency.

After the 1977 loss, a number of developments took place in the party. On 3 June 1977, K. Brahmananda Reddy was elected as the president of the Congress party. Among other things that the new Congress chief did, he spearheaded the dissolution of the IYC, holding both Sanjay and the organization accountable for the election debacle.

Sanjay summoned the IYC state presidents to New Delhi for deliberations. Only a handful of us were left; most others had quit the party. Indira ji and Sanjay had separate meetings with a few of us individually at their residence before a formal meeting took place in a small room of the vice president's house, which was addressed by Pranab Mukherjee. Besides me, some of the others who attended the meeting were Ramachandra Rath (Orissa [now Odisha]), Tariq Anwar (Bihar), Venod Sharma (Chandigarh), Lalit Maken and Jagdish Tytler (Delhi). In addition to the state presidents, other important leaders like D.P. Ray (Calcutta [now Kolkata]) were also present. After having discussions amongst ourselves, we came to the conclusion that since Rath had been elected to the Lok Sabha, it would be appropriate to make him the president. Anwar, Sharma, Ray and I become general secretaries of the IYC.

During the discussion, the general feeling was that of consensus: The onus for the party's defeat had been squarely placed on the IYC and the excesses during Emergency. That being the case, it would be prudent to put the IYC brand on the back-burner for the moment and replace it with another name. Hence, we changed the name of the IYC to Youth Forum.

The Youth Forum continued to conduct some activities but nothing big happened. The IYC was a brand, and the Youth Forum never gained the traction that we hoped it would. In fact, even some of our IYC workers didn't join the Youth Forum. Besides, we hardly had the time to turn the Youth Forum into a success. Most of our time was spent in firefighting. Cases had been filed against Indira ji, Sanjay and other Congress leaders across the country, and we were busy running from place to place in different parts of India and simultaneously reorganizing the party at various levels.

Further, Indira ji was denied permission to use any government accommodation, even ordinary dak bungalows. Even security was denied, particularly by the states ruled by the Janata Party government, during her trips. The Congress party would arrange accommodation for her, and the IYC workers would provide her security. Those were terrible days indeed, both for the Congress party and its leadership.

Then on 1–2 January 1978, the Congress (I) was born, with Indira ji as the president. There had been a split in the Congress, both in the party and its parliamentary wing. The Congress (I) lost its status of LoP to the rival group headed by Y.B. Chavan. After Indira ji took over the presidentship of Congress (I), a few days later on 18 January 1978, the IYC was again revived with Rath as president and I, along with Sharma and Ray, as national general secretaries.

In the later part of 1978, it was felt that the Muslim minority community, as a result of Emergency, had moved away from the Congress party. Indira ji and Sanjay suggested the formation of a new front that would work closely with the minority community and regain the trust of its members. The All India Muslim Youth Conference came into being, and I became its first president; the other office bearers were Tariq Anwar (later to be Union minister), Syed Ahmed (who later died as a sitting governor of Manipur), M.A. Khan (later a member of Parliament [MP]) and Hassan Ahmed (later an MLA). There was another Muslim leader from Karnataka. I ended up holding three positions at a time—general secretary of the IYC, president of the District Congress Committee (DCC), Doda (J&K) and president of the All India Muslim Youth Conference—and had to work double and triple shifts.

I decided to hold the first convention of the Muslim Youth Conference at Mavalankar Auditorium in Delhi. The two-day event was attended and addressed by Indira ji, Sanjay, Giani Zail Singh, then Karnataka CM D. Devaraj Urs, Aziz Seith and Sajjada Nasheen of Hazrat Nizamuddin, besides many senior Muslim leaders from across the country.

Indira ji had suggested that Sheikh sahab, the CM of J&K, be invited for the convention too. She asked Mehmooda Begum, then All India Congress Committee (AICC) secretary and her close friend, and me to visit Srinagar. Armed with a letter from Indira ji to Sheikh sahab, we met him. After reading the letter, Sheikh sahab said that he would depute his son Farooq Abdullah for the event. Around 1,000 delegates from across the country attended the two-day convention. Thus, the very first event of the Muslim Youth Conference was a big success.

Buoyed by the success of the national convention, we had a series of state-level conventions in different parts of the country. A few months later, I decided to organize a Muslim Youth Conference convention for the southern region in Hyderabad. One of my colleagues was rushed to Hyderabad to meet PCC president and then CM M. Chenna Reddy to make arrangements for the two-day convention. The CM not only supported the idea but also extended his full support by saying that he would arrange for boarding and lodging for the delegates. A week later, I reached Hyderabad to meet the CM and discuss with him the final arrangements made for the convention.

After having detailed discussions with Reddy, I informed him that Sanjay too would be making an appearance at the conference, and Reddy's demeanour changed instantly. He flared up and declared that he would have nothing to do with the event, and that I could look elsewhere for help! Unfortunately, Reddy and Sanjay did not get along well.

I was in a fix. My good friend Bhaskar Rao was a minister in the state Cabinet, and he didn't get along well with the CM. When I confided my dilemma to him, he offered to step in and help with the event in any neighbouring state. He suggested that we better shift the venue to Madras (now Chennai) and assured me that he would take care of the arrangements through his friends based in Tamil Nadu. I returned to Delhi and informed Sanjay about the new development.

It was decided that instead of cancelling the programme, we should change the venue from Hyderabad to Chennai. K.V. Thangkabalu was the president of the Tamil Nadu Youth Congress, and as general secretary of the IYC, I was in charge of the southern states. I asked him to help us in making the convention a success and, through his Muslim friends, help in the selection of minority delegates to attend the convention. Thangkabalu was a dynamic, resourceful and dedicated leader, and he had devoted his time and resources to build the IYC in that state, since the 1978 division in the Congress party had adversely affected Tamil Nadu too.

Thangkabalu also suggested that I invite M. Karunanidhi to attend the function; the Dravida Munnetra Kazhagam (DMK) leader was in the opposite camp in those days. Thangkabalu knew Karunanidhi quite well, so he immediately arranged a meeting with the supreme leader of the DMK the very next day. That was my first interaction with the DMK chief; I was impressed by his love and affection as well as the warmth with which he treated me. He promised to attend the conference in spite of being opposed to Indira ji. He also told me that should I need any help, it would be provided without delay. During my meeting with him, Thangkabalu was with me and was privy to this discussion.

After being with Karunanidhi for almost more than 45 minutes, I very politely asked him if I could bring Sanjay to meet him since he would also be attending this convention a fortnight later. He immediately said, 'Yes, why not!' He added, 'My fight is with Indira Gandhi, not with you boys.' Karunanidhi not only attended but also addressed the convention.

When Sanjay arrived for the inaugural function, it was raining heavily, so his clothes were drenched and he didn't have an extra set of clothes with him as he was to return that very day. But somehow because of late flights, and more so since his appointment was fixed with Karunanidhi, he could not return to Delhi the same day. Back in the hotel, he insisted on cleaning the wet clothes himself. Despite others' persuasions to hand them over to the laundry department, he refused to do so. He could have easily ordered a fresh pair of clothes but didn't. Simplicity was his hallmark.

However, the convention could not have been completed without the unstinted support of Arif, a Tamilian Muslim who owned the three-star hotel that we stayed in. During our two-day stay there, a large number of delegates would come to see us and eat and have tea in that hotel. At the end of our stay, Arif refused payment from us despite my repeated insistence. Over the years, I developed a bond with him and his family and, to this day, I stay at his hotel, which is now managed by his son Abu Bucker, since Arif has settled in the US with his other son, a doctor.

After the successful completion of the convention, Thangkabalu and I took Sanjay to Karunanidhi's residence. It laid the foundation for the DMK's support to Congress party in the December 1979 General Elections. Subsequently, his meeting with Indira ji was arranged in Delhi, which clinched the alliance between the two parties. I am lucky to have met Karunanidhi, and our relationship was only strengthened with time. His fatherly attitude towards me remained till his death.

Then came the turning point in 1978. Indira ji contested the Lok Sabha seat of Chikkamagaluru in Karnataka and won. She emerged stronger than before, and that was the signal for the Congress's revival. At the same time, the fissures in the ruling Janata Party had begun to show. Nonetheless, the government was still determined to hound Indira ji as much as possible and ensure that she did not get a chance to be in Parliament despite the public mandate. It called a special session of Parliament. We were not aware of the details of the agenda, but rumours were afloat that the government would do something drastic against her. We had alerted all our state IYC units, especially the Delhi branch, since the action would be in Delhi, to be ready for the occasion. The Delhi IYC unit was headed by the dynamic, resourceful leader Jagdish Tytler, who geared up the organization to meet the impending challenge. Similarly, the two strongmen of Delhi PCC, H.K.L. Bhagat and Sajjan Kumar, were ever-ready to face the consequences and were strong enough to mobilize the crowds.

Our worst fears came true. Parliament passed a resolution on 20 December 1978, dismembering Indira ji from the Lok Sabha for allegedly having repeatedly committed breach of privilege and contempt of the House.[3] The decision to expel her was taken by 279 votes in favour and 138 against.[4] The Janata Party had a majority in the House and could get away with the resolution against Indira ji.

It was clear that the government was using the rules of procedure and conduct of business in both Houses of Parliament, which had evolved over the years with an aim to punish wrongdoing of their members and maintain Parliament's integrity, to settle political scores with its opponents. Not content with the expulsion, the government also resolved to jail her for the offence. The jail term was to be effective till the prorogation of the House session. It was the first instance anywhere in the world of a democratically elected former PM being imprisoned for breach of privilege and contempt of the House.

Tihar Turns the Tide

As soon as Indira ji came out of Parliament after losing her Lok Sabha membership, policemen swooped down on her, arrested her and marched her off to Tihar Jail. H.K.L. Bhagat and Sajjan Kumar and other senior Congress leaders rushed to their respective areas to organize protests against this decision. Tytler and Lalit Maken, too, went to their respective areas to mobilize public opinion and public protests.

I also rushed to Old Delhi where our IYC unit was strong, and urged our Youth Congress workers to start a procession from Old Delhi to Parliament. Thus, I led one group of about 700–800 Youth Congress and parent Congress workers and leaders from the Jama

---

[3]Both the Lok Sabha and the Rajya Sabha have the right to dismember their members under the rules that govern its functioning. In 2005, Parliament expelled 11 members (10 of Lok Sabha and one of Rajya Sabha) in the infamous cash-for-questions scandal.

[4]'December 20, 1978, Forty Years Ago: Indira Jailed', *The Indian Express*, 20 December 2018, https://bit.ly/3lmLpir. Accessed on 19 May 2022.

Masjid side towards Parliament. Our procession was stopped by the police in front of the Daryaganj Police Station. We saw that a few dozen buses were waiting to take us to jail for violating Section 144. Within a few minutes, a large number of police personnel succeeded in pushing at least 500–600 boys into the buses, and three–four of us who were seniors in the organization were requested by the police inspector to get into police jeep. En route, I asked him which police station he was going to take us to. He said, 'Straight to Tihar Jail.' When we came close to South Avenue, where I was putting up with Rath, I requested him to stop in front of Rath's MP flat so that I could collect my clothes. The inspector was kind enough to oblige.

After reaching Tihar Jail, I found many Congress and IYC men and women wandering in the premises of the jail. Some were housed in halls, small and big, and I was lucky to be put in one of the big cells, which had two cemented beds. Five more companions of the parent organization were my roommates. Though many other IYC leaders, including me, who were working with Sanjay had been arrested a number of times in different parts of the country, we were mostly released the same day or at the most the next day. This was the first time I had been jailed in Tihar. It was a new experience for me.

One of our colleagues in the cell was a teacher at a private school and a staunch Congressman. We called him Masterji. He and our three colleagues slept on the floor, while I and another senior leader of Delhi Congress slept on cement beds, covered with thin blankets. On the third day of our stay, Masterji suddenly decided to go on a fast until Indira ji was released. He asked us also to follow suit, which we refused outright. We told him that it was more than enough that we were in jail, but now to go on a fast was too much of a sacrifice for us to make under the circumstances. He, however, proceeded with his fast.

On the second day, an inmate who slept next to him on the floor told us in the morning that he had heard sounds of crunching and munching emerging from under the quilt of Masterji at midnight and suspected that the 'man on a fast' was surreptitiously eating something. We decided to check this out. When Masterji went to the toilet in the morning, we proceeded to investigate the matter. Our efforts unearthed a large amount of sweets, biscuits and dry fruits concealed under the pillow. We confiscated these things. Since we were political prisoners, people would get food for us, and we would go out to pick up that food. Being a local man from Delhi, he must have got the sweets and fruits through some of his friends or relatives and kept them hidden from us.

That night, we heard Masterji twisting and turning in his bed on the floor and walking all through the night inside and outside the cell in an agitated mood. We all were awake but pretended to be asleep! We secretly enjoyed his discomfiture. The following morning, we asked him to end his fast. He immediately agreed, adding that our persistence had impelled him to give up his fast. We then exposed his farce, and all of us had a hearty laugh. Needless to add, we shared the delicacies that he had hoarded.

On her seventh day in jail, Indira ji was released. But my five roommates and I were freed only in January the following year. We six were in that cell from December 1978 to mid-January 1979. We had grown beards during this period, and after coming out of jail, several photos were taken of us with our new look. Some had French cuts, and others sported Chandra Shekhar Azad-like looks. It showed that our youth and childish behaviour was still hidden somewhere in our subconscious.

By the middle of 1979, the feud in the Janata Party had come out in the open. The Bharatiya Jana Sangh (BJS) had quit the alliance, and Charan Singh had revolted and gone his separate way, turning the Morarji Desai-led Janata Party into a minority. Charan Singh became the PM with Congress support and had a short stint—beginning 28 July. Soon, it was time for another general election. Lok Sabha elections were announced for December 1979. In those days, campaigning was allowed for a full month. We could also hold election meetings until the very end. However, all this was later curtailed, and today campaigning has to end 48 hours before voting takes place.

After the Lok Sabha elections were announced, a series of parliamentary board meetings were held at 24 Akbar Road, with Indira ji chairing them, to finalize the list of candidates. The Congress Parliamentary Board (CPB) mainly comprised senior members of the

CWC who had stood by Indira ji throughout but had not been much in the field from 1977 to 1979. Thus, she had to depend mostly on the AICC and the IYC office bearers in New Delhi to cross-check the work done by the candidates so recommended by the PCCs for seeking a mandate. Since the IYC had fought at the grassroots level, it knew about the leaders of both the parent and the youth organization who had been jailed or those who had been active in the field during the crisis period from 1977 to 1979. Since, as general secretary of the IYC, I was looking after the organization and working in the field, Congress president Indira ji would call me to the parliamentary board meeting after every half an hour and enquire about candidates whose selection was a matter of dispute amongst the parliamentary board members, which consisted of Indira ji, Kamlapati Tripathi, Darbara Singh, P.V. Narasimha Rao, Syed Mir Qasim, Chandra Shekhar, K. Karunakaran, M. Chenna Reddy, Arjun Singh, A.R. Antulay and Buta Singh. I would give her the true picture. This would, of course, displease many senior members of the CPB who, as a result, could not get their candidates through. Several IYC leaders got tickets and some rose high in the ranks thereafter, becoming Union ministers, CMs and ministers in different states.

Though Rath, the president of the IYC, was a decent and learned person, a good orator in English, Hindi and Odia and had a deep knowledge of several religions, he was, unfortunately, extremely lazy. He would go to sleep nearing dawn, having read different books, and would wake up only around midday. He would hardly attend the IYC office, leaving the space free for me to operate and take all decisions for the party's youth wing. My other colleagues were Ray, who functioned from Kolkata, and Sharma from Chandigarh. They would visit Delhi once in a while and kept busy with party activities in their respective regions.

Slowly, the tide began to turn in Indira ji's favour. As a result of growing public sympathy following the witch-hunt the Janata Party government had launched against her, and following her own belligerent campaigns across the country to win back public support, a few of the leaders who had deserted her returned to the fold. The Indira ji-led group became the main Opposition and C.M. Stephen, its leader.

I single-handedly conducted all the affairs of the IYC till the latter part of 1978, when K. Vasudeva Panicker, who had joined back the Congress along with Stephen, was made one of the general secretaries. Often, my colleagues and I had to travel to various parts of the country for party work. I would travel to even far-off states including Kerala, Tamil Nadu, Karnataka, Andhra Pradesh, Assam, Bengal, Bihar, besides North Indian states, by second class in trains, and it would take me several days to reach my destinations.

During the travel, I would carry with me reams of typing and carbon papers, and prepare circulars in duplicate or triplicate for our state units, all in longhand, to carry out our further organizational activities. I would put these circulars in envelopes and post them en route whenever the train would stop for few minutes.

Kashmiri Boy Conquers Washim

While the distribution of tickets for Lok Sabha candidates was taking place, there was no question of my asking for a ticket from J&K. This was because of the understanding that had been struck between Indira ji and Sheikh sahab. As a result, five Lok Sabha seats went to Sheikh sahab and only one seat of Jammu to the Congress party. When Mufti and I told her that it seemed to be a one-sided deal, she argued that the arrangement would positively impact the Muslim population across the country. The lone seat from Jammu went to a senior leader and former finance minister of the state, Girdhari Lal Dogra (father-in-law of Arun Jaitley).

On the last day of ticket finalization by the CPB, I got a slip that said I was to come to the room where the CPB meeting was being held. In the meeting room, Indira ji handed over a slip of paper to me and told me to select a constituency to contest from. There were names of three seats. She said that I had to contest from one of them. Two names were from Maharashtra and the other one from Madhya Pradesh. Mir Qasim, who was present in the meeting as a member, wondered why she was sending 'this boy' to contest from an unknown seat far away from J&K. She turned to him, furious, and gave him a dressing down. She told him not to interfere and said, 'You too had been offered seats in Secunderabad (Andhra Pradesh) and Azamgarh (Uttar Pradesh [UP]) on two different occasions to contest two by-elections, but both the times you declined, saying that you would lose, and you know we won both. Actually, you had no courage to contest. Now you want to discourage this young boy.'

Properly chastened, Mir Qasim went silent. I told Indira ji that I was ready to contest from Washim (Maharashtra). There was a reason for my choice. Besides being general secretary of the IYC in charge of Maharashtra, I had earlier served as acting president of the Maharashtra unit too, after the state president Satish Chaturvedi was barred from conducting any political activity in the state for a year by the state government. Chaturvedi was one of the most active IYC state presidents who would organize a number of programmes and stage protests across the state against the functioning of the state government and the Janata Party government at the Centre. As a result, he was made to pay for his aggression and popularity.

Sanjay suggested that I take over as acting president of the state IYC in Maharashtra in addition to my role as general secretary at the national level. He further suggested the post of the president be kept vacant, so that it would not demoralize Chaturvedi and his supporters, and he could ultimately take the charge of presidentship again. As acting president, I had the occasion to interact with a number of state party leaders, both from the IYC and the parent body, and developed a rapport with many of them. My travels across the state had also made me familiar both with the region and its people and their aspirations.

Once I agreed to contest from Washim, Indira ji directed senior leader A.R. Antulay, then general secretary and CPB member, and Jawaharlal Darda, a prominent leader from Nagpur, to take care of me, get my nomination papers filed and help me in my campaigning. There were only two days left to file the nominations, and in these two days, I had to reach Washim, which was about a five-hour journey from Nagpur. Before that, I had to collect from Jammu a certified copy of the voters list in which my name would figure. Thus, I booked my ticket that very night for Jammu. But before going to the railway station, I visited Indira ji's residence to formally thank her.

During that short meeting, she told me that she had, six months earlier, asked Antulay and V.C. Shukla to identify one safe seat for me in their respective states but had directed them to keep the matter a secret. They never revealed this to me. She said that since I had been working so hard, I deserved to contest. Since J&K had been ruled out due to the arrangement with Sheikh sahab, I had to be given a seat from outside.

She also shared with me that it was for the first time that she had a say in the distribution of Lok Sabha seats from Maharashtra. Earlier, it used to be Y.B. Chavan who would distribute all the seats of the state. She further added that Jagjivan Ram would distribute Scheduled Caste (SC) seats for the entire country. I was astonished and realized how wrong people were when they used to say that she was like a dictator. Had she really been one, two of her senior colleagues would not have wielded such power under her party presidentship and prime ministership. It also showed how much she cared for the advice given to her by her colleagues.

The second day after collecting a copy of the voters' list, I flew from Jammu to Delhi. From Delhi, I took a flight to Nagpur, where Darda and his colleagues were waiting for me. They had arranged my five-hour road journey from Nagpur to Akola, where I had to file my nomination papers the next morning. After filing the nomination, I went to Washim, about two hours away from Akola, to stay the night. I put up in the government guest house; this was allowed in those days.

A number of Congressmen met me that night. One elderly person with a Gandhi cap and with a heavy body introduced himself as R.G. Rathi, an advocate. He was a Congressman in his late seventies with a sound legal practice. While saying goodnight to me, Rathi requested me to have breakfast with him the next morning. The following day after breakfast, he came out to see me off and handed me the keys of a new Fiat car driven by his personal driver. He said that the car and the driver were at my disposal till the election was over. He further told me that he had given money to his driver for the entire month for petrol and for his boarding and lodging, and I should not bother on that account. I was overwhelmed by his generous gesture. For the next month, that car was my personal vehicle, and he never bothered me. However, I am extremely happy that after six months of that Lok Sabha election, I could reciprocate the goodwill and generosity shown by him to me by giving him an assembly ticket from a neighbouring constituency, since his own constituency, Washim, was reserved. Happily, he won.

Immediately after the scrutiny of papers, I started campaigning in the constituency. For the first three–four days, I barely attracted a crowd of 1,000 or 2,000 people at my meetings. Meanwhile, Indira ji, through her private secretary and confidant R.K. Dhawan, called from Delhi, saying she wanted to come to campaign for me. I suggested that she should not waste her time, since I was certain to lose. She could instead cover constituencies in UP or elsewhere, which she could turn into winners. The Janata Party and Sharad Pawar's party, Indian National Congress (U), had put up a joint candidate against me. Besides this, there was not a single Congress MLA from Washim parliamentary constituency, which made my chances of winning even more difficult. During the entire election, my opponents highlighted the issue of my being an 'outsider'—not even from the region but from the extreme north of India. But before that sentiment could take root, something unusual happened.

As luck would have it, on the sixth or seventh day of my campaign, Atal Bihari Vajpayee came to address a public meeting for the Janata Party candidate in my constituency. In those days, I did not know him. In his address, he launched a frontal attack on me and my party by saying that Indira ji could not find any local candidate worth contesting from this constituency and, hence, had to import somebody from Kashmir. Vajpayee's public address and aggression turned out to be a blessing in disguise. Now, everybody wanted to see who this Kashmiri boy was that Vajpayee had taken on. As a result, my meeting began attracting huge crowds ranging from 10,000 to 15,000 people.

People now began to consider me more seriously. One or two days later, Pawar came, followed by Jagjivan Ram. By their arrival, they made me more popular and indirectly helped my campaign. The fact that I had come from Kashmir turned into an advantage instead of a liability. More and more people thronged the venue of my public meetings, and there would be lathi charge to control the surge. Over the next 10 days, my name flashed across the state through the media, and I became a celebrity. I began getting requests from candidates from across Maharashtra that I visit their constituencies and put in an appearance! I ended up visiting many areas for my party's candidates across the state, thereby covering almost 20–25 parliamentary constituencies, besides my own.

All through my campaign, I never referred to my opponent—Ade Pratapsing Ramsing of the Janata Party—by name or criticized him, though I robustly questioned the Janata Party and its policies. I spoke of what I planned to do for the development of the constituency if I was elected. I talked of the good that my party had done and would do. I had a very good reason not to speak in public about my political opponent—I was made popular by the tall leaders of the Janata Party, who repeatedly mentioned my name in their public speeches. I came to the conclusion that the more you oppose your adversaries, the more popular they become. Soon, my opponent learnt from his supporters that I never mentioned his name or abused him in my speeches during my entire campaign. So, when he noticed some posters of mine on his residence building, he allowed them to be displayed instead of asking his workers to remove them.

Nothing Personal in My Politics

Throughout my political career, I have had nothing personal against any of my political opponents. I treat political opponents as competitors and not as enemies. How can we treat our own countrymen of other parties as enemies? We only differ politically and ideologically. In politics, every politician has two faces. One is demonstrated through his public posture, which is 'political posturing'; the other is personal. In the first, naturally, when you face political leaders with different ideologies, you counter them politically. But that does not mean you cannot have personal relations with them. In fact, there are examples where members of a family were in different parties. Take the case of J.B. Kripalani and his wife, Sucheta. Their politics was different, their political parties were different, but they stayed under the same roof and shared the same dinner table. There are also instances where father and son or brothers are in different parties, but they don't break their personal and family ties.

In my long political journey, I have had friends in almost every political party and shared warm ties with them. Among them is PM Narendra Modi. A lot has been said about my relationship with him. I have known Modi since the late 1990s, when he was the general secretary of his party and I was the general secretary of mine. Both of us would also occasionally come face to face on television debates. However, before the show or after, we would have tea in the TV studio at the request of the anchors. My first impression about him was that he did not know much. I thought that the BJP had sent just another person from Gujarat for the TV discussion. But when it was his chance to speak, he turned out to be very different. He was vocal, firm, knowledgeable and well-prepared on the subjects being discussed. He did not duck a single question. He was one of the best participants in the subsequent discussions. Still, I never imagined that he would one day be the CM, let alone a powerful PM.

Several years later, as health minister, I got the opportunity to interact with all CMs, including Modi, who was then CM of Gujarat, to ensure that central and state governments are on the same page while implementing health-related schemes. We would also interact with each other when both of us were CMs of our respective states and had the opportunity to have discussions on various issues whenever we would meet at CMs conferences. As CM, Modi would organize an annual kite festival as a means to promote tourism in Gujarat, and he would invite me to the event. However, as I had no interest in kite flying, I never went, though I would thank him for his invitation.

When you have numerous interactions with leaders of other parties, which one does over time, you develop relationships. After all, we are human beings. But, to say that we have come together politically and are plotting something is not only childish but a silly thought. Political leaders who reach a certain level do not mix politics with their personal relationships. Being non-personal is a habit that I have retained all through my political career. Fortunately, Indira ji, Sanjay and Rajiv knew my nature and never objected or misunderstood me.

Perhaps my approach was due to the influence of Gandhian philosophy, which I imbibed from my early student days.

Indira Gandhi Returns

The results of the Lok Sabha election were declared in early January 1980. Indira ji and the Congress had triumphed with a resounding mandate. This was largely due to her extraordinarily impressive and towering personality as well as the aggressive campaigning she led throughout the country.

I, too, had won. When counting for the final four rounds were still due, it was clear that I was winning. Ramsing approached me and said the first celebration of my victory would be at his residence, which I readily accepted. He went home to make preparations. After the results were declared, I left for his house, which was approximately 90 minutes from the counting place. Some of my supporters accompanied me, while others declined to be seen at a rival's home. In all, there was a crowd of around 5,000 people at his place that included his and my supporters. He garlanded me, and there was tea and food for everyone present. I was greatly moved by his large-heartedness and graciousness in spite of his defeat. But what happened soon after floored me.

Ramsing gave a small speech and, at the end, announced that he was joining the Congress party! There was a stunned silence in the gathering. His statement came as a bolt from the blue, which took his party and ours, too, by surprise. He had been impressed by my decency and hard work. He remained with the Congress till his death—may God grant peace to his soul.

As an MP, I worked hard. Every Friday, I would visit the constituency and remain there until early Monday. I interacted with people, listened to their grievances and tried to address them. People saw in me not just their MP but also their MLA, Zila Parishad member and sarpanch. I was told that previous MPs would hardly make an appearance in that constituency. I was a refreshing change for the voters.

I received tremendous love and affection from the overwhelming

Hindu majority in Washim. Their unstinted support has convinced me that we are one nation with one people, and that the divisive Hindu–Muslim narrative has been created by certain elements of the political class to serve their vested interests.

3

SANJAY AND THE DEATH OF HOPE

The year 1980 began on a bright note. The Congress party had stormed back to power at the Centre, Indira ji had become the PM again and I had been elected to the Lok Sabha from Washim constituency in Maharashtra. I was promoted from general secretary to the president of the IYC later in the year.

I was especially delighted that people had rejected the negative image that had been foisted on Indira ji and Sanjay and elected them to Parliament from Raebareli and Amethi Lok Sabha constituencies, respectively. I was happy that nearly 30–40 of our IYC leaders were elected to the Lok Sabha.

The Parliament session was convened in end of February that year, which began with the president's customary address. It was followed by the Motion of Thanks to the president's address, during which members of both sides spoke, using the occasion to take pot-shots at each other. Our group of elected IYC MPs was allotted seats in the centre of the Lok Sabha. On the right side of the Speaker were the PM, ministers and ruling party MPs. On the left sat Opposition members, including Vajpayee. Sanjay sat next to me in the fourth or fifth row in the centre.

The PM was supposed to respond to the discussions on the concluding day of the Motion of Thanks to the President's address. When that happens, the Lok Sabha benches are usually packed, and the media, too, is in full strength. At our party meeting earlier, it had been decided that to gain the upper hand, Sanjay will deliver his address just before Vajpayee's turn, followed by the PM's final address.

That way, Sanjay's speech would receive wider media publicity and attention in the House too.

Sanjay was a man of few words. Even during the election rallies, he would speak for 5-10 minutes at the most and yet manage to convey the essentials. At party meetings, too, he intervened with pithy remarks. His 'yes' was a definite affirmation and his 'no' was an unambiguous rejection. Words like 'dekhenge' or 'sochenge' were not for him.

And so, when he rose to speak in Parliament, we on the Treasury benches knew that he would wind up whatever he had to say under five minutes. He began with a scathing criticism of the Opposition parties but quickly directed his attention to Vajpayee. Thereafter, he launched a frontal attack on the veteran leader, a gentlemanly figure by all accounts. Moreover, Sanjay went on and on, beyond the expected 5-10 minutes, even as members on both sides listened with interest and surprise, as he launched a broadside against the Opposition, particularly the BJP and its leaders, questioning their criticism of the Congress party and Indira ji.

In desperation, I began to tug at the end his kurta, signalling him to call it an end. It was not that I didn't want to listen to him. Rather, his speech had mesmerized the audience. But I was worried that the more he spoke against Vajpayee, the more ammunition he would provide to that powerful orator to turn the tables on Sanjay. But Sanjay brushed aside my efforts and continued. By the time he finished, he had spoken for more than 15 minutes—a record by his standards. He then looked around nonchalantly. It was his first—and sadly his last—speech in Parliament.

Now it was Vajpayee's turn. My heart sank as he got up. He was known to lace his speeches with humour and sarcasm, and bring in them his enormous experience in politics. I wondered if the maneuver of having Sanjay speak just before Vajpayee had been a wise one. I feared, though I did not want to admit it, that the Jana Sangh leader would make mincemeat of Sanjay's address.

Vajpayee surveyed the hall and began. His opening words had made us nearly fall off our seats. He said that he would not speak a word against Sanjay, although the first-time Congress MP had pulled no punches in attacking him. Vajpayee then looked straight at Indira ji and told her that she occupied her post primarily due to the efforts of Sanjay and his team. If Sanjay was responsible for her party's defeat in 1977, he should be credited for its 1980 victory too. He continued, while his own party men listened open-mouthed, stating that Sanjay and his IYC workers had, over the past years, put up a brave fight, matching the Opposition in every way. Sanjay had emerged as a leader in his own right, Vajpayee remarked. He reminded Indira ji that some of her senior leaders had abandoned her just before the 1977 Lok Sabha elections, while a few others left her in the January 1978 Congress split—he didn't take names. But, he added, Sanjay and his band of followers had valiantly battled the challenges and finally emerged victorious.

Vajpayee's speech was a rousing endorsement of Sanjay's leadership qualities and the role of the IYC from 1977 to 1980. Having said all that, Vajpayee then proceeded to touch upon other issues in his address to the Motion of Thanks. As he ended his speech and sat down, I realized what a great statesman he was. It requires courage and magnanimity to not just admit defeat but also give credit to rivals without adding 'ifs' and 'buts'.

Indira ji floored the House with her address and impressed the visitors seated in the gallery with her unparalleled charm. But the day's highlight was undoubtedly Sanjay's 'long' address and Vajpayee's totally unexpected response.

Love Comes Home

There were happy moments on the personal front too. I was to get married in March end in 1980, and my bride, Shameem Dev, was from a family with whom my family members had had a long association. Shameem was a celebrity well before I came to be known nationally. She had sung all the songs in the Kashmiri telefilm *Habba Khatoon* when she was only in high school. Her renditions were a rage on local television and radio stations. An accomplished ghazal and folk singer, she could sing in Kashmiri, Urdu and Hindustani, and even Telugu and Bengali. Shameem was the star performer at her college's cultural events. She did her MA in music from Allahabad

University and was selected by the Jammu and Kashmir Public Service Commission as a music lecturer at the young age of 22. Later, she was appointed to the Government College for Women, Srinagar, the oldest and the biggest women's college of J&K where she had studied up to graduation.

Shameem's father was in the education department and my uncle was his senior. But they were more friends than boss and subordinate. My uncle and the rest of our family used to visit Shameem's home frequently, and they often took me along. I was in college and she was a school-going girl when we first came face to face. We continued to meet each other whenever I would go to their house or they would come to our place. Love blossomed, and we decided to get married when she completed her studies.

Her college principal was one Ms Mehmooda, a Punjabi Muslim whose family was one of the first few highly educated Muslim families in Kashmir. Mehmooda also happened to be Indira ji's close friend. Indira ji used to visit Kashmir often and make it a point to visit the college and attend the cultural events organized in her honour, which were helmed by Shameem. My would-be wife, thus, had begun to interact with Indira ji well before I got to know the latter.

Our wedding ceremonies were to be held from 27 to 29 March 1980. Among the most important rituals is the nikah—equivalent to the 'saat phere' around the sacred fire in Hindu marriages—which was scheduled for 26 March.

The evening before, Sanjay called me up. He informed me that he was supposed to inaugurate a state Mahila Congress convention in Mumbai on 26 March but would not be able to make it because his wife Maneka Gandhi had recently delivered their first child, Feroze Varun Gandhi, and he had to be by her side. He asked me if it was possible for me to go on his behalf. When I reminded him that 26 March was my nikah day, he wondered if some arrangement could be made. He further assured me that he would arrange an aircraft that would take my guests, mostly ministers and MPs, to Srinagar, where the wedding was to happen on 27 March, and bring them back on 29 March after all the ceremonies were complete. He added that I could go along with him in his eight-seater private aircraft and attend the baraat. I was grateful to him for the gesture, but the issue of nikah still remained, though I did mention that the ritual could be done even over the phone, which would be highly unusual.

Finding a way out was now left to me since neither the nikah could be postponed nor the women's convention be missed. I reached out to Mufti and Vijay Dhar, a family friend and son of senior Congress leader Durga Prasad Dhar. The senior Dhar had been one of Indira ji's advisors and was considered the chief architect of the Indian intervention in the 1971 Simla Agreement. Both Mufti and Vijay agreed to be *vakils* (not to be confused with the conventional meaning of a lawyer) who would appear before the maulvi on my behalf, take the marriage proposal to the bride and ensure her acceptance, which is called *quboolnama*.

That arranged, I went to Mumbai and inaugurated the Mahila Congress event on Sanjay's behalf. I could have backed out of this event because I had strong personal reasons, but I did not. Sanjay could have asked for the Mumbai event to be postponed for his own valid personal reasons, but he did not. Both of us were deeply committed to party work even at the cost of our personal and family responsibilities.

Sanjay kept his promise and arranged a small private aircraft piloted by two of his friends. He came along, accompanied by his close relatives. Tytler also accompanied us. Various other Congress ministers and leaders like Vasant Sathe (the then minister for I&B), P.C. Sethi (the then minister for works and housing and petroleum and chemicals) and Mohsina Kidwai took a separate small private aircraft to attend the wedding. More than 100 MPs arrived by passenger flights, for which they paid out of their own pockets.

We landed at Srinagar airport around 11.00 a.m. on the baraat day. CM Sheikh Abdullah had dispatched two senior government officials to the airport to receive Sanjay and inform him that he would be a state guest during his stay in Srinagar. Sanjay asked them whether that courtesy was also being extended to me. On receiving a negative response, he bluntly told them that since he had come for my wedding, he would stay with me. He then busied himself with checking the aircraft and supervising its upkeep since it would be stationed at the airport for the next three days.

The two officials continued to remain on the tarmac, confused over what they should do next. Suddenly, Sanjay turned to them and said sternly, 'May I ask what you people are doing here? You are wasting your time. Don't you have work to do in your offices?' He then told the flustered officials that he would call on the CM later in the day but would not accept the offer of being a state guest.

We stayed at Hotel Broadway in Srinagar, owned by Vijay Dhar's brother-in-law, Krishan Amla. His father Tirath Ram Amla, a Congress Rajya Sabha member, was a fatherly figure and treated me like his son. He was generous enough to not charge anything for boarding and lodging of the guests. Since it was off season in Kashmir, there were hardly any tourists, and we had almost the entire hotel to ourselves.

Having spent three days in Srinagar, we returned to Delhi on the morning of 30 March. The same evening, I hosted a reception in Delhi for guests, mostly parliamentarians, at the spacious Akbar Road official residence of Maragatham Chandrasekar, a Rajya Sabha MP and former Union minister. Both Indira ji and Sanjay attended the reception for two hours. She was pleased to encounter that same young girl Shameem who had entertained her on her many trips to the women's college in Kashmir with her lilting voice but now as my wife.

After we were married, Shameem's singing skills brought her to the attention of well-known music composers of the Hindi film industry, stalwarts such as Naushad, Ravindra Jain and Khayyam. She even recorded songs for them. Naushad sahab particularly took a keen interest in shaping her music skills and provided music to six of her songs. He would devote half a day for a few days for those recordings.

She also sang for quite some time for a number of TV serials, including *The Sword of Tipu Sultan*, *The Great Maratha* and *Jai Hanuman*, which turned out to be big draws. Initially, she would only sing the lyrics penned by others, but during my time as CM, when I was busy and she was relatively free, she began to write and sing her own songs, which turned out to be big hits in Kashmir, particularly the song 'Mere Jannat Mere Kashmir' (My heaven, my Kashmir).

Unfortunately, she was struck by a medical complication that affected her vocal cords. She had to undergo two major surgeries, one in the first week of June 2008 and the other in November 2014, at a hospital in Mumbai. Consequently, she had to give up singing, though her voice remains as sweet as before. Shameem was awarded the Padma Shri by the Government of India in 2005 in recognition of her contribution to the art.

Destiny Strikes a Blow

A few months after our marriage, Sanjay expressed his desire to conduct an extensive tour of J&K in the fourth week of June. The Indira–Sheikh Accord had shackled the functioning of the Congress party there, and Sanjay was keen to revive the morale of our workers. So I proceeded to Jammu and Srinagar in mid-June to prepare the groundwork for his visit. I could hit two birds with one stone during my visit. I had a few family weddings to attend. My wife accompanied me on the trip. I interacted with our party office bearers in the state and gave each one of them a set of responsibilities to ensure that Sanjay's tour was a success.

By chance, we had scheduled our flight back to Delhi on 23 June 1980. On the way to the Jammu airport with my wife, I asked the driver of the vehicle to tune in to the news on All India Radio (AIR); it was 1.00 p.m. The newsreader was already midway announcing the headlines. I caught the words 'died in a plane crash' and continued to listen. It was then that I first learnt of Sanjay's death. It left my wife and I stunned. Speechless and overcome with grief, we reached the airport and boarded the aircraft. A few minutes later, Sheikh sahab entered the plane. He had received the news earlier and had rushed to catch the flight to Delhi.

From the Delhi airport, I drove straight to Indira ji's private office on Akbar Road, where his body lay in state. The place was teeming with people. I could only catch a glimpse of my dear leader before collapsing. That was my last recollection before I awoke and found myself at my residence. Karunanidhi was at my bedside. We hugged each other and cried. When I remarked that we should proceed to the cremation ground, he said that the cremation had already taken place. I wondered at the quickness, and he informed me that I had been in an unconscious state for the last two–three days. I would regain sense in between, only to cry out incoherently and behave erratically, and the doctor had to sedate me. I also had been on drips over the last few hours.

I was still finding it difficult to comprehend the reality, and it would take me days to reconcile to the tragic loss, especially since it was just two-and-a-half months earlier that Sanjay had spent three full days with me during my wedding.

Thereafter, certain unfortunate developments happened in Indira ji's household. The rift between Indira ji and Sanjay's widow Maneka left me disconsolate. I was torn between my loyalty towards Indira ji and regard for the family of my leader, friend and guide, Sanjay, whom I loved dearly. But there were people who exploited the divide for their gains, without caring for the sensitivity of the situation.

4

RAJIV: THE RELUCTANT POLITICIAN

Sanjay Gandhi's untimely death at the young age of 34 had dealt a grievous blow to his mother, wife, brother, other members of the family and friends and admirers like us. It had also adversely impacted the functioning of the IYC. Sanjay had guided the IYC through the best and the worst times: He helped us shape the organization's policies and five-point programmes and assisted in their implementation. His mere presence resolved many of the challenges that we faced along the way, since his word was final. This was not out of fear but respect and his comradeship. We had benefitted from his leadership skills in the post-Emergency period (1977–79) and in the triumphant 1979 elections, but he was gone now. We had become leaderless and rudderless. The void would be hard to fill.

Naturally, we looked to Indira ji for additional support. But in those early days, she too was consumed by the tragedy and had withdrawn from the functioning of the IYC. She would often tell me to go ahead and conduct the business of the organization as I deemed fit. I struggled with the duties; the truth is that even my heart was not in the job. I pined for Sanjay's reassuring presence.

One day, in July 1980, barely 40 days after Sanjay's death, I received a phone call from R.K. Dhawan, saying that the she wished to see me urgently. My office was at Janpath Road, and I hurried to meet her at her South Block office. On reaching there, Dhawan sent a slip of paper with my name to her chamber. I asked him if she was in a meeting. He answered in the affirmative, saying that Pranab da (then minister of commerce, steel and mines and the leader of the Rajya

Sabha) and P. Shiv Shankar (then minister of law, justice and company affairs) were with her. I reconciled to a long wait. Imagine my surprise when I was ushered in within a couple of minutes.

The two ministers and she were deep in some discussion, with several files open before them. On seeing me enter, she asked Pranab da and Shiv Shankar to leave, saying that the deliberations would continue some other time. I felt a little embarrassed that two senior ministers were peremptorily dismissed on account of my arrival. I am sure that they too must have been surprised. Once they left, she signalled me to take a chair and asked me about the activities of the IYC in general. I briefed her on whatever little that was happening. Then, out of the blue, she took out a few newspapers and placed them before me. She asked if I had seen them. I replied in the affirmative.

She asked, 'What did you see?'

'Nothing unusual,' I replied.

'Didn't you notice the news item which said that Maneka had attended a tree plantation programme along with a few other Congress leaders? It is not even 40 days since Sanjay's death and she is already attending events. How could she do it!'

There was no anger in Indira ji's voice. I wondered if I should respond. I decided to keep quiet, considering that it was a family matter in which I should not interfere.

We then spoke of other matters. She suddenly shot another question: 'Don't you think Rajiv should join politics?' I was surprised by the question but also understood the faith she had in me to raise such an issue. One reason for reposing such trust in me was because she knew of my proximity to Sanjay. The fact that he had attended my wedding was also known to her.

I had never given a thought to it and told her so, but added that it would be a good idea if Rajiv was to join politics. 'But that's where the problem is,' she said, 'He's not interested, although I would like him to help me.' Indira ji then asked me whether I knew him well. I replied that I knew him only casually. I had met him on many occasions while travelling from Delhi to J&K and on the return journey or occasionally with Sanjay. Rajiv was a commercial airline pilot and, in those days, piloted the Avro aircraft, which flew from

Delhi to Chandigarh, Jammu and Srinagar and back to Delhi via the same route. We would greet each other when we happened to meet. Rajiv, of course, knew that I was close to his younger brother. He had regard for me and I respected him too.

Indira ji asked me to think over the idea and discuss it further with her the following day, with a caution that I should keep the matter a secret for some time. Possibly, I was the first person in whom she had confided her wish to have Rajiv enter politics.

The 'Bring Rajiv' Plan

I deliberated over the issue through the day and prepared a plan of action. The following day, I met Indira ji and shared my strategy. State IYC units would, through their respective presidents and office bearers, make a passionate appeal seeking Rajiv's entry into politics. It would not be enough, I pointed out to her, for the national office bearers alone to make that request; it should have a pan-India demand. A nationwide buzz would thus be created in favour of the idea over a period of few weeks. Indira ji liked the suggestion.

But the problem of Rajiv's reluctance still remained. Would he accept the appeal? Rajiv had already told her that he would be going to Hyderabad to attend an advanced pilot training course, which he did. However, we did not relent either. The IYC across the country kept the pot boiling, issuing statements regularly in favour of Rajiv's entry into politics. We succeeded in creating an 'environment'.

A few weeks later, Indira ji was on a short visit to Kashmir, and I accompanied her from Delhi. In the aircraft, she asked me to suggest some names on our return, to be appointed as the all-India president of the IYC. When she was returning to Delhi after a two–three day stay in Srinagar, I handed her a list of a few names I had written down at the Srinagar airport. I informed her that I would be staying back for a few more days. I had not written my name in that list. The next day, I heard the news of my appointment as president of the IYC on the radio while I was travelling from Srinagar to Pahalgam.

On my return to New Delhi, I thanked her for my appointment. She told me, 'Henceforth, you should choose your national team and state presidents yourself.' She added, 'There is no need to take my permission.' Since Sanjay had dealt with such matters earlier, she said that she would not interfere in the internal functioning of the IYC. Appreciating my work during 1977–80 as general secretary of the youth wing and earlier as state president of J&K, she said, 'You are aware of the capacity and capabilities of Youth Congress leaders at various levels, so it's better that you select your team.'

Subsequently, I reconstituted the team at the national level and also made some changes at the state level. I think I was the first and last IYC president who had a free hand to appoint all-India general secretaries and state presidents and, of course, other office bearers at various levels too. Sadly, matters have continued to deteriorate to such an extent that today, even the appointments of district-level chiefs are approved by the central leadership and the Congress president, without them even being aware of the people they are appointing.

It is rather ironical that this kind of freedom existed in the organization during Indira ji's time, considering her reputation of being dictatorial in her approach. But my personal experience of working with her, both in the organization and as a part of her Council of Ministers, is contrary to that. On one occasion, she forwarded two names to me, with a recommendation that they be considered for the post of general secretary of the IYC at the national level. One was an office bearer of National Students' Union of India (NSUI) and another was a female corporator and district president of the Delhi Congress. The problem was that they did not meet the criteria laid down for elevation to that post. I, therefore, did not proceed with the process and instead wrote to Indira ji, explaining how the two did not meet the standards for their inclusion and, hence, could not be accommodated.

About four days later, Dhawan called me and said that Indira ji wanted to meet me at her South Block office. On reaching there, I found her busy attending to files. I sat there silently, preparing myself for a scolding that was certain to follow because I had refused to honour her wishes. After a while, she looked up, and I seized upon the chance to launch a spirited defence of my action. She said, 'Did I ask you for an explanation?' I immediately shut up. She continued,

'I asked you to come over so that I could personally compliment you. Keep it up!'

I sat dumbfounded. Indira ji must have sensed my state of utter confusion. She said smilingly, 'You did the right thing. I was not aware of the criteria details, which is why I had authorized you in the beginning to make your own team and appointments, since you know the functioning and working of the Youth Congress much better than I do.' She continued, 'Somebody gave me those names and I forwarded them to you for appropriate action. I cannot be always right. I am glad you declined my request.'

That was Indira ji: She was very accommodating and would listen carefully to any suggestions coming from any quarter and would accept and implement that.

A few months later, it struck me that Sanjay's birth anniversary would fall on 14 December 1980. I told Indira ji that we (the IYC and the parent organization) should celebrate the day in a big way to keep his legacy alive. She was receptive to the idea. I organized a massive gathering at Ajmal Khan Park, Delhi, which was attended by more than 50,000 IYC and Congress workers. H.K.L Bhagat, Sajjan Kumar and Tytler helped me in a big way by mobilizing a huge crowd for the meeting.

A dais had been set up for the PM; Rajiv was also invited for the event. He arrived with Indira ji. The PM was escorted to the dais and Rajiv made his way to the front row on the ground, where a number of senior party leaders were seated.

After receiving the PM and accompanying her to the dais, I rushed towards Rajiv and asked him to come up. As expected, he politely refused. I persisted and he resisted, determined to scuttle my initiative. Then, not-so-politely, I firmly locked my arm into his and practically dragged him up to the stage. The gentleman was so flustered and dazed by my aggression that his resistance crumbled. Indira ji watched the happenings with surprise and amusement; she had no previous inkling that Rajiv would be brought on the stage.

The event began with speeches by Bhagat and Tytler, who recalled Sanjay's contributions to the Congress party, its youth wing and to the society through his five-point programme. His lead role in the victory of the Congress party in the general elections was also prominently mentioned. My turn to speak as president of the IYC came just before the PM's speech.

I had spent the last few days preparing the speech. I wanted it to be unlike my earlier speeches on different occasions, with an aim to bring special focus on Rajiv. I had researched the social, religious and historical environment that had prevailed prior to and during the days of various religious and social reformers centuries ago—how they had succeeded in transforming society by their actions and determination and how they had tackled the challenges that they faced in establishing a just and ethical social order. I had also studied the role played by social and political reformers such as Gandhi.

As I stood up and began my address, I spoke first about the prominent figures of various religions and their roles in reforming society, the country and the world. Rounding that section up with an emphasis on their contribution in changing the social mindset, I similarly dealt with the social reformers and political stalwarts. Thereafter, I spoke about Sanjay's leadership in bringing about positive changes in society through his five-point programme and remarked that he gave the youth of the country a new lead and purposeful direction, restoring them to their rightful place in society through his social programmes impacting the public. I said, 'At a time when we needed him the most, the cruel hands of death snatched him away. Therefore, it is in the fitness of things that Rajiv Gandhi, Sanjay's elder brother, should take upon himself the responsibility to complete the tasks left unfinished by his brother.'

After I finished, the crowd burst into applause, which lingered for a long time. Indira ji clapped the loudest; she seemed pleased. As I took my seat next to her, she patted me on the back and whispered that I had delivered a really good speech. The concluding speech she gave mesmerized the entire crowd and provided us a new energy and strength to rebuild the youth organization once again.

She congratulated me for a second time while approaching her car downstairs. She said that at one point, she had begun to worry that I would equate Sanjay and Rajiv with religious leaders, but I had adroitly steered away from such sycophancy. As she drove away,

I wondered and hoped if a baby step had been taken to induct the reticent Rajiv into politics.

Thereafter, Indira ji, on many occasions, impressed upon Rajiv that she wanted him to lend a helping hand to her in the party's affairs. Rajiv must have also realized that, after Sanjay's death, his mother was overburdened with the task of managing the party and the government. She had been maintaining a punishing schedule, working from 8.00 a.m. right through the day till 2.00 a.m. He must have concluded that he had to help her out. But there was one more hurdle.

Indira ji had once remarked to me that Sonia Gandhi was not in favour of Rajiv joining politics. One of our Youth Congress leaders, Naeem from Hyderabad, had designed a huge poster of Rajiv, with Sanjay's five-point programme depicted on each of Rajiv's fingers. It was an impressive image and Indira ji showed it to Sonia ji, in the hope that she would like it and change her mind about her husband joining politics. I think it worked.

Finally, Rajiv relented and gave up his job to take up the responsibilities of the party. He was persuaded to contest the May 1981 Lok Sabha by-election from the vacant Amethi seat. Immediately after Rajiv filed his nomination, I accompanied Indira ji from Delhi to Amethi by helicopter for a day-long visit. She asked me to get my trusted colleagues to be in charge of each assembly constituency. On our return in the evening, Indira ji asked me to tell Mian Bashir Ahmed, a religious and political leader of the Gujjar community from J&K, to spare few days for campaigning in Amethi, since Amethi had a sizeable Muslim Gujjar population. But she cautioned me that being a *pir* (spiritual guide) of his community, he was used to non-vegetarian food—I had to ensure that he got meat and chicken in his food. She further asked me to ensure good arrangements for his stay. Her attitude showed her concern for her party leaders, so much so she would know and remember each leader's food habits.

On her instructions, I led the campaign with the assistance of five leaders from outside the state of my choice, one in charge of each constituency that made up the Amethi Lok Sabha seat. Rajiv stayed at the residence of Congress leader Sanjay Singh and managed the campaign from there. Singh, being an MLA and erstwhile raja of

Amethi, was of great assistance during the entire elections. Besides my team, three other persons—Arun Nehru, Captain Amarinder Singh and Ajitabh Bachchan, the younger brother of superstar, Amitabh Bachchan—camped at the constituency in their capacity as Rajiv's friends.

The campaign itself had some interesting moments. Once it became known that Rajiv would contest from Amethi, various senior leaders of the party began to fall head over heels to offer their support in campaigning. Haryana CM Bhajan Lal arrived in Amethi by a helicopter. An annoyed Indira ji ordered him to head back to Haryana without a moment's delay. She made it clear that no one from outside would campaign there.

Rajiv, however, was a reluctant politician in the beginning. He only listened to our speeches and would speak just a few words. But he was industrious, intelligent and a quick leaner. Within a few days of the campaign, he became a proficient speaker. Not surprisingly, he won the by-election handsomely and entered Parliament in May that year.

Sanjay's first death anniversary fell on 23 June 1981. To observe the day, I directed all IYC state presidents to organize blood donation camps across the country, right from the district to state levels. Early that morning, as I was about to leave for Shanti Van to offer flowers at Sanjay's samadhi, I received a telephone call from Bhishma Narain Singh (the then minister for works, housing and parliamentary affairs). He said that on the previous night (22 June), Indira ji had asked him to arrange for one mango sapling to be planted on the samadhi of Sanjay. But the next morning, he had received another call from the PM directing that I should plant this sapling instead of her. I was overwhelmed that the PM had chosen me for the task. Within five minutes, I received the sapling from the minister's house and left for the samadhi to pay my respects and plant the mango sapling.

After flowers were offered at the samadhi, where thousands of IYC leaders and workers had gathered to pay homage, we rushed to the Talkatora Indoor Stadium, where a national blood donation camp, one of the largest in the country, was organized by the IYC. Indira ji inaugurated the camp. Besides me, Rajiv, Tytler and other senior leaders donated blood in the presence of thousands of enthusiastic donors, a large number of whom were disappointed by the paucity of the facilities in blood banks.

Immediately after that, I took a flight to Srinagar, where I had to inaugurate another blood donation camp. My wife was the first donor, followed by a few hundred boys. It was possibly the first time that IYC workers in Srinagar had donated blood. By that evening, about one lakh IYC leaders and workers had donated blood across the country. Unfortunately, this type of dedication and social service is totally lacking today in the IYC and other frontal organizations of the Congress party.

Rajiv Fills a Void

After this nationwide initiative, I addressed a press conference in Srinagar, in which I announced the expansion of the national council of the IYC by appointing more than a dozen young MPs as members of the council; Rajiv was one of them. I was of the opinion that Sanjay's death anniversary could be the best occasion to bring Rajiv into the IYC fold. Hence, besides the national-level IYC office bearers and state presidents who normally constituted the national council members, MPs and others people such as Rajiv, Arun Nehru, Rajesh Pilot, P.A. Sangma, Eduardo Faleiro, Arif Mohammad Khan, Ashok Gehlot, Subhash Yadav, Ranjitsinh Gaekwad, N.K. Ramalingam, Rameshwar Neekhra, Chingwang Konyak, Mrityunjaya Nayak, Sukhbans Kaur, Manoranjan Bhagta, Gufran-e-Azam and Biren Mohanty, were included.

After the national council was reconstituted, Indira ji said that I should give more exposure to Rajiv by taking him around the country. I took up her advice with vigour and began to organize national council meetings in various parts of the country, right from Kashmir to Shillong, thus providing Rajiv an opportunity to interact with a cross-section of people in different parts of the country. It also provided him an opportunity to understand the functioning of the party and the proceedings of the council's meeting. It helped the former pilot to come to his own and prepare for bigger roles ahead.

What remained central to all those arrangements was the plan to make Rajiv the leader of the IYC at the earliest so that he could lead the organization from the front. So far, things had gone along expected lines. Rajiv, as member of the national council, had begun attending IYC events, such as blood donation camps, tree plantations, farmer rallies, training camps, slum clearance drives, anti-dowry programmes and many other social and political programmes.

Then, for the final takeover of the leadership, I planned a national convention of the IYC at Bangalore (now Bengaluru) on 29–30 December 1981. Workers and office bearers of the IYC from the district to the national level were to attend in thousands. Invitations were also extended to senior leaders of the parent organization, including CMs, PCC presidents and Union ministers, though the invitation did not mention a word about the proposal to elevate Rajiv to the leader of the IYC. Indira ji was, of course, aware of every detail and accordingly briefed by me from time to time. She had also accepted my request to be the chief guest on the inaugural day of the convention.

On 28 December, when I was to leave for Bengaluru for the two-day convention, I received a message that Indira ji wished to see me, so I rushed to her residence. She pointed out to me that the principal focus was to be on Rajiv's elevation, but that focus would be diluted if she were to be present, since all attention would shift to her. She, therefore, suggested dropping out but added that her absence need not be announced in advance. She had a point that I could not dispute. I left for Bengaluru and did not inform even the officer bearers about the change in her programme; it was announced the next day only hours before the event was to begin.

The convention got off to a resounding start. More than 25,000 delegates were in attendance at a massive ground in the city. Reports were presented by various office bearers, listing out the activities their respective state units had conducted over the past months. Thereafter, a resolution was moved, appealing to Rajiv to become the leader of the IYC. Every single hand in the gathering went up in approval.

Rajiv had been informed about the resolution in advance, and he had not objected. He reconciled to the idea of being an active politician, setting aside his earlier reservations. Moreover, by that time, he was already a Lok Sabha MP. Like Sanjay, he too did not come to occupy any official position in the youth wing but was chosen as the IYC leader. Finally, the void left by Sanjay's tragic death would be filled.

A few days later, Indira ji called me to her Akbar Road residence. Rajiv was present too. She told Rajiv, 'Now both of you have to work together for years to come. Go with Azad (this is how she would address me) to different parts of the country, but remember one thing: He has a mind of his own and calls a spade a spade for the good of the party. If he can say "no" to me, you too will not be spared, but that doesn't means he disrespects you.'

From that day, Rajiv and I worked closely till his death. He neither interfered in my working nor did he suggest any names for appointment at any level in the organization. He remained respectful to the chair of the president, a post I continued to occupy till I became a Union minister in the middle of 1982. Although Rajiv and I had differences of opinion on a number of issues and would argue for hours together, one of us would eventually concede after being convinced by the other. Rajiv never took offence whenever I differed with him, even when he later became the PM and the Congress party president. At times, he would concede; on other occasions, I gave way. It was a great understanding that we shared, premised on mutual respect and trust.

Rao and the Youngster

I was immensely relieved that the leadership issue of the IYC had been resolved at last. It was time to look ahead with fresh vigour and enthusiasm. I then planned to organize an international youth conference in Delhi in January 1982, in which youth leaders and delegates from across the world would participate to discuss issues such as disarmament, conflict resolution, etc. The theme of the convention was 'Problems of Human Survival and Development', and the event was to be held at Vigyan Bhavan.

It was to be a non-government event. I was in touch with almost 100 youth organizations of various countries and had received positive feedback from them. Having done the groundwork, I approached the PM with a request that she inaugurate the international event and give me a suitable inaugural date. She called up EAM Rao on the RAX (phone for internal communication) and asked him to guide me in this regard.

I went straight to Rao with the proposal. He asked me some questions but seemed indifferent. Eventually, he said that I was filling the PM's ears with all sorts of fantastic and imaginary ideas, and that this youth conference would be a non-starter. How could such a huge event be successfully held without government's involvement? Even with the government's participation, functions of that kind were difficult to organize, he said, and virtually dismissed the suggestion.

He had probably thought that I would bury the matter, but I was not going to give up easily; I went to the PM and reported the matter to her. She said, 'You go ahead. Leave him out. This is the problem with these seniors. They don't encourage younger people to take on responsibilities.' She added that if participants from more than 20 nations came, she would inaugurate the event. She further said that I should keep her informed about the progress.

The PM told Dhawan to give me a date for the inauguration, and I proceeded accordingly by writing letters to various international youth organizations, seeking their participation. Rao was kept out of the loop. I was determined to make the event a success; after all, it was now a matter of prestige for me and my team. I jumped into action and started the preparations. D.P. Ray, a general secretary, and Anand Sharma were of great help in drafting the resolutions. However, the contribution of Anil Mathrani, in charge of foreign affairs in the IYC, cannot be forgotten. He was the main person who coordinated and ensured the participation of maximum number of countries. He worked practically 24 hours a day for a month, since the delegates of some countries were only available in the night, given the time difference.

More than 500 delegates from nearly 75 countries, including a few dozen youth affairs ministers and MPs from different countries, participated. Each country was represented by five–six delegates. Countries aligned with the two superpowers of the time, the Union of Soviet Socialist Republics (USSR) and the United States, were equally represented, to the extent that two countries hostile to each other, Iran and Iraq, were also represented by their youth affairs ministers at the event. When the confirmation from more than 20 countries was received, I informed the PM, and she directed the foreign secretary to vet the resolutions that were to be adopted, so as to ensure that they were non-aligned in nature and in accordance with the Government of India's stated policy on international relations.

The three-day convention was held from 22 to 24 January. On 21 January, around 10.00 p.m., I met Indira ji at her residence and asked her whether I should pick her up in the morning from her residence. She suggested that I should be at Vigyan Bhavan and attend to the foreign delegates; she would join us there. I had walked only a few steps out of the house when she called me back and asked about my speech. When I said it was ready, she enquired as to who had prepared it. I informed her that it had been done in-house by the international youth affairs cell of the IYC.

She thought for a while and said I should send the draft speech to her in the next 15 minutes, so that she could have a look at it. Since my house at 1, Rajaji Marg, was a couple of minutes away from her residence, I sent across to her a copy of the speech through Dhawan. I received it back past midnight from one of her staff members. The PM had read it thoroughly and made appropriate changes by her own hand. I felt proud that the PM of the country had taken the trouble of going through my speech and improving upon it. Unfortunately, I did not preserve the draft speech with her corrections.

Being the president of the host country's Youth Congress, I was designated as the chairman of the international conference. The IYC delegation was represented by former IYC chief Ramchandra Rath; Rajiv Gandhi, member of the national council; Arun Kumar Singh Munna, general secretary of the IYC and Vimal Negi, joint secretary of the IYC. Rao was not present for the event; he had not been invited.

After my brief speech, the PM delivered a well-received inaugural address, with cheers from the international delegates. She was extremely happy and repeatedly congratulated me and my team. Later, she hosted a dinner for the delegates at Hyderabad House, for which she invited Rao too. Needless to say, the foreign delegates were delighted to have her amidst them. While everybody was busy with the food, she took me aside and said with a twinkle in her eyes, 'Call him (Rao) for the concluding function.'

Meanwhile, the EAM had got positive feedback about the first day's proceedings from his officials. At the dinner at Hyderabad House, I went to him and sought an appointment for the next morning before the start of the second day of the conference. He called me over straightaway. He greeted me warmly, congratulating me on the success of the conference and remarked, 'But you did not invite me.' It was a direct question, but I could not give a direct reply, as that would have been improper. Rao was an erudite and soft-spoken man, and he had been good to me. I had enormous respect for his scholarly bearing—he was deeply knowledgeable in Indian and Western philosophy, religion, culture and spirituality, and was proficient in a dozen languages.

I replied that I did not wish to burden him, since he had expressed disinterest in the event. However, diplomatically, I added that because the inaugural day had the PM's address, he would have had no role to play. I added that I had come to invite him for the concluding day's event and address. He sportingly agreed and, rather sweetly, admitted that he had underestimated my ability to pull off a function of that proportion. 'Such large-scale events require an entire government's might to succeed, but you did it without our help. I am delighted that youngsters like you and your colleagues have matured to shoulder future responsibilities.'

I was touched by his remarks. I am sure his initial tepid response was not borne out of any ill-will. He must have genuinely felt that the conference would not turn out to be so big, and that involving the PM with a minor function would have been inappropriate.

The Muslim Face in Indira's Council of Ministers

A few months later, the Soviet ambassador to India, Yuliy Vorontsov, met me at my residence and extended an invitation to my wife and me to visit the Soviet Union on a two-week holiday, courtesy of the youth division of the Communist Party of the Soviet Union. I accepted the invitation subject to my visit being cleared by the PM.

When I met her, she unhesitatingly gave the permission and insisted that I must take along Shameem unfailingly.

The invitation had come with an added 'attraction'—spending 15 days at the Black Sea. According to the host organization, most of the senior office bearers of the Communist Party would go for a holiday there. My wife and I arrived in Moscow and were received by representatives of the Youth Federation, besides a few Indian embassy staff. Saiyid Nurul Hasan was the then Indian ambassador to the Soviet Union, and he hosted a dinner for my wife and me on the very first day. A historian with a taste for literature, he was gracious and always treated me with great love and affection. I addressed him as chacha (uncle).

The following day, my wife and I proceeded to the Black Sea from the Moscow airport by a special Russian State aircraft. Even though we nurtured romantic visions of the place, we were to be terribly disappointed. It might have been a nice place for the retiring political types in the twilight of their life, but not for young people like us, who had been married for only two years. We could see nothing else but the enormous expanse of the sea. We began to tire of the place within a couple of days and decided to amend our programme.

A friend of mine, Pritam Thukral, had been pestering us to visit him and his family in London. Having come that far, I told my wife that we could use the rest of our vacation time to explore the UK and Switzerland for good measure. She was delighted, and I decided to call Hasan chacha and requested him to ask his staff to book our tickets from Moscow to London, for which we would, of course, pay.

That evening, the landline at my resort room rang. It was Hasan chacha. He was chuckling at the other end. I wondered what the joke was. He said that my vacation stood curtailed and that I should forget about my trip to London, since Indira ji had summoned me back to Delhi immediately. When I enquired about the reason, he said that I was to be sworn in as a junior Union minister. I was taken aback and told him that if the PM had entertained such a thought, she should not have allowed me to take the vacation. 'You know madam's way of work, she would never disclose anything before time,' he responded. Now, this was a new problem. I told him that I had no desire to become a minister, since I had a few more years to continue in the IYC—in those days, 35 years of age was the limit fixed to remain in the youth wing of the party.

I requested him to convey to the PM my inability to return. Besides, I added, I had no desire to be a minister. Scandalized by my impetuosity, he flatly refused to be an intermediary, explaining that it would be against protocol for him to directly convey such a message to the PM. I requested him to at least send a telegram to the Prime Minister's Office (PMO) under my name, saying that I didn't want to become a minister and hence I was not returning. This, he agreed to do. Meanwhile, I informed the leaders of the Youth Federation and the protocol officer accompanying us about the change in programme, and they promptly arranged a special aircraft for our return to Moscow.

The following morning, my wife and I were back in Moscow by the same special aircraft that had brought us to the Black Sea, and from the airport, we went straight to the ambassador's residence to collect our tickets to London. In London, we stayed with my friend Pritam Thukral and his gracious wife Mona. They ensured that we saw the best locations in the UK and Switzerland, and they drove us through almost all important regions of these places. Both husband and wife were good drivers too. We had a memorable time.

A fortnight later, I landed in Delhi and, the very next day, met the PM at her South Block office. She enquired about my vacation, and I gave her the lowdown. She had a good laugh over my opinion of the Black Sea and said, 'You did the right thing going to Switzerland.' She then added, 'This is the age for you to see new places.' I was relieved that she was not annoyed by my refusal to return early when I was asked to take oath.

Then she dropped the bombshell. She said that I was to take oath as minister the next day, subject to the availability of the president! I looked at her open-mouthed. I had presumed that I had deftly wriggled out of the situation. There was no escaping the inevitable now. I made one last-ditch attempt, suggesting that she should instead induct the veteran leader from Jammu, Girdhari Lal Dogra. The PM said that he had already served for almost three decades as a minister in J&K. Besides, she added significantly, 'I want a Ghulam Nabi from

J&K.' Implicit in her remark was that she wanted a Muslim face from the state in her ministry.

I took oath of office the following day. The next day, I learnt that I had been made deputy minister for law, justice and company affairs. My troubles didn't seem to end. Law and justice was Greek to me! It is true that I had done my LLB, but it was through a correspondence course, and I had got through by learning the syllabus by rote. In reality, I understood nothing of the subject. I explained all of this to Indira ji. She said, 'I had asked Dhawan to tell me about your degree and he, quoting from *Who's Who* (a book of MPs), told me that you were MSc LLB. Hence, I gave you law and justice.' Finally, after hearing me out, she suggested that I make do with the portfolio until she affected a reshuffle six–seven months down the line.

Incidentally, when I got elected a second time to the Lok Sabha from Washim and when the time came for a revision of Parliament's *Who's Who* in 1985, I promptly deleted the LLB part from my name and retained the MSc in zoology, which I had passed in first class from Kashmir University, thus ensuring that I did not fall into the law trap again anytime in the future!

My Cabinet minister was Jagannath Kaushal, a former Advocate General and a lawyer of repute who had earlier been a district and sessions judge as well as the governor of Bihar. He was a kind soul and, understanding my dilemma, did not burden me with much work.

However, he asked me to handle all Waqf-related work, which came under the law ministry; it was a subject with which I was familiar. I was also aware that large chunks of Waqf properties across the country had been appropriated by various people, including government departments both at the Centre and in the states, and many of those were lying vacant for future encroachments.

Subsequently, I told the PM that state and central governments should relinquish their hold on at least those properties that were lying unused. On my request, she agreed to write letters to all CMs in this regard. As a follow-up measure, I visited a number of states and met their CMs. Within six months, I succeeded in retrieving a few hundred properties from the possession of state governments and various organizations. It is an achievement that I remain proud of. But, unfortunately, following a change in my portfolio after six months, most of these properties were encroached by private and other agencies, thus depriving the Waqf board of these precious pieces of land. My idea was to construct schools and hospitals for the community, but that dream remained unfinished after I left the law ministry.

My stint as deputy minister also gave me a glimpse of Indira ji's far-sightedness. There are several incidents that are worth narrating, but the one that stands out in memory had to do with my trip to Sri Lanka as deputy minister in 1982. It was around September–October 1982, and I was in Shillong canvassing for a party candidate contesting for assembly by-elections. I received a message from the governor's office that I had been summoned by Indira Gandhi and had to reach Delhi immediately. Wondering about the urgency, I rushed back to Delhi via Guwahati and met Dhawan, who informed me that the PM wanted me to attend a forthcoming international law ministers' conference in Sri Lanka.

It had so happened that when Law Minister Kaushal had sought permission for himself from the PM to attend the conference and the relevant file landed at the PM's desk, she struck down his name and replaced it with mine, with a noting that I would gain some experience of international government events by attending the Sri Lanka function. Besides, I would also get an opportunity to reconnect with the SSM leader Dr Ariyaratne, with whom I had spent weeks together in 1973 as a student. I was pleasantly surprised that the PM had remembered the incident, which I had narrated to her a few years ago. After attending the conference, I was pleased to meet Ariyaratne. He was delighted by my progress in politics.

Some seven months after my induction into the law ministry in 1983, there was a media buzz about a ministerial reshuffle. I rushed to the PMO. It was around 1.00–1.30 p.m. As I entered, Indira ji asked me if it was something urgent, since she was heading home for lunch. I reminded her about the change in my portfolio. She smiled and asked for my choice. Without the slightest hesitation, I requested her to give me the charge of the I&B ministry. She smiled again and agreed. In those days, the I&B ministry was considered an important assignment. There were no private channels, and the I&B minister was a much sought-after person for public functions because the organizers knew that the I&B minister's presence assured them wide publicity on state-run Doordarshan (DD) and AIR. The I&B minister would also develop contacts with mediapersons, which is always useful to a politician.

Thus, I got the portfolio of my choice. My Cabinet minister was H.K.L. Bhagat. I had a good equation with him since my early days in the IYC. According to the distribution of work, he handled television-related matters, while I took care of the various other arms of the ministry, such as field publicity, songs-and-drama division and radio in particular. He had little time for ministerial work in any case, busy as he was with Delhi's politics. Besides, he was also the Cabinet minister for parliamentary affairs.

During my student days in Kashmir, BBC Urdu dominated the listeners' space since it relayed, among other things, hourly news bulletins. In contrast, AIR had just three news bulletins in a day—one each in the morning, afternoon and evening. I used to think that if I had a chance someday to change this situation, I would do it. That opportunity had now arrived. In the first month of my tenure as junior minister for I&B, I floated the idea of an hourly radio news bulletin on the lines of the BBC, put the proposal on a file and sent it to my senior minister, Bhagat, for his approval. Unfortunately, the Cabinet minister promptly shot it down. The file went back to the secretary concerned, who brought it to my notice and said that the senior minister had rejected my proposal.

Unfazed, I called up Dhawan and sought an appointment with the PM. Dhawan was a wonderful person, unquestionably devoted and loyal to Indira ji. He was aware that his boss had a soft corner for me, so he always accommodated my request for meetings with her. I was called that very evening, and I narrated the entire episode to the PM. She asked Dhawan to get Bhagat on the RAX, and told him sternly, 'Bhagat ji, this is the problem with old people like you and me. We don't think of anything new and will also not let others think and do something novel. I envy this boy for having thought of the idea of hourly news on radio. I wish it had occurred to me when I was I&B minister (in Lal Bahadur Shastri's government).' Then she abruptly disconnected the phone. Bhagat, I am sure, must have stuttered and stammered at the other end.

When I returned to my Shastri Bhavan office, I learnt that Bhagat had been fervently enquiring about my arrival back to office. But before I could go to meet him, he entered my cabin and said, 'Arrey, you got me a dressing down from madam! You should have come to me and persuaded me. I would have agreed. You are free to do anything, mere baap!' He called for the file and observed that my suggestion was excellent and ought to be immediately implemented. Thus, I got my student days' dream of hourly news implemented on the AIR.

5

THAT OCTOBER OF 1984

My tenure as the deputy minister for I&B was a great learning experience. It was also a revelation of the importance the portfolio attracted. Although a junior minister, I had direct access to the PM. But that was not the reason why people wanted me to attend their functions. The real reason was that my presence as I&B minister ensured them publicity on radio, DD and the print media.

A delegation of an association of paan sellers once approached me and requested my presence at one of their national conferences to be held in New Delhi. I smiled and told my visitors that I understood that they were looking for some free publicity on the state-run television channel. Taken aback by my candour, they sheepishly admitted to the plan behind the invite. Since I did not wish to embarrass them further, I assured them that the event would get the required coverage but also expressed my inability to attend. I warned them that if I went, I would speak against the paan-chewing habit.

I then narrated to them an incident that had turned me fiercely against paan and tobacco. The first and only time I consumed betel leaf in my life was in 1976, when I was the president of the J&K Youth Congress. I had come to Delhi to attend the national council meeting and stayed at Jammu and Kashmir House at Chanakyapuri. Across the road was Madhya Pradesh Bhavan, where my friend and general secretary of the IYC from Madhya Pradesh, Gufran-e-Azam, was put up. The day after I arrived, he picked me up from Jammu and Kashmir House to attend the meeting at 10, Janpath, then the national headquarters of the IYC. At the end of the party's deliberations, Gufran suggested that we spend some time at Connaught Place (CP). He had a car, and we drove there.

He had coffee, and I settled for tea. He was addicted to paan, so we made our way to a well-known paan shop in the area. While I stood at a distance, he went to the counter and asked me whether I too would have one. I said yes—after all, paan was nothing but a leaf, and no harm could come out of consuming it for once. Gufran enquired as to what 'number' paan I would have. I had never had paan before and was least informed that the supposed delicacy was known by its numbers. I told him to bring whatever he had chosen for himself.

After a while, both he and I put the nicely wrapped product in our mouths and began to walk around CP. Soon after, not knowing that I had to spit it out, I promptly proceeded to chew and swallow the paan and its constituents, of which I had no knowledge. Within five minutes, I went into a tizzy and collapsed on the ground. When I opened my eyes, I found myself in an alien surrounding. Gufran was by my side, relieved that I had come around. I was in his room in Madhya Pradesh Bhavan.

He narrated that after I had fallen to the ground unconscious, certainly due to the devastating effect of the tobacco in the wrapped betel leaf, and he had quickly bundled me in his car and brought me to his room. A doctor was summoned, and I came to my senses, only to begin talking incoherently. I was then sedated. Nearly 12 hours had passed since the incident before I had woken up in a normal state of mind. I went back to my room in Jammu and Kashmir House, freshened up and said to myself: Never again! Nothing to do with paan in any way! No more of such experiments in the future!

On hearing the tale, the delegates laughed and appreciated my principled refusal. In fact, they were glad that I had excused myself because had I gone, I would have surely ruined their conference with my anti-paan speech.

Bonhomie amid the Biting Cold

One of my tasks as the deputy minister was to oversee and ensure the setting up of new TV transmitters within the prescribed period of one year in a bid to extend the coverage of DD across the country. With elections scheduled for the year end (1984), Indira ji was keen that the 126 low-power and high-power TV transmitters planned were made functional well before the code of conduct for the polls was announced. Work on their installation and commissioning had begun on war footing. It so happened that two such transmitters had come up in Kargil and Leh, and I was to inaugurate them.

Knowing that Rajiv loved to travel and dabble in photography, I asked him if he would like to accompany me. There would be ample time for exploring the region once the official work was done. He immediately agreed. He was especially keen on seeing and photographing the wild horses found in the heights, visiting Pangong Lake (Pangong Tso) and Chushul, the last point on India's side before the India–China border in the region. He suggested that we take our spouses along, as it would be a good change for them as well. It was to be a week-long trip beginning 9 October 1984.

The plan was finalized. Three days before our departure from Delhi, on my way back to Delhi from my constituency Washim, where I had been on a short trip, while I was at the waiting room of the railway manager of Akola railway station, a call came for me from Dhawan; Indira ji wanted to speak with me. She had heard from Rajiv about our trip to Ladakh and advised me to drop the idea of taking our spouses along. She said she wasn't comfortable with the idea of Sonia ji and my wife Shameem having to brave the heights; they could have problems adjusting to the drop in air levels. I had no option but to relent. Finally, Rajiv, his friend Arun Singh and I left for Srinagar on the morning of 9 October, minus our spouses.

We arrived in Srinagar via flight from Delhi, and from there, we were accompanied by Krishan Amla, our common friend. That night we stayed at Sonamarg, a two-and-a-half-hour road journey from Srinagar. Incidentally, Indira ji and Feroze Gandhi had, a month after their wedding in 1942, come on one of their honeymoon trips to this popular tourist place and stayed in one of the huts.

That evening, Rajiv expressed a desire to have bhuttey (corn). I approached Haji Mian Bashir Ahmed, a religious and political leader who was close to Indira ji and Sheikh Abdullah and was equally respected by me. We dispatched a jeep to his place, and he sent it back loaded with not just corn but also several glasses of lassi (butter milk) and loads of butter. Bhuttey, if overeaten, could have a deleterious effect on the digestive system, and lassi is considered a good antidote to that possibility. We roasted the corn on fire and ate it, sipping lassi alongside, until two in the morning. Each one of us must have had at least six to seven corn shoots! Having had stomachful of corn, we had to miss the *wazwan* (multi-course Kashmiri meal) dinner waiting for us, arranged by the *tawaza* (hospitality and protocol) department on the advice of the then CM G.M. Shah (brother-in-law of Farooq Abdullah).

The next morning, we were escorted to the tourist hut located on a small hilltop where Indira ji and Feroze had once stayed. We went through the register, which had the signatures of both, along with a small write-up about their stay. We also entered our remarks in that old register about our journey. That hut and register were preserved and protected by the state government and were attractions for tourists. Unfortunately, in the 1990s, when militancy raged across the state, that hut, along with many other huts, was torched by militants, and nothing could be saved.

After breakfast, we proceeded to Kargil. Rajiv himself drove a Jonga (Nissan Patrol P60, a heavy-duty off-road vehicle formerly used by the army) on the five-hour drive from Srinagar, while other vehicles followed. At Kargil, I inaugurated the TV transmitter and addressed a public meeting. We stayed in Kargil for the night and headed for Leh, an eight–nine hour drive in those days, indulging in a lot of photography en route. After inaugurating another TV transmitter and a radio expansion programme followed by a public meeting, we stayed at Leh for the night.

On that night, we met a number of local delegations, which provided us an opportunity to learn about the hardships the people of the region encountered, especially during winter, due to lack of essential commodities and other facilities, infrastructure and communication and particularly electricity. We had received similar feedback the previous night in Kargil too.

On the third day, we left for Pangong Lake. An army officer of the rank of major general accompanied us from Leh, since we would now be entering a military-dominated area and the army would be our host. The army organized a boat ride on the lake, which was a memorable and nostalgic experience. It provided us an opportunity to see the recently much-talked about patrolling points Fingers 4 to 8 on one side of the Pangong Lake. The waters of the lake were crystal clear, and we could actually count the pebbles deep down.

After lunch, we headed to Chushul. The five-hour drive tested the level of our physical endurance, and I was glad that we had not brought our spouses along. It was not a road in the real sense, just a path paved with pebbles. As we rattled along, every single bone in our body creaked in protest. Never had I been so glad to end a journey. After having dinner and before retiring for the day, we discussed with the army officers and jawans various issues with regard to their physical and mental well-being and security-related problems, and understood from them the extremely tough conditions they brave (cold of -20 to -30°C) to keep our country safe. We thanked them for their sacrifice, and after extending our full cooperation and appreciation for the service they render to the nation, we made our way to our respective rooms.

The 'rooms' were actually bunkers, and the ones allotted to us had a cot generally found in villages. The door was a massive single-flap one, outside which I found a guard posted when I entered the room. On a small table stood a contraption that seemed to be a telephone, but it looked strange, as it had no keys or rotary numbers. The surface was simply blank. I presumed that it had been placed there as a showpiece—the army's definition of decoration! The following day, we were to explore and talk to more jawans on the border to boost their morale, with a special interest in knowing more about Jawaharlal Nehru's visit to this army post a few decades back. We were also looking forward to spot those wild horses that were known to survive in the harshest of climates.

Unfortunately, around 2.00 a.m., when the outside temperature dipped to -10, -15°C, I developed a high fever (maybe because of our hectic four-day road journey). All energy seemed to have drained from my body. I needed help and quickly. Remembering the guard outside, I somehow dragged myself to the door and opened it after much effort. A chilly draught blew in. The guard was not there. The wind gushing in made it impossible for me to shut it. Summoning whatever strength I had, I crawled back, with the door left open. In desperation, I lifted the phone's cradle and immediately heard a voice at the other end, 'Yes, sir?'

Never before had I been so relieved to hear a human voice. I identified myself and informed the jawan of my plight. Within five minutes, some army men arrived along with a doctor. One look at me, and doctor declared that I was in a bad shape and needed to be airlifted to Leh for treatment. He gave some medicines for early relief. Rajiv was informed, and he immediately came to my bunker. He was greatly worried at my condition. The PMO, through the army, was informed, and permission was sought to airlift me in an army helicopter.

The following morning, two helicopters arrived and took us to Leh. Miraculously, I had begun to feel much better by the time we reached Leh. From there, we took a commercial flight to Srinagar. I had completely recovered since the problem had been one of shortage of oxygen. Rajiv grumbled that I had ruined the last leg of our journey. Our visit to Ladakh concluded on 13 October.

Who knew that in just a little over a fortnight, Rajiv would be the country's PM! The messed-up trip, however, had one advantage. After Rajiv became the PM, I took up the issue of allowing some more regions in Ladakh to be opened up for civilians and tourists. I argued that this could be done without compromising security considerations and would be a major boost to the tourism sector in J&K, particularly Ladakh. Since he had seen the place for himself, he immediately agreed and granted permission.

The Last Meeting

Back in Delhi, it was in the last week of October while I was attending to office work that I received a call from Dhawan around 4.00 p.m. from the PM's residence, asking what I was doing. I laughed and counter-questioned, 'What does one do in office?' He said that 'madam' had asked me to meet her if I was not too busy. As if being busy would have stopped me from honouring her summons! But this was her way of calling her colleagues, even if they were juniors.

Dhawan informed me that the PM wanted to see me at her residence at Safdarjung Road. On arrival, I was ushered into the drawing room. It was for the first time that I had entered her residence for a meeting. I still remember that all the sofas in the room had pristine white covers. I normally used to meet the PM at her private office at Akbar Road, her South Block office or her Parliament office.

After a while, Indira ji entered. She was dressed casually, and little black droplets were dripping down her forehead. I brought it to her notice as diplomatically as I could. Similng, she said that she had just coloured her hair. She said it so disarmingly. With a motherly touch, she continued, '*Tum to bachon ki tarah ho* (You are like a child), else I would not have come out in this state.' After enquiring about my wife and family, she told me that she desired to go to Srinagar on a two-day vacation. Since Lok Sabha elections were to be held in the next few months, it would be difficult for her to make the trip later. She told me that in her childhood, she loved to go to Kashmir in the months of October and November along with her father to see the changing colours of Chinar tree leaves—from green to yellow to red and then to flaming red before autumn. She wanted my opinion on whether it would be safe to go.

There was a reason for consulting me. In the previous year, 1983, during the assembly elections, she had extensively canvassed for Congress candidates in the Kashmir Valley. Unfortunately, on the last day of her campaign, while she was addressing a public meeting at Iqbal Park at Srinagar, some miscreants had misbehaved, stripping naked and yelling, 'Indira Gandhi murdabad!' We all were disappointed and angry—so was she. It was rumoured that the miscreants were goons of the NC. However, NC leader Farooq Abdullah had apologized and publicly stated that his party had nothing to do with the incident.

I assured Indira ji that the incident of the previous year during the public meeting had happened in the heat of electioneering. The situation was normal now. Moreover, she would be on a private trip.

She felt reassured. I further informed her that I would not be able to accompany her, as I had to go to various places in southern and western parts of India for the inauguration of a few dozen television transmitters, which had been pending for the last few months. I suggested that, to be on the safer side, her office should inform the J&K administration about her visit only an hour before her departure from Delhi. An hour would be too short a time for any demonstration to be organized. She liked the idea and briefed Dhawan accordingly in my presence.

Having dealt with her Kashmir visit subject, she then asked me if I had prepared the list of campaigners for the forthcoming Parliament elections, which she had asked me to do a week before. I was entrusted with such exercises when I was the IYC president. She was aware that I knew the geography and demographic profile of the country, besides knowing the capacity and capability of leaders and their standing in public, which is why she had told me to submit a draft list of campaigners who would take part in the national campaign.

On earlier occasions, during my visit to different parts of the country along with her, I used to get opportunities to discuss such issues in the aircraft. In those days, senior leaders and good orators were supposed to be part of national-level and state-level campaign committees. The 'star campaigner' phrase was not in vogue then, and we did not have to inform the Election Commission of India about those names, unlike today.

I told her that the list was ready but was at my residence. I would give it to her on her return from Kashmir and on my return from my trip. However, I mentioned a few names that I remembered. After listening to me, she said all the names, except two, were good; she mentioned the names of both. She commented adversely on the capacity and performance of those two senior leaders. Her observations were scathing. She was not an ordinary leader; she was a perfect, down-to-earth politician who knew everything about her own colleagues, their activities, qualifications, disqualifications and their capacity for work in office and for the public. After her death, I had an occasion to check on them and discovered that she was right in her assessment.

Top: Youth and idealism—With my friend Basharat Ahmed in Kashmir in the early 1970s.

Bottom: Speaking at a seminar on Gandhi's life in Ganderbal garden, Kashmir, in 1973. Also seen is Mirza Mohammad Afzal Beg, who signed the Indira–Sheikh Accord in 1975 on behalf of Sheikh Abdullah.

Top: The Sanjay I knew—Welcoming Sanjay Gandhi to the All India Congress Committee (AICC) session at Gauhati in 1976. Ramachandra Rath is also present.

Bottom: Sharing the stage with Giani Zail Singh at the Muslim Youth Conference organized in New Delhi in 1979.

Top: Sanjay and I share a laugh during my wedding in Srinagar in March 1980.

Bottom: Receiving India's Iron Lady—Prime Minister (PM) Indira Gandhi gets a warm welcome from me, the president of the Indian Youth Congress (IYC), at an event organized by me in 1980.

Top: At an event organized by Delhi Pradesh Youth Congress to mark the first death anniversary of Sanjay Gandhi in 1981. With me on the stage are PM Indira Gandhi, Maneka Gandhi and Jagdish Tytler (seated to my left). Congress leader H.K.L. Bhagat is speaking.

Bottom: The making of a leader—Presiding over a National Council Meeting of the IYC in 1981. Seated next to me are Rajiv Gandhi, Anand Sharma and Venod Sharma (right to left).

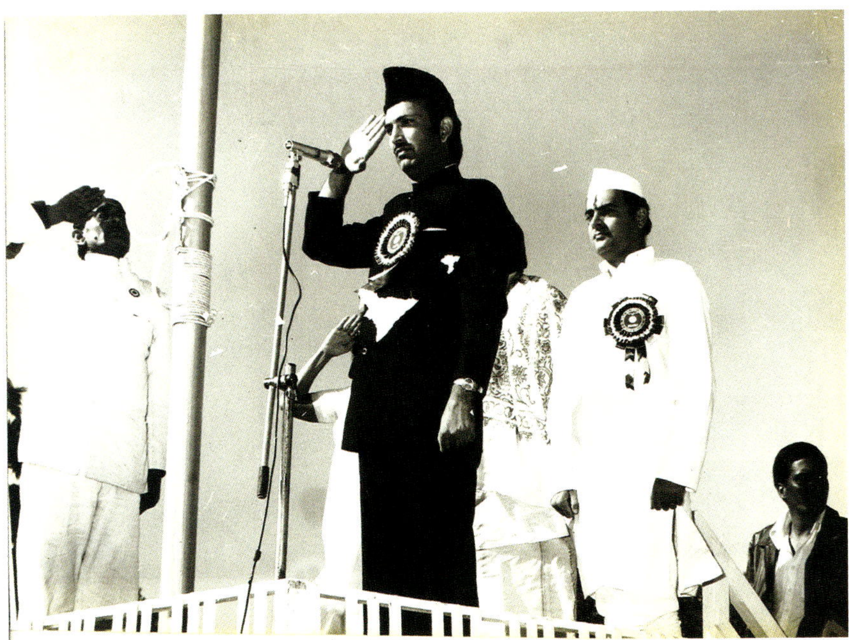

Taking the salute as the president of the IYC at a Congress Seva Dal event in Bengaluru in December 1981. Rajiv, along with R. Gundu Rao, chief minister (CM) of Karnataka and the PCC president (partially seen), is standing behind me.

Top: Introducing delegates to Indira ji at a dinner hosted during the International Youth Conference organized by the IYC at Hyderabad House in New Delhi in January 1982.

Bottom: Stepping into Sanjay's shoes—Rajiv is accorded a warm welcome at IYC's National Council Meeting in Srinagar in 1982.

Top: A great understanding, premised on mutual respect and trust—With Rajiv at Srinagar Airport. Arun Nehru is also seen.

Bottom: Hosting a lunch for a visiting Russian delegation in the early 1980s as the general secretary of the AICC. Sitaram Kesri, treasurer of the AICC, is also seen.

Top: Leading an all-party delegation of parliamentarians as the minister of parliamentary affairs in a meeting with Bob Hawke, former PM of Australia, in 1991. Sushma Swaraj, Member of Parliament (MP), and Shivraj Patil, Speaker, are seated first and second from the left, respectively.

Bottom: Paying tribute to the Mahatma on Church Street outside Pietermaritzburg Station on my first visit to South Africa in 1993 as minister for civil aviation and tourism.

Visiting Siachen, the world's highest battlefield, as parliamentary affairs minister along with Defence Minister Sharad Pawar in 1991–92.

From political wilderness to prime minister: With P.V. Narasimha Rao.

Top: *Juley, Juley*—With locals during a visit to Ladakh as minister of civil aviation and tourism in 1994.

Bottom: With a newborn child born to migrants from Kahal Jugesar, Bhadarwah, rescued from caves in the Chamba region of Himachal Pradesh in the summer of 1994. Having fled their home after a militant attack, I took them back to their homeland after providing security and all necessary requirements.

Top: Receiving a memento at the presentation of Bodhi tree at the Guryongsa Temple in Seoul, South Korea, as minister of civil aviation and tourism in October 1995. Ms Mayawati, then CM of Uttar Pradesh, and Shashank, the Indian ambassador to South Korea, are also seen.

Bottom: Braving bullets—Speaking at a mass contact programme in Punjab in the 1990s as the general secretary in charge of the state. The Pradesh Congress Committee (PCC) president Beant Singh, who was the CM from 1992 to 1995, is seated along with Congress leader, R.L. Bhatia.

Top: Receiving President Dr A.P.J. Abdul Kalam as minister of parliamentary affairs and urban development at the inauguration of the 10th Annual Convention and National Seminar of Indian Building Congress on Energy Management in Buildings and Services at Vigyan Bhavan, New Delhi, in June 2004.

Bottom: Attending a CM's conference on internal security in New Delhi in December 2007 as the CM of Jammu and Kashmir (J&K). Seen here with Bhupinder Singh Hooda, CM of Haryana, Virbhadra Singh, CM of Himachal Pradesh and Narendra Modi, CM of Gujarat (from left to right).

Courtesy: Ministry of Home Affairs, Government of India

Top: Visiting border areas of J&K as CM along with former CM Farooq Abdullah.

Bottom: Attending Dusshera celebrations in Jammu as the CM. To my left is statesman, educationalist, philanthropist, author and poet, Dr Karan Singh.

Top: A dream come true—Sonia Gandhi inaugurates the Indira Gandhi Memorial Tulip Garden in Srinagar in March 2008. Shameem Dev Azad is also present.

Bottom: A walk through the garden with Sonia ji and Shameem.

Top: The people's CM meets the people's president—In conversation with Dr A.P.J. Abdul Kalam

Bottom: Empowering my people with education—President Pratibha Devisingh Patil inaugurates the Bhaderwah Campus of the University of Jammu in May 2008, as Lt Gen. (Retd) S.K. Sinha, the chancellor of the university, and I, as CM, look on.

As planned, Indira ji went to Kashmir. Thereafter, she visited Odisha, where she addressed her last public meeting in Bhubaneswar before she was assassinated.

India Loses Her Iron Lady

It was 31 October 1984. After completing a week-long official visit, I landed at the Delhi airport from Mumbai around 9.00 a.m. In those days, cars used to drop and pick up ministers right from the aircraft ladders. The moment I came out of the aircraft, a woman ground staff member, who had come to receive me, informed me that the PM had been shot just a few minutes back and had been taken to AIIMS. I was aghast and went straight to AIIMS from the airport. A huge crowd had gathered outside the hospital, and more people continued to pour in as the news spread like wildfire. There was no clarity on her medical condition.

The medical superintendent of the hospital was Dr A.N. Safaya, a Kashmiri Pandit and a family friend. I went to his room, and through the rear lift, he escorted me straight to the floor where Indira ji had been taken. On reaching there, I saw Vice President R. Venkataraman and Arun Nehru in an adjacent room. They hugged me and wept, saying that she was no more.

It was the greatest shock of my life. I cried bitterly outside the room and could not dare to see her body. I had experienced a similar moment four-and-a-half years ago when I had seen Sanjay's remains and lost consciousness for hours. There were several senior ministers and leaders who were waiting in one of the halls on the ground floor of the hospital, since they were not allowed to go upstairs where the body lay. While upstairs, I was privy to the discussion between Venkataraman and Arun on 'what next'. We waited for President Zail Singh to return from a foreign visit and for Rajiv, who was on a tour of eastern India, to arrive in Delhi.

At that point in time, the vice president was the senior-most official in the country. He took me aside and pointed out to a constitutional crisis: There was no PM and no head of state. We could not announce the death until a new PM took charge, he said. He suggested that I, being the deputy I&B minister, must direct DD and the AIR to not relay the news of Indira Gandhi's death for now.

He had a point. Rajiv, along with senior leader Pranab Mukherjee and some other leaders, arrived from West Bengal around 3.00 p.m. Meanwhile, the president had also arrived. Rajiv, the president and the vice president had discussions in the hospital itself, and it was decided that Rajiv and Indira ji's entire Council of Ministers should be immediately sworn in at Rashtrapati Bhavan. That was done; meanwhile, Indira ji death was made public.

Rajiv's succession to prime ministership became the subject of much speculation. It was rumoured that Pranab da wanted to become the PM and had even lobbied for the position. Even if Pranab da had nurtured the ambition, there was no way he could have become the PM. The entire top brass of the party had known for long that Rajiv would one day succeed his mother. He had been groomed for four years for the responsibility—since he quit his job as a pilot, joined the IYC, became an MP, led the IYC and took over as general secretary of the parent organization. Not a single senior leader or MP would have backed Pranab da, particularly in the circumstances that prevailed then. There was also an outpouring of sympathy for Rajiv after Indira ji's assassination.

Moreover, Rao was more senior and experienced than Pranab da, and he could have staked claim for the prime ministership. But he did not, perhaps for two reasons. The first was that he was not ambitious enough. The second was that he may have been consumed by guilt over his failure as home minister to prevent the massacre of Sikhs in the wake of Indira ji's assassination. There were murmurs in the party that he was, to some extent, responsible for the terrible tragedy that befell innocent Sikhs. He must have had a lurking fear that, even if he pushed his name for prime ministership, it would have been rejected, and he would have lost face.

All through those horrific moments, Rajiv was busy receiving people who streamed in to pay their last respects to the departed leader, whose body lay in state. He was also occupied with the anti-Sikh riots in Delhi and elsewhere, and I was occupied with the completion of an important formality—collecting signatures of

Congress MPs for a resolution that would name Rajiv as the Congress Parliamentary Party leader. I had been assigned this task by some senior parliamentary board members of the party. The less senior MPs were requested to visit the party office where their signatures were taken. However, I would visit the homes of the more senior leaders for their endorsement to the resolution. In the wake of the assassination, most of the MPs had arrived in Delhi.

Had I not been busy with collecting signatures, I would surely have been in the field, providing refuge and help to our Sikh brethren and dousing the fires. Even so, I found time to provide shelter to several Sikhs. They were so frightened that they were willing to cut their hair and shave their beard, but I dissuaded them and promised them that they would be safe.

Reliving Her Memory

Indira ji had, over the years, discussed many issues with me, but the militancy issue in Punjab, which claimed her life, was not one of them. Perhaps she believed that the matter was too complicated for me to understand. The leaders she leaned on most on the subject were Buta Singh, Zail Singh and Darbara Singh. She also consulted Balram Jakhar, P.V. Narasimha Rao, Pranab Mukherjee and P. Shiv Shankar.

The problem was that Darbara Singh and Zail Singh had their own political differences and 'camps'. That must have made Indira ji's task of finding a solution to the Punjab problem even more difficult. Buta Singh remained neutral and did not have the support that Zail Singh and Darbara Singh had. I do not wish to go into details on the matter because I was not privy to its intricacies.

However, a few days before Operation Bluestar, Indira ji called a meeting of the Council of Ministers, which included both Cabinet and junior ministers, and sought the opinion of each minister on ways to deal with the situation of flushing out the terrorists from the Golden Temple complex. When my turn came, I suggested that instead of taking any harsh action, water and food supplies could be stopped immediately, which could force the militants to surrender. But another senior minister countered me by pointing out that there were tube wells inside the temple and also enough food stocks for years to come. The Council of Ministers left the final decision to the PM and her advisors and experts.

While in the hospital, my thoughts went back to the years I had spent with the assassinated leader and the memories associated with them. Particularly, I remembered a trip with her to Andaman and Nicobar Islands. It was a mix of an official and a sightseeing visit to the islands. After we arrived at the Port Blair airport and reached the city, the trip within the city was in an open jeep, with thousands of people lined up on both sides of the road to welcome her. Indira ji made me stand by her side in the open vehicle. I was touched by her magnanimity and respect afforded to me at that young age, when I was only the national president of the IYC. While we were staying at Raj Bhavan, I got to know Indira ji more intimately as PM, a caring person, a mother and a great human being.

One day, we were taken to an island that was out of bounds for the public, since it was inhabited by a tribal community that had its own traditional and cultural ways, and the government did not want them to be exploited for tourism purposes. Both men and women of the tribal group wore no clothes. It was a natural way of living for them, but I was deeply embarrassed, more so in the presence of a woman. We sat on a dais, watching a dance performance, when some of the performers came up and affectionately requested Indira ji to join them. She obliged and jigged along with them. I had kept my eyes fixed to the ground most of the time! After a while, the PM came to me, dragged me down from the dais, brought me in the midst of the tribal men and women and made me dance with them. You can imagine how red I must have gone in the face!

I recalled another incident that showed her affection for and confidence in me. It was during the AICC session in Kolkata in December 1983. On the dais were members of the CWC and the CPB. I was seated in the front row below along with ministers and other senior party functionaries. Meanwhile, a Seva Dal worker came to me with a slip from Indira ji. She had called me on the dais. When I went up, she enquired if I knew the industrialist Dhirubhai Ambani. I replied that I knew him only casually.

I had wondered why she had suddenly brought up the topic and got the answer soon enough. She said that Ambani's daughter Deepti was getting married that very evening and she had been invited to attend the event. But she had forgotten about it and now it was not possible for her to go to Mumbai. Since it would not be proper for her to merely send a congratulatory message, she suggested that I take a flight to Mumbai and attend the wedding function on her behalf. She then asked Dhawan, who was lurking behind, to inform Dhirubhai that I would be in attendance as her representative.

I was greeted at the Mumbai airport by my ministry's personnel as per protocol and also by representatives of the industrialist's family. At the wedding venue, I was received with great warmth by the Ambani family—not because I was a minister or a political leader but because I represented PM Indira Gandhi.

Incidentally, I knew the bridegroom, Dattaraj Salgaocar of Goa, from my IYC days since he too was associated indirectly with the organization. However, one habit that I had right from the beginning and that I have continued till date is that I don't keep close relationships with industrialists; the same is true with the Ambani family too.

There were several other instances when Indira ji bestowed honours on me. In 1983, the I&B secretary, M.S. Gill, came to my office with a file. He said that Indira ji had noted on the file that I should lead the Indian delegation at an international film festival scheduled to be held at Tashkent; she had struck down Bhagat's name, who was my Cabinet minister. Not just that, she had also written that the official delegation should include Shameem Dev since she was an artiste of eminence. Gill did not know that my wife was a singer and had been intrigued by her inclusion in the list. Indira ji had told Gill that she felt somebody young should attend the film festival, so I was the right choice!

Those happy memories transported me to the past even as the party's senior leaders around me grappled with the tragic present.

6

BATTLES ON MANY FRONTS

Indira ji's assassination was followed by another tragic event—the massacre of thousands of innocent Sikhs across the country. Terrorists and militants have no religion, but since Indira ji had been shot dead by two of her Sikh bodyguards, the incident triggered a wave of mindless revenge among various sections of people, incited by certain individuals and compounded further by the mob mentality against innocent Sikhs in general. In Delhi alone, unfortunately, a large number of Sikhs lost their lives. The country, which was already in mourning over their beloved PM's tragic end, now also grieved the catastrophe that befell innocent Sikh men, women and children. Much has been written about it, and I would not like to elaborate further, except express deep sorrow and anguish on the uncalled-for happenings.

Shameem, then visiting my constituency Washim, faced the wrath of a rampaging mob as a result of a misunderstanding as well—she escaped by the skin of her teeth. It was my practice to visit my constituency once a week while I was an MP from there. However, there were times when my prior engagements in Delhi would not allow me to visit my constituency. On those days, Shameem would go out and interact with the locals, party workers and voters there, and fill me in when she returned. She ended up becoming a well-known face in Washim.

When she heard the news about Indira ji's assassination, Shameem cancelled all her programmes and proceeded to Delhi by car, which belonged to one of my Sikh friends from my constituency and was being driven by his son. The local MLA, a bearded Papa Lal Dandole, also accompanied her. En route, she noticed a large number of trucks abandoned by the drivers on the roadside; she was unaware that Sikh security personnel had assassinated the PM.

When the car reached Amravati (the divisional headquarters), located equidistant between Washim and Nagpur, a large crowd tried to stop her car, shouting that a Sikh family was in the vehicle. 'Maaro maaro (kill, kill)', they shrieked. The crowd believed, judging by the attire of the people in the vehicle, that they were Sikhs: My wife was dressed in a salwar kameez, which Sikh women normally wear; the MLA had a beard and a Sikh youth in a turban was driving the car. Sensing trouble, all three of them exited the car and began to run towards the city, looking for shelter. When they were coming out of the car, some people in the mob had managed to snatch my wife's purse, her gold bangles and her necklace. As my wife ran for her life, she kept shouting that she was Mrs Azad and not a Sikh. Fortunately, they were all young and able to outrun the rampaging mob.

My wife was saved by a stroke of luck. A Congress woman, probably a Seva Dal worker, who was watching the incident from the terrace of her house, recognized my wife. She came down and ran towards her and took her and the other two gentlemen into her house. Then she cried out loudly, 'Mrs Azad is being attacked by a crowd.' Within a few minutes, people, both Hindus and Muslims, came out of their homes in large numbers, armed with lathis, and chased away the mob. My wife and her companions got away. However, their car was torched.

Meanwhile, the news of the attack on her spread. When I received a telephone call from Amravati, I immediately called the police commissioner. My wife was then escorted in police protection from Amravati to Jawaharlal Darda's house at Nagpur. Darda was a minister, family friend and a fatherly figure to us. That night, Shameem and her companions stayed with the Darda family. The following day, she flew back to Delhi, while the other two were escorted back to Washim under police protection.

To this day, my wife shudders to think of the consequences if that woman in Amravati had not identified her. Thankfully, the senseless violence across the country receded after a few days, though leaving behind traumatic memories for thousands of families—scars they bear even to this day.

Triumph of Democracy

Immediately after this episode, I got busy with preparations for the Lok Sabha elections scheduled to be held in two months. Rajiv asked me not to contest because he wanted me to be free to campaign across the country and not get tied to my constituency alone. When I suggested that I could contest and still be free to canvas elsewhere, he replied that it would be risky because I could lose for want of adequate attention to Washim. But I assured him that even if I did not campaign in my constituency, I could win, and that I would file the nomination papers and return to the constituency only after the results were out. Seeing my confidence, he relented.

Rajiv informed me that he would be kicking off his national campaign from Mumbai, a day after the last day of filing nominations, and would pick me up from Washim early in the morning; I would be done with my nomination by 4.00 p.m. the previous evening. The evening before leaving for the constituency, I tried to dissuade him, explaining that the trip would be long—he would have to fly from Delhi to Nagpur by aircraft, from Nagpur to Washim on an hour-long helicopter journey, then back to Nagpur and then to Mumbai. But he insisted that he would reach Washim between 7.30 and 8.00 a.m., even though it would be inconvenient for him to start early from Delhi.

While discussing the issue, an idea occurred to me. I suggested to him that since he was coming to Washim anyway, he might as well address a public rally there between 7.00 and 8.00 a.m. That would also be my first and last campaign in my constituency. He looked at me as if I had lost my mind. Who would come for a rally at seven in the morning, that too mid-winter, he wondered. However, he left the decision to me.

The next day, after filing my nomination, I told the waiting media, party leaders, workers and the crowd at the Akola district headquarters that the PM would be addressing a public rally at Washim at seven in the morning the following day. The word spread like wildfire. I also instructed my workers and local leaders to begin the task of getting people to the venue. The next day, the crowd began to gather from 6.00 a.m., and by the time Rajiv arrived, accompanied by CM Vasantrao Banduji 'Vasantdada' Patil, who had joined him from Nagpur, the crowd had swelled to 50,000–60,000!

My speech was short and to the point. I told the gathering that it was my first and last appearance for campaigning in the constituency as party president Rajiv had given me the responsibility to canvas for other candidates across the country. I added, 'If you are satisfied with the work I have done over the last five years, please vote me back to the Lok Sabha again. If I have failed, you can reject me.'

After we were done with the public meeting, I accompanied Rajiv from Washim to Nagpur and finally to Mumbai. En route, he asked me and Patil to give him some points for the campaign to be launched from Mumbai, to ensure that the party secured the maximum number of seats. Patil suggested two or three points. But Rajiv did not appear to be impressed with them, though he said nothing.

Patil's suggestions were eventually rejected because they would have impacted only certain regions of the country. Also, the fructification of those suggestions would have taken a longer time—that would not do because general elections were going on. On the other hand, my suggestions promised a positive effect on both rural and urban regions of India and they could be immediately implemented, with the results evident in the short period of next few months.

I offered two suggestions. The first was to pass a subtle message in his very first public meeting and press conference that, if any of our Lok Sabha candidates trailed in any assembly segment of his Lok Sabha constituency, the MLAs concerned would be denied renomination in the forthcoming assembly elections to be held within the next few months. I explained to Rajiv that it had generally been seen that Lok Sabha MPs worked against their MLA candidates during assembly elections, if the candidates were not of his choice. When it came to the Lok Sabha election, the MLA candidates, whether elected or defeated, paid back the Lok Sabha candidates in the same coin. This was how we were losing most of the MLA and MP seats in most cases, I explained.

The second suggestion I gave was even more radical. I pointed out that an overwhelming number of Lok Sabha MPs and the MLAs belonging to the rural constituencies often relocate their families to bigger cities and state capitals or even to the national capital after getting elected, and thereby spent more time with them than in their respective constituencies. This way, they lose connect with the people of their respective constituencies. Hence, I suggested that the party must give tickets to only those candidates who were prepared to have their families and houses in the constituencies they represent. As a result, once Parliament or assembly sessions are over, they would have to go home to their respective constituencies. This would provide an opportunity for workers and voters to have access to their representatives.

Rajiv liked both ideas but agreed to implement and announce the first during the ongoing elections. The second idea, he said, would be implemented five years later for the next Lok Sabha elections. On arriving in Mumbai, in the first press conference there, Rajiv announced the first point and went on to repeat it throughout his campaign across the country.

While in Mumbai, we divided the Lok Sabha constituencies among ourselves. He would campaign in almost 60 per cent of the constituencies, and I would take care of the remaining 40 per cent. During campaigning, besides talking about a number of public-related issues, the main point for the party cadres was the first suggestion that I had made. The clear messaging helped many of our candidates to win. The sitting MLAs not only worked hard but also spent their own money to ensure the victory of the Congress Lok Sabha candidates! They realized that the winning Lok Sabha candidates would automatically help them in their re-nomination.

The Congress party registered a historic victory by getting 414 seats, including the one for my constituency Washim, in the Lok Sabha, a feat that remains unrivalled to this day. Three factors were attributed to the massive win: one, the hopes and aspirations that a fresh-faced Rajiv invoked; two, the sympathy for the party following Indira ji's assassination and three, a reason not discussed in the public domain till date, which is the announcement of the first suggestion that I had made to Rajiv.

Later on, the PM conducted an assessment, with inputs from the Intelligence Bureau (IB) and through the party functionaries, and came to the conclusion that one of the major reasons for the party winning the 414 Lok Sabha seats was the first suggestion I had made, which had made a difference of an additional 80–100 seats. Four months later, when assembly elections took place, more than 200 sitting MLAs were denied tickets across the country where our Lok Sabha candidates had fallen behind in their assembly constituencies. Even in my constituency, one sitting MLA was denied the ticket; although he was one of the hard-working ones, his adversaries ensured that I lost in that segment, and thereby ensured that he was denied the ticket.

Now installed as an elected PM, Rajiv set about forming his ministry. I was made the minister of State (MoS) for parliamentary affairs. Justifying his decision, Rajiv told me that he was not yet fully conversant with the functioning of Parliament, nor did he know the majority of his MPs. I would have to help him along and ensure proper floor coordination, management and proper feedback, not just about our own MPs but also the Opposition benches, particularly the performance of both ministers and MPs on the floor of the House, which I did faithfully and reported to him accordingly. He told me that once he got a grip on the matter, he would give me a ministry of my choice.

However, I was perfectly content with the portfolio. In fact, I was happy, as I had a chance to interact with parliamentarians across the political divide. Moreover, it was very close to my heart because it was similar to organizational tasks I always had a knack for.

In the process, I built some very precious personal relationships cutting across the political divide. My Cabinet minister was, again, H.K.L. Bhagat, but as usual, he was too busy with Delhi's politics. Besides, he also held the tourism ministry portfolio. Thus, I had pretty much a free run of the parliamentary affairs charge. I would even nominate members in various committees, such as chairpersons or committee members of the Public Accounts Committee, public-sector undertakings and many others organizations without any interference from the PM or my senior ministers. If the PM had any names in mind, he would pass them on to me with merely a suggestion that it could be considered on merit. I would directly report to him as many times as I desired during the session or off session.

Though Rajiv constituted his first ministry based on his own understanding, in all subsequent reshuffles and expansions of the ministry in his capacity as the PM, he consulted me and included most of the names that I had suggested right until the end.

Reshuffles were quite frequent in his tenure. Six months after forming the government, he asked me give him a few names to be included in the Council of Ministers on the basis of their performance in Parliament. I passed on the names of about half a dozen hopefuls. He said that he would reshuffle the ministry in the next two days. Two days went by, and there was no reshuffle. A week passed, and yet there was nothing. I would meet him often, sometimes three–four times a day, especially during the Parliament session, but I never raised the matter, nor did he say anything about it. One day, he finally said that he would be including all the names that I had suggested for the reshuffle that would take place the next day—he did.

I casually asked him about the delay. He laughed and said that I had made quite a few 'enemies' for myself. When I looked puzzled, he narrated the story. Apparently, he wanted to test my capacity of keeping things secret. He had told a few of the hopefuls whose names I had recommended that they would be included in the ministry. When they were pleasantly surprised, he let it slip that I, as MoS for parliamentary affairs, had been already been intimated about it well in advance and wondered if I had told them about it! They all denied it and added that perhaps I had not wanted them to be made ministers. He wanted to check if I had told the candidates and sought to take credit for their eventual inclusion.

This was the first and the last time Rajiv tested me. Thereafter, until the very end, he trusted me implicitly. As general secretary of the party and after having worked with Indira ji, he had noticed the tendency of some of her close aides to appropriate certain honours, make others beholden to them and enhance their own reputations as members of the 'inner circle'. Rajiv was happy that I had not fallen to such temptation.

Elevations and 'Demotions'

In 1986, I became MoS for home affairs. It was a big responsibility for me. My Cabinet minister was Buta Singh. I was given charge of Union Territories (UTs) and of the implementation of the Punjab, Assam and Mizoram Accords, two of which had been signed before I took over. Before me, no minister had given much time to the affairs of the UTs (the number of UTs was almost double back then as compared to today). I oversaw and brought about several administrative changes in these places, at times ensuring that the people of far-off UTs received justice and fair deals.

None of the accords were easy to implement. The Rajiv–Longowal Accord of 24 July 1985, for instance, went for a toss after the assassination of the Akali leader Harchand Singh Longowal barely a month after the agreement had been struck. As part of the agreement, the Union government accepted most of the demands of the Shiromani Akali Dal (SAD), which included referring the part of the Anandpur Sahib Resolution that dealt with Centre–state relations to the Sarkaria Commission, continuing with the Sutlej Yamuna Link Canal (SYL) work, and passing an all-India Sikh Gurdwara Act for structured governance of Sikh shrines across India. The SAD agreed to withdraw its agitation following the agreement, but the militants believed that Longowal had 'sold out' to the Centre. On 20 August 1985, he was shot by Sikhs who opposed the accord.

The Assam Accord was a memorandum of settlement signed on 15 August 1985 between the representatives of the Government of India, government of Assam and leaders of the Assam movement led by All Assam Students' Union and All Assam Gana Sangram Parishad. The protesters had been demanding, among other things, identification and deportation of all foreigners (mostly Bangladeshi immigrants) staying in Assam illegally. Through the settlement, the Union government acknowledged the political, social, cultural and economic concerns of the Assamese people; it agreed to revise the electoral database and identify and deport any and all refugees and migrants who had settled there after 25 March 1971.

In the case of Mizoram, the Mizoram Accord, 1986: Memorandum of Settlement was inked on 30 June 1986. It was signed by Laldenga, who had spearheaded a civil unrest in the region for decades under the banner of the Mizo National Front (MNF) and a representative each of the Centre and the Mizoram administration. The insurgency outfit had earlier demanded that all MNF members be freed from criminal charges, that no Act of Parliament would be legalized in Mizoram unless the state government approves it and that Mizoram should be a separate state and given a university and a high court. The accord accepted the demand of statehood (to be given at an appropriate time) and agreed to the continuation of the inner line system, which restricted unauthorized stays in or visits to Mizoram. But the agreement also laid down that the MNF would surrender all arms, ammunition and other such equipment to the Government of India and also amend its constitution to conform to the Constitution of India. Accordingly, CM Lal Thanhawla and his Cabinet resigned, and Laldenga was appointed the CM. As the MoS in charge of UTs, I recommended statehood for Mizoram and Arunachal Pradesh; at a later stage, both received statehood in 1987.

A study of these accords would make it evident that Rajiv was committed to establishing peace through all legal and reasonable means. For him, the country's integrity was more important than his party's rule. In Punjab, he reached out to the SAD; in Assam, to the All Assam Students' Union and in Mizoram, to the MNF.

Besides the implementation of these accords, I also took an important decision with regard to Lakshadweep. A policy existed in those days by which no locals could be recruited in the police force above the rank of a constable. Even assistant sub-inspector- and inspector-level officers were exported from Kerala. This had caused a great deal of heartburn among the locals, as the constables had nothing to look forward to in terms of career progression. I scrapped this regressive policy and allowed police officers to be selected from Lakshadweep.

Some seven months after becoming the MoS for home affairs, I requested the PM for a change in my portfolio. He was surprised and remarked that I wanted to give up a plum charge that many others desired. I told him of whispers I had heard—that minority and SC community members had grabbed both the Cabinet minister and the MoS rank in home affairs. Since it was not right for me to suggest Home Minister Buta Singh's transfer as he was a Dalit, I told the PM that it would be best if I were given another charge. Reluctantly, Rajiv agreed, and I was moved to the food and civil supplies ministry.

However, he was gracious enough to ask me for a name to replace me. At my suggestion, an upper-caste MP from Odisha, Chintamani Panigrahi, was brought in my place. There was talk thereafter that I had been 'demoted', but I never clarified the issue; this is the first time I am doing so. As MoS for food and civil supplies, I took the initiative to create food storage facilities in far-flung regions of the country, such as Leh, Kargil and the Northeast.

Shooting Off a United Opposition

By the middle of 1987, Rajiv had begun to face the heat of the Bofors controversy. Many of his trusted aides had left his side and even quit the Congress party to float their own outfit. The exodus was led by V.P. Singh, his one-time finance and defence minister, and included Arun Nehru, Arun Singh, Arif Mohammad Khan and Mufti—all Union ministers—and many more. On one occasion, when Parliament was in session and the PM was out on an official trip abroad, Opposition members launched a broadside against the government over the Bofors issue. As one Opposition leader after the other slammed the government in general and Rajiv in particular, senior ministers of our Treasury bench remained mute spectators and listened silently, not bothering to counter the charges. I was deeply upset and hurt.

One reason for their meekness was perhaps that there was complete confusion within our ranks due to the friction between PM Rajiv Gandhi and President Zail Singh. There was one group within our party, led by a particular MoS, that was fuelling misunderstanding between the two constitutional heads. This person would tell Singh that Rajiv wanted to impeach him and the same person would feed Rajiv information that the president wanted to dismiss him over the

Bofors matter! The man was playing both ways. Congress MPs did not know how things would eventually turn and preferred to stay neutral. A few senior ministers saw in this confusion an opportunity to occupy the post of PM and kept quiet, preferring to keep the pot boiling.

The situation had become so tense that even I was apprehensive and avoided attending functions hosted at the Rashtrapati Bhavan, although I enjoyed very cordial relations with Singh. In fact, I knew him well before I got to know Rajiv. I remember the day when the votes were to be cast for the election of the president—Singh was the Congress's candidate. But he had refused to vote, wondering how he could vote for himself. Indira ji learnt of it and asked Dhawan to contact me. She said that only I, then president of the IYC, could persuade Singh to vote. I went to his residence and asked him to sit in my car and come for the voting. He said in mock anger, 'You are ordering me!' I too replied in the same vein, 'Yes. Now please get into the car.' Such was our relationship. Needless to add, Singh came to Parliament in my car to cast his vote, after which I dropped him back to his residence.

There was a reason why Indira ji had such faith in my ability to persuade Singh. In 1977–78, when a number of Congress leaders had either quit the party or disassociated themselves from it, I would meet Indira ji often. The buzz was that Singh was also planning to jump ship. During one such meeting with her, she mentioned that she had heard that I got along well with him. I confirmed the same, after which she asked me to bring Singh to meet her. A few days later, I came to her with him and the latter assured her that he would stand with her no matter what.

In many ways, Singh was a simple and down-to-earth person. I would invite him to my house on various occasions and he would unfailingly be there. One hilarious occasion deserves recall. It was late evening when the doorbell to my Rajaji Marg residence rang. One of my domestic helps opened the door and told me that a bearded man had come to meet me. I came out, and to my surprise found Zail Singh, the then home minister of India, at my doorstep. I expressed delight but also curiosity on his sudden arrival. He said that I had invited him over for dinner. With acute embarrassment, I reminded him that the invitation was for the following day! He exclaimed that he had already relieved his security personnel and asked them to return after a couple of hours. I told him warmly that since had come nevertheless, he should have dinner. The situation was thus saved.

However, it wasn't that easy to deal with the tense situation arising out of the supposed cold war between Singh and Rajiv. On one occasion, the PM was at the Rashtrapati Bhavan. I also happened to be there and was seated at a distance from the two. During tea time, an aide of the president came and said that the president had asked for me. When I went to the president, Rajiv was still with him. Singh turned to the PM and complained that I had stopped attending functions at his house, adding that we had known each other since my Youth Congress days when Sanjay was the leader. Rajiv said he did not know of that. After that, I resumed my visits to the president's house.

Around this time, there was speculation that the government wanted to impeach the president and that the president wanted to dismiss Rajiv. He wondered who was spreading such falsehood and said that some people were being mischevious and creating bad blood between Singh and himself. I personally believe that somebody who wanted to replace Rajiv as the PM or somebody who had harboured hopes of becoming the PM after Indira ji's assassination could be the troublemaker.

I had the unenviable task of briefing the PM about the political firestorm triggered by the Bofors issue in Parliament during his absence. He called a meeting of the Council of Ministers and raised this issue. A senior minister from UP remarked that it was not the job of the ministers to defend the government and Rajiv; the party should take a lead in the matter. An infuriated Rajiv banged the table with both his palms and told the minister, 'Why don't you then quit the government and work for the party?' He then rose in a huff and walked out, heading straight to his car.

I ran after him to persuade him to return. I chased him up to car but he didn't agree. Rajiv asked the driver to step aside and took the wheels; he asked me to sit beside him. He then drove to his residence. Tea was called for, and when he had calmed down a bit, I said that a sort of Kamaraj-type plan would be appropriate, where resignations of ministers could be called, and they should be inducted for party work.[5] I wrote down my own resignation on a piece of paper then and there and handed it over to him.

Although Rajiv liked the idea, he wondered if the plan would work. Nonetheless, he agreed, and it was decided between the two of us that I should make it known to the ministers that Rajiv wanted their resignations from their respective ministries so that they could work for the party. I gave lot of publicity to my resignation and my offer to work for the party in the hope that other ministers would follow suit. The media, too, projected it as yet another Kamaraj Plan. Days passed, but no resignations came. A few ministers said they were willing to be drafted for party work but would not give up their ministerial portfolios voluntarily.

I, however, stood firm on my resignation and requested Rajiv to give me the charge of worst-affected states like Punjab and UP, the two states where the Congress party faced deep problems—Punjab because of militancy and UP because of V.P. Singh and company almost taking over the entire state of UP. He agreed, albeit half-heartedly, knowing the landmine I was walking into, particularly Punjab.

In UP, our state unit president Chaudhary Balram Singh Yadav and CM Veer Bahadur Singh had gone underground. They had no capacity to match the Opposition overdrive led by V.P. Singh, Arun Nehru, Arif Mohammad Khan and Mufti, who also had the support of the likes of Mulayam Singh Yadav, Kanshi Ram and a host of tall BJP leaders of the state. After taking charge of UP as general secretary, I spoke with Veer Bahadur, and he appeared despondent and resigned to doom, saying that the Congress party was hopelessly placed in the face of V.P. Singh's onslaught. Nothing that I said could enthuse him. Veer Bahadur was a hard-core grassroots Congressman and a perfect gentleman, but he was a poor orator, less of a vote-catcher and hardly a crowd-puller.

Unfortunately, it has always been the tendency of the Congress's national leadership to have weak CMs in UP. For instance, H.N.

[5]The Kamaraj Plan, proposed in 1963, called for the voluntary resignations of high-level national and state officials in order to devote their efforts to rebuilding the Congress party at the grassroots level following India's humiliating 1962 war with China.

Bahuguna was elected CM in mid-1970s and was acceptable to every section of the society, irrespective of caste and religion. However, he was replaced by a far less acceptable CM, N.D. Tiwari, during Emergency and a second time again after the removal of Veer Bahadur. The tendency of having pliable leaders in key positions continues till date in the Congress. This practice of appointment of PCC presidents and CMs in particular, and other functionaries of the party in general, has virtually finished the party.

However, the party could afford to have weak CMs under the leadership of both Indira ji and Rajiv, since both had charisma and the ability to bounce back after setbacks. Their pan-India acceptance and appeal, the hard work they put in and their connect with grassroots leaders and workers meant that the party gained ground both at the Centre and in the states. People in those days voted in national and state elections keeping in mind the national leadership of Indira ji and Rajiv—just as they do today, with Narendra Modi as the central figure. But after Rajiv's assassination, there has not been a single leader in the Congress who could match either him or Indira ji. In such a situation, a weak Congress CM was a further blow to the party's rise.

This was a phenomenon I had to deal with when I landed in the state of UP. I told Veer Bahadur that I would like the Congress party to organize 1,000 public meetings across the state in the coming year to counter the lies being spread by V.P. Singh and his colleagues. After hearing me out, he said that it was not possible even to organize one, let alone 1,000 public meetings. I had to tell him that in a democracy, people would like to hear from both the sides. Since V.P. Singh and his people were moving across the state, only their version was being heard and reported by the media. If we didn't counter that, the public was bound to accept his viewpoint unchallenged. Hence, we should counter that publicly through public meetings and be equally heard and reported in the media.

After hearing me, he wanted the presence of the PCC president Balram Singh Yadav in the meeting as well. Thus, Balram Singh was asked to come from Lucknow to Delhi to discuss the issue in detail. Both Veer Bahadur and Balram Singh were perfect gentlemen but lacked courage and initiative, and neither of the two were able to make decisions about organizing the first meeting. Hence, I had to come forward and tell them I would organize the first meeting that they had to attend. I told them that I would confirm the venue and date within the next two–three days.

The following day, I called a meeting of leaders from Moradabad, led by a family friend and Lok Sabha MP Hafiz Mohd Siddiq, at my official residence in Delhi and told them that I wanted to hold a public meeting of at least one lakh people in their city. I further told them that it was a question of my prestige. They were not only supportive but also overwhelmed that I was giving them an opportunity to arrange the first meeting after taking over as general secretary in charge of the state. Siddiq was close to me and a highly respected person both in religious and political circles. After meeting with these leaders, I informed the CM and PCC president about the date and venue of the public rally.

A fortnight later, hovering over Moradabad city in a helicopter, accompanied by the CM and the PCC president, we came across the stadium where people had gathered for the meeting. The CM looked down at the vast crowd and remarked that the pilot had come to a wrong place and that it seemed like one of V.P. Singh's meetings. I immediately corrected him, saying that it was *our* meeting. We landed outside the stadium and had our first public rally of about 40,000–50,000 people. It was indeed a big success given the situation.

Veer Bahadur and Balram Singh were now completely transformed. In comparison to their earlier lack of enthusiasm during my initial meeting with them regarding rallies, they now remarked that if an 'outsider' could organize a public meeting in UP, they would no longer lag behind! From then on, there was no stopping us—we ran a year-long public campaign in the state and had one public meeting in each block in an attempt to fulfil my target of 1,000 meetings in one year.

Determined Fight-Back in Punjab

I would simultaneously attend public meetings in Punjab, where I had planned a six-month schedule as part of the first phase of my mass contact programme. I was at five public meetings in each assembly constituency every day, thus attending more than 600 meetings in six months. I had drawn the roadmap for Punjab for six months with the help of PCC president Beant Singh, PCC vice president Rajinder Kaur Bhattal and former PCC chief S.S. Randhawa.

Punjab posed a different set of challenges, both in terms of risk of physical harm and political breakthrough. Our state unit had become inactive. Leaders and workers were scared to even enter the villages, forget about holding meetings, since militants had killed many leaders and innocent people. The other major party in the state, the SAD, had lost the courage to speak out against militants. Even the elected MPs and Union ministers of the Congress couldn't enter Punjab, let alone go to their respective constituencies.

My first meeting thus began from Dera Baba Nanak in Gurdaspur district bordering Pakistan. I addressed the sparse crowd at the venue in the presence of Singh, Randhawa, Bhattal, firebrand state Youth Congress president M.S. Bitta and many other leaders. I was the last speaker, and as I was about to get up to address the crowd, a slip of paper was passed on to me by a leader seated on the dais. Since the writing was in Punjabi, I handed over the slip to Singh. Once my speech was over, the PCC president told me that the gurdwara near our meeting venue had invited me and wanted to present me with a *saropa* (a robe of honour).

I asked everyone, including Singh, for advice. The local leaders accompanying us advised me against accepting the invitation; they were fearful of physical harm to me in the shrine. After all, nobody knew what kind of elements were in the vicinity of the gurdwara so close to Pakistan, which was complicit in the separatist Khalistan movement. After thinking for a while, I told my Punjab leaders that I had two options: 'If I accept the invitation, I run the risk of physical death. If I refuse the invite, it would be my political demise.' My refusal to accept the invitation would be a surrender to fear and also be a political setback to me and my party, and an insult to the sentiments of the Sikh community. 'I prefer physical death to political death,' I said.

On hearing this, Singh, who was far older than me, remarked that if a young man like me was willing to risk my life, he would not lag behind. He offered to accompany me. We climbed the long flight of stairs to the gurdwara. We were received with great warmth. I gave a short speech exhorting the values of peace and brotherhood. I told them of the inner peace I experienced whenever I visited the Golden Temple in Amritsar. My address was well received and I was loaded with saropas by members of the shrine.

After that, there was nothing to stop us from going ahead full steam with our Punjab campaign. Not surprisingly, by the end of the first phase after six months, our last meeting at Ludhiana attracted a crowd of 50,000 people. I was just 38 years old, full of hope, courage and enthusiasm, bearing the great responsibility to turn around the situation in Punjab. As general secretary in charge of the state, it was now for me to retrieve the situation, leading from the front. I ensured that all PCC office bearers, MLAs and DCC presidents would accompany me and the PCC president in their respective areas for the next six months. I also announced in the PCC meeting that should any PCC office bearer not participate in the programme, they would be dropped from the list of officer bearers. My decision was appreciated by party president Rajiv Gandhi.

Immediately after the meetings of first phase that lasted six months, keeping with my earlier announcement, I suspended six office bearers of the PCC from the party for their failure to participate in the programme. Most of the leaders who had not participated had high connections in Delhi, but I dropped them without bothering about their contacts.

Two days later, when I was in Delhi, I was told by Rajiv that two–three senior leaders, including Union ministers, had come to him with the complaint that I had suspended their nominees or supporters from the Punjab PCC. But what was heartening to know was Rajiv's response: 'I told them that it was said that they themselves didn't go to Punjab and also wanted their supporters to remain silent and not participate in the mass contact programmes.' He categorically told them, 'Ghulam Nabi Azad has risked his life, resigned from the ministry and taken upon himself to be in Punjab till the situation improved. You people sit in Delhi and defend those who could not work. I feel sorry for you.'

This is the kind of support Rajiv would give to his colleagues. I had not sought the permission of the Congress president to sack those six general secretaries and vice presidents, yet Rajiv had supported my move and appreciated it too. The advantage of this decision was that for next three years, each and every leader was in the field with me in Punjab, and together, we succeeded in bringing back normalcy, followed by fair elections.

However, this normalcy came at a huge price. In the first phase of six months, while we addressed more than 600 small and big meetings, we lost more than few dozen of our party leaders, which included office bearers, MLAs and block presidents, in attacks by militants. But our drive against militancy continued unabated. Rajiv had instructed the IB to work closely with me and warn me of any impending terrorist attacks. He had also kept a six-seater aircraft at my disposal through Captain Satish Sharma because I had to commute between Punjab and UP to carry out the programmes simultaneously, sometimes with first half of the day devoted to UP and the second half to Punjab. In effect, in the initial days, we were addressing our own leaders and security men accompanying us, since the general public was scared to take part in gatherings where militants and their supporters were criticized.

I would keep Beant Singh's and my overnight stays a complete secret, and our programmes were not known even to the security personnel accompanying us. I must confess that both Singh and I owe our lives to the IB officers who tipped us off on several occasions, otherwise, both of us would have been assassinated long back, like our fellow Congressmen. The IB's timely information about the places and dates the militants had planned our killing saved us from militant attacks on more than two–three dozen occasions.

One such close escape was in January 1988 in Tarn Taran, then a militant hotbed. I was to reach there by road from Amritsar. A day before, I was in Delhi and had gone to the airport to see off the PM, who was leaving for London on a long foreign tour. But before the flight took off, he received a message at the airport that Khan Abdul Ghaffar Khan, also called Frontier Gandhi, had died in Pakistan. Rajiv decided on the spot to visit Pakistan immediately to place a wreath on Frontier Gandhi's mortal remains and return to Delhi airport and, thereafter, proceed with his scheduled trip.

Frontier Gandhi's last rites were to be performed the next day at his native place in Afghanistan. After his return from Pakistan, Rajiv announced at the Delhi airport that a high-level Indian delegation comprising Vice President Shankar Dayal Sharma, H.K.L. Bhagat and Farooq Abdullah would attend Frontier Gandhi's final rites in Afghanistan on behalf of the Indian government.

On his way, aboard the aircraft, Rajiv must have realized that the delegation did not have any leader of the Congress party. On reaching London, he immediately sent a message to the PMO that I was also to be part of that delegation. The PMO informed the vice president accordingly. According to my programme, I was to take a flight next morning for Amritsar and from there to Tarn Taran, but after receiving the message from the PMO to accompany the vice president to Afghanistan, I got busy with making the arrangements.

On reaching Kabul, our delegation, led by the vice president, met Afghan President Najibullah. He said that the deceased leader's native village was some distance away at Jalalabad and another aircraft would take us there. He said that the take-off would be at night and the local pilots knew the navigation better—even the aircraft's inner lights would be switched off while take-off to avoid possible attacks from militants. After attending the funeral, we returned to Kabul, again in the dark.

Earlier, while still in Delhi, in the rush of getting ready for the early morning Kabul trip, I had forgotten to inform Punjab leaders and workers in Amritsar about the change in programme and the cancellation of the Tarn Taran tour. On return from Kabul after three–four days, I contacted them and went to Amritsar. When I was about to land, I saw a mass of security people at the tarmac and began to wonder which important person was about to land there! As soon as I touched ground, hundreds of security personnel surrounded me and escorted me to the airport terminal.

They informed me that they had apprehended a bunch of militants the day I had left for Kabul, who, during interrogation, revealed a plan to kill me along the road journey from Amritsar to Tarn Taran.

To ensure that they did not fail, like on many earlier occasions, traps had been laid at three spots, one after the other, on the way. Had I stuck to my original itinerary and not gone to Kabul, it is possible that I would have been killed in one of the militant attacks.

I owe my life to two people: Rajiv and Frontier Gandhi! Had the latter not died, I would not have gone to Afghanistan and had Rajiv not made me part of the delegation at the last minute, I might not have survived the militant attack.

Nearly two years ago, on 2 October 1986, while I was the MoS for home affairs, an assassination attempt had been made on Rajiv at Raj Ghat, when he had gone there to pay homage to the Father of the Nation. President Zail Singh was there too. While they were putting on their shoes after paying homage, I was standing right behind them. Rajiv was accompanied by his wife Sonia. Meanwhile, a gunman behind a nearby bush had fired from a crude pistol. In a matter of few seconds, security persons in and around the area fired thousands of revolver shots. I ensured that both the dignitaries were safely escorted to their respective cars, after which I returned to oversee the search for the culprit, who was ultimately found.

That incident had led me to begin reading books on how various international leaders, who were constantly targets of assassination bids by some big powers, managed their safety and security. Leaders such as Yasser Arafat, Muammar Gaddafi and Fidel Castro were the subjects of my study. I realized that the key to safety was to keep one's movements secret and never follow a set pattern of visiting places or office. I made use of those learnings during my Punjab campaign days, never staying at one place for long and not taking anybody into confidence about the last-minute change in my plans, especially on overnight stays. My first three-year constant presence in Punjab was a difficult time, and I was faced with the possibility of death at the hands of militants at every moment.

Walking with Destiny

Rajiv had stormed to power in the 1984 Lok Sabha Elections after achieving a feat like never before in India's political history. Despite this, he was clear that the 1989 Lok Sabha Elections would be tough and that the Congress would have to go the extra mile to win. He said that party general secretaries at the national level should not contest elections but devote their time to party electioneering and campaigning. 'And you certainly will not contest,' he told me, adding that I would have to share his burden for nationwide campaigning, as I had done five years earlier.

Over the years, I had, at some point in time or the other, held the charge of nearly every major state as AICC general secretary and, therefore, had an intimate understanding of their issues. I also had a rapport with senior leaders of those states. Besides, I was now counted among the 'seniors'—of course not in terms of age but by virtue of being the general secretary of the AICC and holding charge of maximum states, being a member of the CPB, besides being a member of the CWC. The 'real' seniors had quit the party during the 1977 General Elections and when the Congress split in January 1978. Some of them returned later, but they no longer enjoyed the seniority they had earlier and also lost their following in the party. I was lucky to have more acceptability in the party across the country by the virtue of being general secretary of the IYC from 1977 to 1980.

Unfortunately, the Congress party lost the 1989 General Elections, and V.P. Singh became the PM, heading a National Front government. But we were not decimated and were confident of a comeback soon since we did not believe that Singh would last long with his ragtag alliance that was supported by the Left, the Right and the socialists.

Even after the Lok Sabha election defeat, Rajiv continued to be the party president and LoP in the Lok Sabha. However, he could now spare more time for party affairs. I was still battling to bring peace and normalcy in Punjab. After completing the first, second, third and fourth phases involving various programmes between 1987 and 1990, things had begun to look better for the party. People's participation in our meetings had increased manifold, and militancy and militancy-related incidents had reduced to a great extent.

During this period, Punjab police chief K.P.S. Gill was also able to control militancy to a great extent. Gill's job was to fight militancy and the militants, and my task was to ensure public participation and the mobilization of people's opinion against militancy by visiting almost each village at the grassroots level along with my party colleagues. Fortunately, both of us succeeded in our respective missions almost simultaneously.

A few months later in October–November 1990, I suggested to Rajiv that since things had improved largely, he too should meet political leaders of Punjab, district-wise, at his official residence at 10, Janpath. He readily agreed, and the process of meeting Punjab's leaders continued for almost 10 days, with each district taking a few hours every day. Rajiv was a great listener and always liked to go into the depth of the problems.

But I was far from physically fit to attend these meetings, which I had proposed and arranged. I had been suffering from black motions, which was a result of the neglect of my health for three years, shuttling between Punjab and UP during that period. I would have just one meal a day and suffered from lack of sleep. Initially, I had developed acidity, followed by ulcer; the ulcer then started bleeding. Thereafter came black motions.

It was during one of those meetings at 10, Janpath that I had to visit the toilet more than three times. After one of the visits, I looked visibly pale and exhausted. When Rajiv enquired about my condition, I told him about my ailment. He was greatly agitated and also angry at the manner I had neglected my health. He cancelled all the meetings and directed me to return home and consult a doctor. I had two family doctors, a physician and a surgeon from AIIMS and Dr Ram Manohar Lohia Hospital (RML), visiting me twice a day: once in the morning before I left home for the meetings and once in the evening after I returned. The doctors had prescribed medicines and advised me complete rest. But the moment they left after their morning round, I would get dressed to attend the meetings with the Punjab leaders at 10, Janpath without their knowledge.

On the day I was asked by Rajiv to go home, the meeting had continued a little longer. After I arrived at my residence with great difficulty, I saw that both doctors were waiting for me. They checked my pulse and blood pressure and found that the pressure had dipped alarmingly. Just then, I rushed to the washroom and collapsed there. I had suffered an ulcer burst. Half an hour later, I gained consciousness and found myself in bed. My legs had gone numb; my jaw seemed to be in a state of paralysis and I could not speak. However, I could clearly hear the doctors talking; an ambulance that had been called for had got stuck in the traffic. Somehow, I was loaded in a car and taken to RML. I don't know what happened thereafter, and when I opened my eyes after a few hours, I found myself in a hospital room.

I was told that my operation had lasted six-and-a-half hours, and parts of my bleeding intestine and stomach had to be removed. While I was recovering on the third or fourth day of my operation, around 12.30 a.m., I felt a sharp pain on the left side of my chest. The resident doctor on duty somehow thought that it might have been a heart attack, and without checking up with his seniors and fulfilling other formalities, he treated me for a heart attack. As a result, I lost almost the entire water content of my body; my blankets and bed were soaked.

Now, a new complication had cropped up with the wrong medication, which continued through the next day. That night, it was touch and go. Rajiv would visit me thrice a day: morning, lunchtime and around midnight. On the night my health condition deteriorated, I found Rajiv, PM Chandra Shekhar and the doctors of AIIMS and RML discussing among themselves as to how my life could be saved.

I could hear everything but was unable to speak; I had oxygen tubes in my nose and IV channels in my arms. They were discussing the possibility of shifting me to London. The PM offered his aircraft for the purpose. However, Rajiv, being an ex-pilot, said that the aircraft could not directly fly from Delhi to London since it would have to land and take-off in Dubai. The doctors refused to take the risk of additional take-off and landing, and ultimately it was decided that the best possible treatment would be to continue being treated at RML.

Luckily, I survived and was discharged from the hospital after 29 days of hospitalization. The doctors and God had come to my rescue, but I felt that no sacrifice was greater than one that brings peace and normalcy in Punjab.

Barely a week after I returned home, I accompanied Rajiv on his four-day visit to Gujarat and Odisha, since I was in charge of both these states. Ahmed Patel was the PCC president of Gujarat. At the very first meeting in Gujarat, I fainted. Clearly, I had not fully recovered from the operation I had undergone just a few weeks ago. I was brought to Vadodara for a night halt. Doctors were called, and the next morning, I was flown back to Delhi, while Rajiv continued with his programme.

But little did I know then that destiny would have its own ways, something that mere mortals like me could not comprehend. Before a tragedy that none of us had imagined occurred, the deteriorating situation in J&K caused widespread alarm across the country. I, too, was impacted by it.

7

A NATION IN MOURNING

Few people realize today that one of the devastating fallouts of the Congress's defeat in the 1989 Lok Sabha Elections was the explosion of militancy in J&K. The political instability there made matters even worse.

Prime Minister V.P. Singh had little understanding of the state. It is true that he had Mufti, a Kashmiri, as the Union minister of home affairs. But even with the status of *mufti*,[6] he was ill-placed to handle matters of his home state. Besides, he faced challenges from the NC's Farooq Abdullah and, of course, the Congress party. He did not get along well with either of them, and that clouded his judgment. Moreover, Mufti had not worked much at the national level and, thus, had to first grasp the nuances of national politics and learn about the internal problems being faced by this huge country. All this left him with little time for his home state.

Though Mufti had quit the Congress party and had become our political opponent, I still maintained excellent personal relations with him. There were two reasons for me not opposing him. One, he had been responsible for keeping the Congress party alive in J&K after the Indira–Sheikh Accord in 1975; he had laboured hard for more than a decade and made huge sacrifices for the party. Two, he had helped me in my initial days in politics when I was in the Youth Congress.

Although I had a personal rapport with Mufti, I did not intervene when he quit the Congress in 1987. It would have been futile even

---

[6]Muslim legal expert who makes decisions based on religious laws

if I had tried because there were deep differences between him and Rajiv. In fact, at some level, he had become disenchanted with the Congress back in 1975, after Indira ji came to an understanding with Sheikh Abdullah. Mufti, then a Congress leader, was miffed over the Indira–Sheikh Accord but had agreed to abide by Indira ji's decision with a heavy heart. Indira ji was then not only the PM but also the party's supreme leader. There was no question of challenging her decisions.

However, once she was ousted in the 1977 General Elections, Mufti, then the PCC president of J&K, probably thought that she was politically finished for good and decided, in a way, to challenge her authority. The party unit, which he headed in the state, announced the withdrawal of support to Sheikh's government. Indira ji was furious, since the decision was taken without her approval, but there was little she could do then.

Assembly elections were held in June 1977, following the withdrawal of support. Mufti was projected as the chief ministerial candidate of the Congress party, but he lost both constituencies he contested from. The NC, under Abdullah's leadership, came back to power with an overwhelming majority. Clearly, the voters had not liked Mufti's betrayal of both Indira ji and the accord. This made Mufti even more unpopular, and the gap between the Abdullah family and Mufti further widened.

At the Centre, the V.P. Singh government was in power because of the BJP's support. He was, thus, totally dependent on the BJP, which had its own agenda to manage the affairs of J&K. In January 1990, Jagmohan Malhotra was appointed as the governor of the state against the wishes of CM Farooq Abdullah. Both did not see eye to eye; they never did even during Jagmohan's earlier stint in 1984 when Rajiv was the PM and the NC was then in alliance with the Congress party in the state. It was during this first stint of Farooq as the CM that his government was toppled by a rebellion led by G.M. Shah, his brother-in-law, who was also a senior minister. The NC split into two groups, one owing allegiance to Farooq and the other to Shah. Shah did not have the majority to form the government, but Mufti, who was the state Congress president and also bitterly opposed to Farooq, extended support to Shah. These developments had happened under Governor Jagmohan's watch.

During CM Shah's tenure, the government remained unstable, and Jagmohan exploited the situation to exert his authority and became more assertive. Even after the coalition of the NC under Farooq's leadership and the Congress party coming to power in November 1986, Jagmohan continued to throw his weight, which angered Farooq. In the midst of Jagmohan's over-assertiveness, three horrific massacres of civilians took place in the state. The governor was held accountable and removed within a few months.

Jagmohan's second-time arrival compounded the problem for both the Centre and the state. Farooq was against Jagmohan's appointment as governor. He was correct in saying that he couldn't have fought militancy without the full support of the governor. He decided to quit against the appointment. With Farooq's resignation, J&K again came under Governor's Rule. With this decision, the Congress party and NC completely lost connect with the state administration headed by Jagmohan; at the national level, the Congress party was already in Opposition since December 1989.

My Paradise Lost

It was a crucial period for the state and its people; militancy had arrived in a big way. Some 17 months earlier, Kashmir had faced its first major militancy attack when two bombs exploded in Srinagar in late July 1988. Nobody realized then that it was only the first of many strikes to come. The Jammu and Kashmir Liberation Front (JKLF) was at its peak.

Kashmiri Pandits became the first targets of the militants for three reasons: one, because they were staunch Congress supporters; two, because they were pro-India and did not support the separatists and militants and three, because the Kashmiri Pandits held several important positions in the Union government offices in Kashmir, so targeting them was the militants' way of challenging the Centre.

Soon, the unfortunate persecution of the Pandits began; the militants used loudspeakers to spread the message, asking Kashmiri

Pandits to leave Kashmir. Contrary to general belief, not all the clerics in charge of the mosques were supportive of the militants; in fact, most of them actually supported Kashmiri Pandits. Some of them made those announcements out of fear of the militants rather than out of sympathy for them. However, the fact remains that the Pandits were harassed and many lost their lives at the hands of militants. Fearful of their lives, the Pandits began leaving Kashmir, ultimately abandoning their homes and hearths.

The Centre's mismanagement of the problem led to the mass exodus of Kashmiri Pandits, which remains a blot on the people of Kashmir in general and the Janata Dal government in particular, whose representative, Governor Jagmohan, was heading the government of J&K at that time. The Pandits could have been relocated to some other parts of Kashmir with adequate security cover. Instead, they were not only allowed but also facilitated to migrate to Jammu in public transport arranged by the then government, thus making their return to their homes even more problematic.

The Pandits had every reason to be afraid and flee, since prominent members of their community, such as Judge Neelkanth Ganjoo (sitting high court judge), Lassa Kaul (director, DD, Kashmir), Prem Nath Bhat (advocate), Tika Lal Taploo (BJP leader) and many others occupying important positions in government, were killed by the militants in the initial days of militancy.

The well-off businessmen and professionals also had been targeted by the militants and had no option but to leave the Kashmir Valley. Several of them, particularly doctors, engineers and businessmen, relocated themselves in Gulf countries. Unfortunately, the less privileged relocated themselves in Jammu. Most people, including the Pandits, thought that the migration would be a temporary matter, and once the situation normalized in six months or so, those who had left would return. That never happened because the situation in Kashmir turned from bad to worse in the coming years. Some of them could afford to rent houses, but a large number of Kashmiri Pandit families were accommodated in tents, both in the summer and biting winter. Their condition was really pathetic. However, I must admire the courage of the 600-odd Pandit families and the overwhelming majority of Sikhs who stayed back in Kashmir despite the threats to their safety.

The targeted killings also led to a 'political exodus' from the Kashmir Valley. The leaders of all mainstream political parties, be they national or regional, right from district to the state level, fled to Jammu, since they had now come under the radar of militants. Even within Jammu province—in rural areas of Chenab Valley, and Pir Panjal in particular, and some areas of Reasi, Udhampur and Kathua districts—both Muslim and Hindu leaders and prominent people from the Muslim-dominated districts shifted to Jammu city because of the targeted killings.

Thereafter, it was the turn of prominent Muslims in various fields to be targeted. Academics like the sitting vice chancellor of Kashmir University Mushir-ul-Haq, former Assembly Speaker Wali Muhammad Itoo, religious leader Maulvi Umar Farooq and many others were killed by militants. This led to the flight of thousands of Kashmiri Muslims from the Kashmir Valley, a fact that did not get as much prominence as the Kashmiri Pandits' exodus. A large number of these Kashmiri Muslims, like their Hindu brethren, settled in Jammu and in different parts of the country.

The influx of people into Jammu city from Kashmir and neighbouring districts of Jammu province had both negative and positive impacts on Jammu city. The negative impact was that the exodus caused immense stress on the city's resources, particularly power and water supplies. The positive impact was on the economy in general of Jammu city; more people pouring in resulted in more business of all kinds. The arrival of the migrants expanded the local market by nearly three times and economic activity grew manifold almost overnight. The demand for rental accommodation also increased. This resulted in good business for locals who had residential premises to hire out.

The migration of both Hindus and Muslims gave rise to an interesting by-product, the cosmopolitanism of Jammu city, with both Hindus and Muslims living side by side and sharing the province's resources. Over time, a number of families from Ladakh would also settle down in Jammu for six months of the winter season. Although there was no militancy, they came to escape the chilling cold of Ladakh.

Here, I must salute the people of Jammu for their exceptional tolerance and capacity to accommodate people from outside the districts, without any hesitation and while maintaining peace and harmony.

Unfortunately, the same cannot be said about some political parties, which took full advantage initially of the chaos and the migration and exploited the situation politically. These parties not only backed the Pandits settled in Jammu but also instigated them to routinely issue anti-Kashmiri statements, which made the possibility of the Pandits' return to the Kashmir Valley even more complicated. In time to come, however, the very same political parties that initially exploited religious sentiments began to demand that they be shifted back to Kashmir because the local Jammu population, among whom the parties had established support, had begun to resent the demands on scarce resources and jobs as a result of the large-scale migration of the Pandits.

However, it broke my heart that the once-peaceful paradise on Earth had been torn apart by violence. I strongly felt then, as I do today, that Kashmir was and is incomplete without Kashmiri Pandits, since they are the original inhabitants of the region and are an inalienable part of a composite culture that we are proud of. The fact is that the Kashmiri Pandits lost their native place, were uprooted and totally ruined.

Sadly, I was witness to this ruin and destruction during my subsequent visits to J&K as a Union minister. These visits were usually in less happier circumstances. I would go in the aftermath of a serious terror strike by the militants or when clashes between the security forces and militants resulted in collateral loss or loss of lives of innocent citizens.

I still recall my first trip to Srinagar as a Union minister. I reached the state guest house at Sonwar under an elaborate security cover from the airport. I was given the *salami* (salute) by Central Reserve Police Force (CRPF) jawans in the lawns of the guest house. I also heard hundreds of bursts of gunfire from Shankaracharya Hill, just a short distance away. A police officer present told me that it was a signal from the militants holed up high above on the hill to say that they had noted my arrival. The officer further said that the militants had sophisticated devices that enabled them to intercept conversations on the police wireless equipment, and it was from those interceptions that they had learned about my arrival from the time I landed at the airport!

Nevertheless, I started visiting the Kashmiri Pandit camps in Jammu regularly; they were still in tented accommodations, and I would support them by providing them with more tents and typewriters and setting up typewriting training centres. I helped the Pandits in other ways too, like filling up job forms and giving them access to forms of the Staff Selection Commission, the Indian Railways, etc. Many years later, as the CM of J&K, I took a number of initiatives for their settlement in Jammu, particularly accommodation and employment, after taking up the issue with PM Manmohan Singh. However, all this was far from being enough.

During my visits to the state in the early 1990s, I found the political space completely empty in the Kashmir Valley and most parts of the Jammu province. There was hardly any mainstream politician left with whom I could discuss the situation in Kashmir. In fact, there was just one mid-level NC leader, Mohammad Syed Akhoon, with whom I could speak. He, too, lived under massive security cover. Whenever I visited Srinagar, I would send my bulletproof vehicle to fetch him from his residence in the dark, and he would come to the guest house where I was lodged. After discussions, he would be dropped at his place in my vehicle.

Such was the atmosphere then that it was not conducive for not only Kashmiri Pandits but for any nationalist Indian, whether a local or outsider, be they Hindu, Muslim, Sikh or anybody else, to roam around freely. Such was the sorry state of affairs that the Union home minister's own daughter was kidnapped from the streets of Kashmir by the JKLF, who demanded the release of some imprisoned terrorists in lieu of the lady's safe return. Thankfully, the episode ended on a happy note, with the militants letting her go unharmed.

The situation was so bad that even for a common man, coming out of his house meant risking his life. No one was sure of a safe return, even if they had gone to the local market. In fact, many who went for day-to-day work never returned. Even I, whenever I would visit the Kashmir Valley, was not sure of returning to Delhi alive.

My family, too, had been targeted by militants belonging to the Al-Umar Mujahideen. They abducted my youngest brother-in-law, Tassaduq Dev, then aged just 22. The militants demanded the release of some of their jailed men. I issued a press statement that there was no question of succumbing to the militants' demand even if my brother-in-law was to lose his life. The demand was 'unacceptable', I added. My father-in-law, Mohammad Abdullah Dev, supported my position when he, too, came out openly in favour of non-negotiation. Our remarks were widely reported in the media, including leading newspapers such as *The Times of India* and *Qaumi Awaz* New Delhi.[7]

While my brother-in-law was still held captive, a package was found at the doorsteps of the Srinagar office of a news agency. In it was a severed thumb and a note claiming that the body part belonged to Tassaduq—a revenge for the failure of the government to concede to Al-Umar's demand. His family and I remained firm on our position that no exchange should be done with the militants. Eventually, he was released the following year after five–six months in captivity, with both his thumbs intact. Apparently, the severed part in the package belonged to some other unfortunate victim.

The targeting of my family by militants did not end there. There were three more subsequent cases. Mohammad Amin, my wife's cousin, was the administrator of Srinagar Municipal Corporation. One day, while he was coming out of his office after work hours to return home, a militant lying in wait at the main gate fired several bursts of fire from his AK-47. Amin was rushed to a nearby hospital, where he was administered first aid. But since the wounds were of a serious

[7] *The Times of India*, New Delhi edition, dated 2 October 1991, reported:

> Mr. Ghulam Nabi Azad, parliamentary affairs minister and AICC general secretary, has stated that the demand of his brother-in-law abductors for releasing detained militants in lieu of the hostage was unacceptable to the entire family. Mr. Mohd Abdullah Dev, father of the 22-year-old kidnapped Tassaduq has expressed similar sentiments. Mr. Azad said the family was aware of the gravity of the situation. Yet, they were prepared for the worst in order to uphold the value they cherish. Even if Tassaduq is cut to pieces and slain, the Azad family wouldn't urge the government to release detenus as demanded by the kidnappers. Mr. Azad clarified that he was speaking only for his family. It may be recalled that in recent years militants have killed 10 ministers and MLAs belonging to the National Conference.

nature, he was airlifted to RML in Delhi. Doctors operated on him and retrieved a number of bullets from his abdomen. He was discharged six months later. It was a miracle that he survived after being shot multiple times from such close range.

After these two incidents, I had to shift my two brothers-in-law to Delhi and the other two to Bengaluru for almost a decade; they returned only when things improved slightly, but this shift ruined their future lives.

Similarly, my younger brother, Ghulam Abbas, was also the victim of militant violence against my family members. Abbas managed a shop close to our ancestral home in Soti village of Doda district. He would always move about with two armed security men provided by the government, given the threat perception that existed. One day, while he was walking downhill from the residence towards his shop, militants hiding in the nearby maize fields accosted him and opened fire. Fortunately, they missed, but the bullet hit one of security men in the leg. My brother jumped into the maize fields, in which the crops had grown full size in the season. He managed to hide himself effectively. He was also well versed with the topography of the area, unlike the militants, and eventually managed to give the militants a slip. Following this scary incident, my brothers had to be shifted from there to Jammu city for safety concerns and that shop remained closed for good.

The fourth incident involved my father. My parents had stayed behind in Soti. They lived in a three-storey house built in a terraced manner, given the uneven nature of the land in the hilly region. While the main entrance was on the ground floor, there was also a rear door that opened out into the maize fields from the second floor. One day, the household help informed my father in an alarmed voice that he had noticed a large group of armed militants approaching the house; this group included more men than the security forces guarding the house and my parents.

My father immediately had a look at the approaching militants and realized that the security forces on guard were no match for the militants both in number and arms and ammunition they were carrying. Hence, he asked my mother to stay behind (hoping that the militants would not harm an elderly woman) and rushed out of the rear door from the second storey and straight into the maize fields. He walked for around half a kilometre and hid himself at a spot from where he could keep an eye on what was going on at his house. Meanwhile, the militants, not finding my father and dissatisfied by my mother's response that he had gone out for some days, stayed in the house for two full days and nights. Unfortunately, the security forces guarding them had laid their arms before militants.

Realizing the grim nature of the situation, my father walked for nearly 30–40 km during night to reach Thatri, the neighbouring tehsil headquarters, and spoke to me over the phone from the post office. I got in touch with the inspector general of police, S.S. Wazir, who immediately dispatched a strong contingent of police and CRPF to my father's residence. Meanwhile, the militants, perhaps fed up of waiting, and after seeing large number of security forces coming towards them, fled into maize field and ultimately disappeared from that area. Post this incident, my parents had to be shifted to Jammu.

Other leaders including Farooq Abdullah had left the country and had temporarily settled in London with his wife, while his son Omar was still staying in Mumbai. Mufti was relocated to Delhi with family.

On a Path to Nowhere

Clearly, things were worsening with each passing day. PM V.P. Singh and Home Minister Mufti could not do anything, and everything was left to Governor Jagmohan. Mufti, too, was fed up and expressed his helplessness every now and then.

Part of the reason for his inaction was that he belonged to a minority party at the Centre, headed by V.P. Singh, which was struggling for survival on a daily basis. The government was supported from the outside by two polar opposites, the Left and the Right, which were pulling the government in different directions. As if that was not enough, there were fissures within the ruling alliance, with the likes of Devi Lal and Chandra Shekhar constantly snapping at V.P. Singh's heels. It was only a matter of time before the internal contradictions in the V.P. Singh government eventually led to its downfall.

Chandra Shekhar, backed by Devi Lal, wanted to quit the Jan Morcha-led alliance. Rajiv asked me to open channels of communication with Devi Lal. The Haryana strongman was represented by his son, Ranjit Singh Chautala (presently the minister for power, new and renewable energy and jails in Haryana). However, there were other intermediaries working to clinch the issue.

After several rounds of discussions, the Congress decided to support a government led by Chandra Shekhar. The party did not want to form the government with the support of parties that were themselves unstable, nor did it want another general election so soon. Besides, we wanted to concentrate on strengthening the party. It has been my experience that a party in power for a long period of time tends to lose focus on strengthening the party and concentrates more on governance, as it happened with the Congress party between mid-2004 and mid-2014.

A few months later, Chandra Shekhar, who had been the PM for only a few months, had to undergo rather unfortunate circumstances. In March 1991, the Congress party took exception to two constables of the Haryana police keeping an eye on Rajiv's residence and demanded that the PM sack the Haryana government on the charge of spying. Chandra Shekhar refused, saying it would be unconstitutional, and clarified that he himself had nothing to do with the so-called spying episode. The Congress did not relent. Once it became clear that the Congress would withdraw support, Chandra Shekhar resigned on the floor of the House, leading to the general election that we wanted to avoid.

I believed then, and I still believe today, that the Congress party's stand to withdraw support was not wise. I have no idea who advised Rajiv to escalate the issue. I don't think he would have done it if he was left to himself. The issue over which the furore was raised was not of much importance, and matters should have been allowed to rest after the PM's clarification. Further, the PM had been supportive of our demands, like extending Scheduled Tribe (ST) status to Gujjars, Bakarwals and the shepherds in J&K. He had always been an independent-minded person, even taking on Indira ji once upon a time.

At that point in time, I was out of Delhi on party work. Had I been in town, I would have spoken to Rajiv and persuaded him against the withdrawal of support and precipitate action. Had Chandra Shekhar not been pushed to the wall and made to resign, general elections would not have been called and Rajiv would not have lost his life, the fallout of which the party and the country face to this day. I strongly hold the leaders who had advised Rajiv to withdraw support responsible for his death.

Campaign Strategy: To Win and Save India

It was time for another general election in 1991. Since the withdrawal of support took place suddenly, the Congress was not geared up for elections. The entire campaign, therefore, fell on the shoulders of Rajiv and me.

We formed a strategy committee, which included R.K. Dhawan, M.L. Fotedar and me, besides Rajiv. We would meet for long hours, discuss constituencies, conduct SWOT analysis of each constituency and arrive at conclusions on the way ahead. It was decided that Rajiv and I would go to different parts of the country for campaigning and return to Delhi after every two–three days. Meanwhile, in our absence, Dhawan, Fotedar and Vincent George, Rajiv's personal secretary, would seek feedback from our state leaders' candidates and party leaders about the prospects of the party winning. When Rajiv and I would return, they would share the data with us, and we would sit late into the night, sometimes up to 2.00 a.m., discussing the same. The next day, Rajiv and I would again go to different directions to campaign and return to Delhi on a pre-fixed date and time.

George was helping Dhawan and Fotedar. He played an important role in backroom research and coordination. He had a good understanding of the political situation in the country and was well read and knowledgeable. George had earlier worked as staff member with Indira ji when she was in the Opposition from 1977 to 1980. He rose to prominence after Rajiv assumed charge and was the most competent private secretary after Dhawan. Both Dhawan and George knew about every Congress leader of the country and would solve most of the problems at their end without bothering the leader unnecessarily on every issue.

There is a perception that Rajiv's friends interfered in politics and governance, but that is not true. Even during electioneering, his friends were not involved at any stage, and least of all in government work. The involvement of one of his closest friends, Captain Satish Sharma, was limited to campaigning in Rajiv's constituency.

It was the third week of May, and voting had begun in phases. Some parts of the country had already voted, while others were yet to cast their ballots. As usual, Rajiv, Dhawan, Fotedar and I met to fine-tune our strategy for the forthcoming crucial rounds of voting. It was late into the night when we split.

The following morning, Rajiv was to go to some states of the north and then to the south, including Tamil Nadu, while I was to proceed to western India, including Maharashtra. Rajiv asked me to come to 10, Janpath early in the morning and wake him up. When I arrived around 6.00 a.m., I found him awake and pacing the lawns of the residence. Since there was still time before we left for the airport, we spent around half an hour together, walking and talking about various apolitical issues. Then we proceeded to the airport. While I boarded my flight to Nagpur, he left for his programmes.

At the airport, I chanced upon P.V. Narasimha Rao, who, too, was flying to his constituency near Nagpur to pick up his books and other items, which were to be transported to Hyderabad, where he had planned to spend his retirement days, reading and possibly engaging in spiritual matters. Earlier, during the distribution of tickets, Rajiv had asked Fotedar and me to meet with Rao and convince him to contest, since he had declined to do so. The two of us went to Rao's residence late in the night. He was surprised to see us at that hour. We tried to persuade him, but he refused, saying he had had enough of politics and wanted to retire peacefully in his home state. He said, 'You people are young. If you lose, you will still have a political life. But if Congress party forms the government, you can give me some *likhne padhne ka kaam* (reading and writing work) for the party.' He added that contesting elections was an expensive affair, and he did not have the money for it. During those days, the party's coffers were nearly empty. We were in the Opposition and, therefore, had difficulty raising funds for elections. Things had taken a turn for the worse in 1989 after we lost power. Realizing that Rao had made up his mind, we returned empty-handed and reported the matter to Rajiv.

Anyway, at Nagpur airport, nearly 1,000 people had come to receive me. Unfortunately, nobody had come for Rao. Since he was not contesting elections, he had become a nonentity overnight for opportunist Congress workers who go where the 'winds of power' blow. This is the unfortunate aspect of Indian politics—you are in demand when in power and are ignored once you are not. It happened with Indira ji initially in 1977, when she was refused permission to stay even at dak bungalows. However, she was a mass leader and bounced back. Rao wasn't a mass leader, unlike Indira ji. Seeing Rao struggle with his luggage, I stopped and shouted out to our party workers that instead of hanging by my side, they should help the veteran politician Rao with his bags. I personally rushed to him and made him comfortable in his car, which had come to pick him up. Who knew then that this man's fortunes would change almost overnight.

A Dream Dies, an Era Ends

From Nagpur, I visited different parts of Vidarbha region over the next two days. On the evening of 21 May, I had dinner with one of our local leaders and former minister Azhar Husain in Akola. On this tour, I was accompanied by actor-director and friend, Sanjay Khan. That same evening, I was to catch a train from Akola to Mumbai for further electioneering. On reaching Akola railway station, we were told that the train was running late by half an hour. We made ourselves comfortable in the station master's office.

At 9.15 p.m., Hussain called me up with the tragic news of Rajiv's assassination that day at Sriperumbudur in Tamil Nadu. I was stunned and banged the telephone receiver in despair. I also cried out loudly, and people at the station rushed towards me. Soon, the news of Rajiv's assassination spread like wildfire at the station. Grief-struck commuters gathered at platforms. When the train arrived late that evening, I was lifted physically by our workers and seated in the train, accompanied by Sanjay.

I sobbed throughout the overnight train journey. The ulcer that had been operated on just six months ago was exacerbated because of my emotional response to Rajiv's death. I was vomiting blood while coughing. Sanjay gave me sleeping pills for relief. At Mumbai station, a large crowd of Congress workers received me. From Mumbai, I took a flight to Delhi and went straight to Rajiv's place, where his body was lying in state.

It was a traumatic experience, and words cannot explain my grief. Rajiv and I had worked together in the IYC and then in the party and the government. We worked as colleagues, friends, brothers. He was my leader too. His death was a huge personal loss for me. My interest in politics waned; I felt like quitting. But then I thought that it was my responsibility to accomplish his mission.

I restarted the second part of the campaign. I was again accompanied by Sanjay and another friend, S.N. Chaturvedi, from Mathura. Both Sanjay and Chaturvedi were wonderful speakers. Sanjay was a celebrity, and a large number of people would come to see and hear him in pin-drop silence. He had the capacity to keep pace with me. During those days, I used to campaign for days on end and would travel by road for at least for 16–17 hours a day, with hardly one meal during the day. So, only a few leaders would accompany me. But Sanjay and Chaturvedi withstood this physical torture, for which I shall always remain indebted to them. I must admit that I feel extremely sorry that after coming to power in 1991, we could not do anything for them; of course, they never asked for anything, which was so gracious of them.

However, nothing could take away the pain and trauma of Rajiv's death. His assassination was a big loss for the party and the country. Rajiv was dynamic and charismatic and had a vision to take the country to the twenty-first century, which he had made clear way back in 1985, immediately after taking over as PM. A dream, which we all had dreamt, would not come true. I knew then that the entire political scenario of the country had changed forever. Equally important, the scenario for the Congress party had changed too. After Rajiv became the PM, all of us in the party believed that we had got a leader who could take the party from strength to strength for the next several decades. We did not have a second rung of leadership; most of the senior leaders were in their sixties and seventies. After his tragic death, the party simply collapsed. Although the Congress-led United Progressive Alliance (UPA) won the general elections in 2004 and 2009, the party never had a majority of its own and the government had to depend on others for survival. And today, its return to power in the foreseeable future appears to be a bleak possibility.

8

RAO: FROM POLITICAL WILDERNESS TO PRIME MINISTER

With the Rajiv Gandhi era unfortunately over, that too so suddenly and in the midst of a general election, we were left without a charismatic and youthful leader in the second and third phases of polling. The task of nationwide electioneering for the Congress fell on me. I was already neck-deep in work, holding charge of a number of states. I was looking after the organization as AICC general secretary and was in charge of AICC sessions; the CWC and member secretary of the CPB and handling publications, publicity, work of frontal organizations and various AICC cells, including foreign affairs.

We did have a good number of senior leaders, but most of them were contesting elections themselves and could not devote time to national-level campaigning. Unlike most of them, I had the advantage of having known each state since my IYC days and more so as general secretary of the parent body. After each reshuffle of the AICC, which took place quite often, I would get the charge of different states. Thus, I had handled nearly all the states and UTs.

Luckily, being a CPB member secretary, I also knew most of our candidates' contesting elections. The CPB was the party's apex body involved in the selection of candidates for both the Lok Sabha and Rajya Sabha. It was headed by Rajiv and included Kamalapati Tripathi, Darbara Singh, P.V. Narasimha Rao, Virbhadra Singh, Arjun Singh and Maragatham Chandrasekar as members. I, too, was a member and also general secretary in charge of the CPB. Since I had been closely involved with the distribution of tickets and in charge of elections, eventually, after Rajiv's death, I ended up campaigning in nearly 120 parliamentary constituencies.

Voting for the first phase was held on 20 May. The second and third phases of voting were conducted on 12 and 15 June, respectively.

When results were declared, we had both good and bad news. The good thing was that the Congress had emerged as the single-largest party and was within striking distance of forming the government. It won 232 seats out of the 487 that it had contested, doing particularly well in Maharashtra, Karnataka, Andhra Pradesh and Tamil Nadu. The bad news was that we did not do well in the crucial states of UP and Bihar.

The main reason for the poll debacle in UP and Bihar was that the Congress was squeezed out in the 'Mandal and Mandir politics', both being potent issues in the two states. While V.P. Singh's National Front had appropriated the gains arising out of implementing the Mandal Commission's recommendations for reservation to the Other Backward Classes (OBCs), the BJP had benefitted from the Ayodhya temple agitation and won as many as 51 seats from UP.

Since we could not reach the magical halfway mark, and more so because we did not have any pre-poll alliances with other parties, we had to depend on smaller and regional parties to run a minority government. It was clear that we would lay claim to form the government. But with our prime ministerial candidate and leader Rajiv not amidst us, we had no one to lead the government and the party. Hence, the question that remained was: Who would be the PM?

Rao, meanwhile, had still not shifted to Hyderabad for his post-retirement life. After the results, he was in constant touch with me. He was a shrewd politician. He was aware that since I had been involved in the selection of Lok Sabha candidates, besides having been close to Rajiv for over a decade, the winning MPs would not only listen to me but also honour my wishes. He never directly expressed his desire to be PM but would indirectly say that I had the advantage of putting behind my weight to decide on the prime ministerial candidate. To the best of my knowledge, he did not approach any other leader of the party to push his claim, tacitly or otherwise. I understood his intent; after all, I too was a politician!

I shared a good rapport with Rao for a number of reasons. On many past occasions, as general secretary of the party, I would seek his help in drafting political resolutions that were adopted in the AICC sessions. Rao was considered a master of drafting as his language skills to prepare nuanced texts were acceptable to all members. We also shared a common language—Urdu. Often, he would converse with me in chaste Urdu, and I must admit that sometimes his Urdu was even better than mine.

There were several other things in his favour. One, he did not belong to any faction or camp—he was seen as 'neutral'. Two, he had been a loyalist since Indira ji's time. Three, he had vast administrative experience, having served as a minister in Indira ji's and Rajiv's governments; he had also been a minister and CM of Andhra Pradesh earlier. Four, he was well-learned and a master of at least a dozen languages. Last but not the least, he was a dignified figure.

High Drama, with Twists and Turns

There were also other names doing the rounds for prime ministership including those of Arjun Singh, Sharad Pawar and N.D. Tiwari. But each one of them had plus and minus points. Some of them had the support of MPs in their respective states, while others were being opposed by the MPs of their own states.

Arjun Singh, though a capable administrator and popular national leader, was at loggerheads with other senior leaders of his own state of Madhya Pradesh, such as Madhavrao Scindia, Motilal Vora and the Shukla brothers—Shyama Charan Shukla and Vidya Charan Shukla. Another reason against him was that only two-and-a-half years earlier, he had had to give up the chief ministership of Madhya Pradesh on the advice of the CPB because of the Churhat Lottery controversy. Although the state had elected a good number of Congress MPs, yet the name of Arjun Singh could not be considered.

Another strong contender was the strongman of Maharashtra, Sharad Pawar, who was experienced and a down-to-earth leader. He had a number of points in his favour. One, age was on his side. Two, he represented one of the biggest states of the country, Maharashtra. Three, he was a resourceful leader with national appeal. Four, most importantly, he had good relationships with the leaders of other political parties across the country. Unfortunately, he could not qualify as a candidate. It was pointed out that he had joined the Congress party only two–three years back. Doubts were raised on whether he would gel with the party rank and file and whether he would be able to carry everybody along. Another thing that went against him was that a few of his close friends became more active in their campaign to choose him as the PM candidate, and this campaign, instead of helping him, went against him. However, Pawar being who he is, a powerful leader yet polite and gentle, did not pursue his candidature beyond a point, even though his leadership would have provided stability to the Congress party in the long run.

There were also talks of N.D. Tiwari nurturing ambitions of becoming PM, but his candidature was a non-starter. He was soft-spoken, politically sound and affectionate and could strike friendships even with his rivals. His plus point was that he belonged to UP, then the biggest state of the country. However, there was huge resentment against him for destroying the party and ensuring the defeat of his own government both in the Assembly and in Parliament elections in 1989 while he was CM. The reason behind this was that when he was made CM in 1988 by replacing Vir Bahadur Singh, instead of being happy, he became hostile against the leadership. As a result, from mid-1988 till the November 1989 Lok Sabha and Assembly Elections were held, instead of working hard to ensure the return of the Congress party to power, he openly defied the leadership and worked hard against party interests. He virtually paralysed the state government, which finally resulted in the huge defeat of the Congress party in UP, in both the Assembly and the Lok Sabha.

Thus, in 1989, the Congress got only 15 Lok Sabha seats and a little over 90 seats in the Assembly, which was one of the major reasons for the party not returning to power in 1989. As a result, the members of the CPB, the CWC, senior leaders and Congressmen of UP were angry with Tiwari. This defeat in UP had adverse short-term and long-term effects on the performance of the Congress party. The short-term effect was that in the 1991 elections, the number of Congress MPs further dropped from 15 to five. The long-term effect continues till date. With these matters in mind, no one was ready to consider the name of Tiwari for prime ministership.

During this period, many people were in touch with Sonia Gandhi. Although she was not in politics at that time, yet people would interact with her out of respect for the family. I, too, met her in this regard, being general secretary of the organization. Though my association with the Nehru–Gandhi family began from Sanjay and Indira ji's time, I was hardly in touch with Sonia ji during those days. I only began to know her later, when Rajiv joined politics and I got to interact with him. Rajiv would make it a point to attend the Diwali Milan and the Eid Milan parties that I would organize at my residence every year. Sonia ji would accompany him. Even when Rajiv became the PM, the tradition continued. Both Sonia ji and he would my place as main guests and would stay back well after others had left.

The last such party in which Rajiv was present (but without his family) was the Eid Milan in April 1991, almost a month before his assassination. At that time, the CPB meeting was in progress at 10, Janpath to discuss ticket distribution for the Lok Sabha elections. Rajiv suspended the meeting for an hour to attend the event at my place! He could have continued the deliberations while excusing me, but he made that touching gesture at my request and asked all the CPB members to attend the function.

After it was certain that a broad consensus in the party had formed in favour of Rao, I met Sonia ji and discussed the issue with her. She said that Rao was a fine man and a good choice. Rao—who had refused to contest Lok Sabha elections in 1991 and had decided to retire from politics, who had not even campaigned for the party—was persuaded to become the country's PM. No one knows when politics and life can take new turns.

With Rao's name finalized, a meeting of the parliamentary party was called, and he was formally chosen as the leader in the Central Hall of Parliament. Soon after that, he asked me to join him on his drive back to his residence. I suggested to him that he first visit Raj Ghat and the samadhi of other leaders in the vicinity. He liked the suggestion, remarking that the thought had not occurred to him. We proceeded to pay our obeisance, after which I accompanied him to his residence. He asked me for help in choosing his Council of Ministers. I gave him a number of names but did not suggest portfolio allocations, saying that it was the PM's prerogative to do so. Rao was pleased with the response.

Once the ministerial list was finalized, Rao asked me to inform the candidates. I replied that it would be improper for me to do so. Instead, either he or his senior staff member should do the needful. After a few hours, I accompanied him to the Rashtrapati Bhavan where ministers were to be sworn in. As Rao and I were driving to the premises, I was surprised to see one of our Dalit MPs from UP, Ram Lal Rahi, exiting the Rashtrapati Bhavan. I asked the driver to halt, much to Rao's amazement. I told Rao that the man was in the list of ministers he had submitted to the president. 'Oh!' he muttered. The MP was apparently not aware that he had to take the oath! I spoke to him and made him head back to Rashtrapati Bhavan.

At the time of distributing portfolios, Rao said that he wanted me to handle parliamentary affairs. He gave me the same reason that Rajiv had given in 1985. He said that I should take the portfolio since I knew both our party MPs as well as those of the Opposition parties very well, which would help in the smooth functioning of Parliament and would be able to bring stability to the minority government. I had a good relationship with senior Opposition leaders such as Atal Bihari Vajpayee, L.K. Advani, Harkishan Singh Surjeet, Somnath Chatterjee and Indrajit Gupta, Chandra Shekhar, Sharad Yadav, George Fernandes as well as second-line leaders like Nitish Kumar and Ram Vilas Paswan.

Rao hardly had any social contacts, unlike Indira ji and Rajiv, who would organize Iftar parties and invite people from various sections of society across party lines. This would include not just politicians of different hues but also people drawn from academics, arts, media (both national and regional), literature and theology. For the Iftar parties hosted by Indira ji, the task of selecting invitees, especially scholars, intellectuals and editors of Urdu papers from across the country, was generally given to me. She would also attend similar functions organized by party colleagues. She personally knew people and regularly interacted with many of them. Both would also attend other social functions organized by party colleagues.

Rao's belief that I was adept at managing matters in the House was not misplaced. Within a few months, I had made friends with a large number of Opposition MPs. I would go to those who were elder to me; I would invite those of my age group to my house for dinner, lunch and tea or get-togethers. There were occasions when, as the parliamentary affairs minister, I even helped some Opposition party MPs without any immediate gains. Once, for instance, a bunch of Opposition leaders, including Nitish, Paswan and another one from the Biju Janata Dal (BJD), complained to me that the time allotted to their parties was entirely consumed by just one person who represented their block in the Lok Sabha, George Fernandes. He would go on and on, and when he was done with, no time was left for the other leaders of his group to speak.

I played a little mischief here to help them out. I told the complainants of his party that when Fernandes rose to speak, they should simply walk out of the House—one by one, not at the same time. I would also ask my MPs to do the same. The tactic was implemented, which led to a lack of quorum and suspension of proceedings a couple of times for three–four minutes each time, thus disrupting his speech and ensuring that he would lose more time. The trick was played on a few occasions, and Fernandes's speech would end abruptly. Perhaps the senior socialist leader got the message. Thereafter, Fernandes stopped delivering long speeches and others got their chance to speak!

There were also moments when I would consult senior Opposition leaders like Vajpayee and various others from the Left parties and Janata Dal on contentious issues, with a view to avoid those matters being raised or to delay their mention. I would frankly request the senior Opposition leaders to not bring up issues that could create problems in society and were not in the overall interest of the nation, and they would agree provided the matter was avoidable. At times, they would gently persist with a request that the Opposition be given a chance to make a point that could put the government on the defensive, and I would concede to their demand. There was, thus, a lot of give and take to run Parliament smoothly while accommodating one another's viewpoints.

I haven't seen such floor management happening in recent years, which is most unfortunate. There is hardly any camaraderie left; the Opposition and the government behave like each other's worst enemies, and the blame lies on both sides.

The essence of this camaraderie and mutual respect is evident in an incident involving Rajmata Vijay Raje Scindia and her son Madhavrao Scindia. The mother and son shared strained political and personal relations. She knew that I was close to Madhavrao, and that must have led to her resentment and dislike towards me. On one occasion, while the Parliament session was on, Vajpayee was the leader of the Opposition, the Rajmata was the deputy leader, M.L. Khurana was the chief whip of the BJP and L.K. Advani was the party president.

The Rajmata got up to speak during the Zero Hour and sought permission of the Speaker. She said that a delegation of BJP leaders from Jammu had told her that I had helped in the release of three militants from my home district, Doda. On hearing this, the Treasury bench members as well as those from the Left and other like-minded parties rose in protest. There was pandemonium in the House. I requested members of my party and others to take their seats and hear out the Rajmata. After she was done with her short speech, I sought the permission from the Chair to respond.

I said that one, I had not even visited my home district in the last few years. This was because of militancy and I had been busy with party affairs and government work. I was also caught up attending to my constituency in Maharashtra. Two, if I had at all made any such recommendation for the release, then I must have spoken to some high-level officials in J&K—the governor, the chief secretary, the director general (DG) of police, the inspector general of police, the development commissioner, the superintendent of police, a station house officer or somebody. I challenged her to name one person that I had interacted with.

I then requested the Speaker that since an allegation of such a serious nature had been levelled against me, the House should take note of it and that there should be a high-level inquiry. Hence, on behalf of the government, as parliamentary affairs minister, I proposed a four-member parliamentary committee, comprising Advani, the Rajmata and Khurana, with Vajpayee as the chairman, to probe the charges and submit its report to Parliament at the earliest.

Just as I was announcing the panel, Vajpayee walked into the House. After I completed my submission, he got up and asked the Speaker what sort of a committee he was supposed to head. Since he had not heard the earlier part of my speech, I then narrated the incident to him.

He expressed regret that a baseless allegation of such grave nature had been levelled against me and added that perhaps the Rajmata did not know 'who Ghulam Nabi Azad is'. Had she known, she would not have made such an accusation, he added. His response touched my heart and resulted in a huge applause from all sides of the benches.

On hearing this, the Rajmata walked out of the House in a huff. When Khurana followed her in a bid to placate her, Vajpayee stopped him from doing so! It was a great gesture from the statesman. Though he was close to the Rajmata, he did not allow their personal relationship to come in the way of truth and took a principled stand in my favour, as the allegations made against me by the Rajmata were totally unfounded, baseless and politically motivated.

The Rajmata was a sober, dignified and intelligent lady. I am sure that she must not have believed in the allegations either. However, perhaps her dislike for me because of my close friendship with Madhavrao and maybe pressure from some of her party leaders from Jammu clouded her judgment. Later on, when we met one day in the Central Hall, she apologized to me and clarified that she had been misled by some of her party workers from Jammu.

Outside Parliament, PM Rao got off to a cracking start with economic reforms. Along with his finance minister, Manmohan Singh, he helmed what would turn out to be the most comprehensive revamp of the economy—the fruits of which the country has reaped for decades thereafter. We successfully pushed through these changes in Parliament despite heading a minority government, and it was my duty as parliamentary affairs minister to get reform Bills passed, although we did not have a majority of our own or any alliance with any party. We sailed through the votes of no confidence on a number of occasions. Parliament functioned smoothly, helped by the personal rapport I enjoyed with senior Opposition leaders. I made sure to include maximum number of Opposition leaders as part of parliamentary delegations abroad and also in some foreign visits that the PM would make.

Apart from ensuring the smooth conduct of business in Parliament, I managed another important achievement—that of introducing the system of parliamentary standing committees. It was originally the idea of a senior party leader and the then Speaker of Lok Sabha, Shivraj Patil, but it needed the Cabinet's approval. When I first brought the proposal before the Cabinet, it was rejected. However, when I presented it before the Cabinet a second time, the suggestion gained acceptance and was approved in 1993.

Shivraj Patil, in my opinion, was one of the best Speakers we have had. Tactful, considerate, well-informed and affable, he was also the first Speaker of the Lok Sabha who had been Deputy Speaker and Speaker of both the Maharashtra Assembly and Parliament—a rare honour. I can say with authority that he was also one of the most honest politicians I have come across. He was a landlord with modest holdings and routinely sold off his property to fund his politics rather than depend on donations from the corporate world. He would unfortunately come under unfair attack in the aftermath of the 26/11 Mumbai terror attacks in 2008, not only because he was the Union minister for home affairs but also, of all things, for his sartorial taste. I don't understand how wanting to dress well can be a subject of criticism.

Floor Management of a Different Kind

Despite the excellent relations I shared with members of the Opposition, there were some within my own party who were forever scheming to cut me to size. They believed that if they could not rise in stature on merit, they could bring me to their level. Perhaps they were frustrated that I continued to be in the PM's good books despite taking him on, even if indirectly on number of occasions. One such devious move to embarrass me was made in April 1992 at the Tirupati session of the AICC, where, besides other things, the elections for the CWC was to take place.

Usually, elections for the CWC are held simultaneously with the conduct of the AICC plenary session. Of the 20 members of the CWC then, 10 were to be elected by the AICC delegates, while the remaining 10 were to be nominated by the Congress president. The list of 10 members to be elected are generally chosen in consultation with the party president 'unofficially' and circulated in advance among the AICC members for their endorsement through voting. However, besides this, any member can contest and, if they have the support of members, can get elected. The elected candidates, however, are considered higher in stature, since they are chosen through the ballot, as opposed to the ones nominated by the party president. My name was naturally among the 10 candidates seeking election and also in the panel unofficially approved by the Congress party president.

During sessions, the party president presides over the session. He also takes time-off in between to attend to other work or meet different delegations in a separate room specially meant for the party president attached to the venue of the session. During his absence, a senior CWC member presides over the business. In the 1992 AICC session, Rao excused himself and went to the adjoining room and asked me to preside over the session. I was still the general secretary in charge of the organization and the AICC session, in addition to being a Union minister. While proceedings of the session were on, the election for 10 CWC members was also happening simultaneously.

After sometime, while I was still presiding over the session, my friend and then CM of undivided Andhra Pradesh, N. Janardhana

Reddy, came on to the stage. He whispered into my ear, 'Brother, why have you withdrawn your name from the contest?' For a moment, I could not grasp the remark. He repeated the sentence, adding that my name had been struck off from the list of 10 members to be elected and replaced by another Muslim candidate.

I was shocked. I told him that I had not withdrawn from the race. He then told me that two senior leaders, one from J&K and the other from MP, had told Rao in his room that Azad stood no chance of winning because no AICC members had been elected from J&K due to the issue of militancy there. This was a silly reason since there were just 13 AICC members from J&K out of a total 1,100; the figure was a drop in the ocean in comparison. They told the PM that my name could be added in the nominated list since I was a senior leader. Rao had categorically asked them to seek my consent before going ahead, Reddy told me.

It was obvious that these two leaders had ignored the PM's directive and proceeded to strike off my name without bringing it to my notice and seeking my consent. I had to do something to salvage the situation. I handed over the charge of conducting the proceedings to another senior member, Sitaram Kesri, and reached the place where the polling was on. I dragged a chair and stood on it. Waving a copy of the list, I told the gathering in a loud voice that my name had been removed and replaced without my consent and that I was very much in the race; hence, I requested them to vote for me. That caused a commotion, and the AICC members surrounded me. By then, 40 per cent of the polling was already over. After making my point, I came down, asked some of my close associates to keep an eye on the elections and went back to attend the session.

Finally, with the grace of God and the support I enjoyed within the party, and despite all the mischief, I was lucky to win and was number five in the order of votes secured. But for Janardhana Reddy, I would have become the victim of a dirty game. I later told Rao about the incident. He was deeply upset and shocked.

Rao showed sincerity and impartiality in conducting the elections for the CWC, and even for the post of presidents of PCCs. This, to an extent that in his own home state of Andhra Pradesh, V. Hanumantha

Rao, who belonged to his rival camp, was elected as the PCC chief.

One day, after the CWC and PCC presidents' elections were held, Rao told me that only I could help him since the elected Andhra Pradesh president was close to me. When I was the IYC president, Hanumantha was the state president of the youth wing and we had bonded well. Rao asked me to seek his resignation and said that he would ensure that Hanumantha would be made a minister in the state government. I went to Hyderabad, met my old colleague of the Youth Congress days and sought his resignation. He tendered it without hesitation and another candidate amenable to Rao was appointed as the president. But the unfortunate part is that Rao did not keep his word and Hanumantha was not made a minister.

When a Dome Fell

I soon realized that this would not be the only occasion when the PM would not honour his word. It was 6 December 1992. The Babri mosque in Ayodhya was demolished by a rampaging mob. The incident led to large-scale violence in many parts of the country—riots broke out and a few terror attacks took place. The country went through traumatic times, and the Rao government as well as the party in general, and the PM in particular, came under serious attack. In fact, I believe that the demolition was the only black spot on the Rao government; otherwise Rao's tenure was one of the best in terms of performance. The economy was in good shape and the poor, the middle-income and high-income groups were all happy.

The demolition presented a major crisis for the Rao government. People held the government, especially the PM and Home Minister S.B. Chavan, responsible for being a party to the demolition, directly or indirectly. But in my view, the government could not be held responsible because the Supreme Court had given permission to the Kar Sevaks to gather there. Nonetheless, there was a strong buzz within and outside the Congress party that, notwithstanding the court permission, Rao and Chavan should have anticipated the worst since thousands of people in a frenzied state of mind would be gathering at the disputed site. Anything could have happened. No doubt, the Kar

Seva was being led by senior and responsible members of the BJP. But once the mob goes wild, even the leaders find it impossible to control it. The government could have, as a matter of abundant precaution, ordered the deployment of central paramilitary forces at the disputed site and nearby well before the incident. They could have intervened to save the situation. Unfortunately, that was not done.

What was even more unfortunate was that the PM and home minister were not reachable from the morning when the demolition of the mosque began: They could not be contacted over the phone. It was only after the demolition that the Cabinet was convened at four in the evening. When it became clear that the mob, equipped with all sorts of tools to demolish the mosque, was getting aggressive, had the home minister been accessible or the Cabinet convened earlier, steps could have been taken to rush paramilitary forces. It is possible that by the time the forces arrived, the damage would have been done. But at least the government, especially the PM and the home minister, could have been absolved of the allegation that they did nothing to stop the demolition.

Further, the Union government had no control over the state police machinery, and trusting the word of the state government headed by Kalyan Singh—that everything would be under control on 6 December at the Ayodhya site—was not justified. And so, in the Cabinet meeting in the immediate aftermath of the demolition, it was decided to dismiss the four BJP-ruled state governments—UP, Madhya Pradesh, Rajasthan and Himachal Pradesh—for their complicity in the demolition.

The winter session of Parliament was on when the incident happened. The Opposition parties demanded Rao's resignation for his alleged failure to prevent the demolition. The Opposition did not allow Parliament to function. As the parliamentary affairs minister, it was my responsibility to find a way out. The solution was not an easy one. I held several meetings, both with senior Opposition leaders and other like-minded parties, in groups and one-on-one. I explained to them that demanding the PM's resignation was neither reasonable nor acceptable. If he quit, the government would fall. Since no other party or group had the numbers to replace the Rao government, elections would have to be called, which the country could not afford in such a charged atmosphere.

I suggested a way out, saying that instead of the PM, Home Minister Chavan could tender his resignation. After all, law and order was his subject. After much hemming and hawing, the Opposition parties and other like-minded leaders agreed. I extracted a commitment from them that once the decision was made, they would let the House function. The PM was not a part of these discussions, nor did he even once take the initiative to break the impasse.

I went to Rao's residential office with the formula. Rajesh Pilot, MoS for communications, who was by chance in my room at that time, accompanied me. The PM heard me out and asked me to contact Chavan and convey the decision. I declined, saying that he, as the PM, should seek the resignation. However, he insisted that I must go to Chavan's residence and 'prepare' him for the resignation and then ask him to see Rao at his Parliament office at 4.00 p.m. The PM also told me to be present at the meeting.

I requested Pilot to accompany me to Chavan's residence, but he politely declined. Hence, I left for Chavan's residence alone. I met him around 12.30 p.m.; he was asleep and had to be woken up. After having a general discussion, I told him that the PM desired that he step down so that Parliament could resume its work. He readily agreed. I also conveyed to him about the 4 p.m. meeting to be held at the PM's Parliament office. After leaving Chavan's residence, I went to see the PM again and told him Chavan had agreed to resign, so I could tell the waiting Opposition leaders to resume the functioning of Parliament after lunch. The PM agreed to the proposal, and I informed the leaders accordingly. Post lunch, the Parliament session resumed its work, three–four days post the demolition.

At 4.00 p.m., as decided earlier in the day, both the PM and I were in his office in Parliament House, waiting for Chavan to turn up. We waited until 6.00 p.m., having many rounds of tea and calling the home minister's residence and office every 15 minutes, but there was no trace of Chavan. I was very upset since after my meeting with the PM and Chavan, I had to convey the decision of his resignation to the Opposition parties.

When Chavan did not turn up, Rao threw up his hands and said that we could not wait any longer. He suggested that we return to our respective homes. Parliament had already conducted the business of the day. The PM added that he would contact the home minister later in the night and ask him to resign and that I should take the Opposition into confidence and ensure the smooth functioning of Parliament. I did as he said, and from the next morning, again with my assurance of my previous day that Chavan would resign, the House resumed normal functioning. However, I was cautious not to make that commitment on the floor of the House.

One day passed, two days went by and then three, but there was no sign of Chavan's resignation. The Opposition began getting restless, and I rushed to the PM. He told me with a straight face that Chavan had 'disappeared'. He could not contact him! 'Let's forget it,' he remarked.

I had to cut a sorry figure before the Opposition leaders who had taken my word at face value and allowed the House to function smoothly. It goes to their credit that despite feeling cheated, they did not make an issue of the deal that I had struck with them to elicit their cooperation. Had they done so and proceeded to disrupt the House yet again, I would have had a hard time explaining the situation to the Opposition and the public. Anyway, things ended well for our government. Neither Rao nor the home minister had to quit, and the House resumed functioning normally. Consequently, both saved their chairs; only the masjid got demolished and four BJP state governments were dismissed. In retrospect, I feel strongly that in politics, personal relations matter the most. Had I not had personal relations with the Opposition leaders, they would not have spared me. Unfortunately, such camaraderie is missing today.

Today, when I think about it, I realize that Rao had played a crafty trick on me. After I left his residence at noon to meet Chavan with the commitment that I would seek the home minister's resignation on the PM's direction, he must have contacted Chavan, with whom he shared a great personal rapport and friendship since their student days, when Marathwada, the hometown of Chavan, was part of Hyderabad State before Partition. Rao must have advised him to go underground for some time and resurface after the storm blew over.

Behind Rao's soft and scholarly demeanour lurked a shrewd political mind. He could have sacked his minister, regardless of Chavan's unavailability, but he did not do so. He could have called up the minister in my presence and asked him to quit, but he did not do that either. Clearly, the PM was buying time as he had no desire to axe Chavan. It reminds me of Rao's famous quote: 'Not taking a decision is also a decision!'

Not just decisions, Rao was also reluctant to implement the suggestions given by his ministers. This was in sharp contrast to Indira ji and Rajiv, who would always take my suggestions seriously and implement them. I realized Rao was a different kettle of fish. In 1992, the president of the United Arab Emirates (UAE) Sheikh Zayed bin Sultan Al Nahyan visited India. The PM had hosted a dinner in his honour at Hyderabad House. I, too, was present on the occasion. Prime Minister Rao and the UAE leader were seated opposite each other and I was made to sit to the right of the president, as per protocol. There was also an Indian interpreter just behind the two of us.

After a few minutes went by with Rao and the UAE head of State discussing something, the UAE leader asked about me. I introduced myself. On learning that I was from J&K, he immediately turned his complete attention towards me. In no time, he was asking me several questions and I began replying to them. Rao would intervene but was met with monosyllabic responses from the guest.

The visiting dignitary told me that he had heard negative things about Kashmir from Pakistan—that it was isolated from the rest of India and that its residents did not have even basic amenities. I said that this perception was not true at all. I added that former PM Indira ji's emphasis had been on food, shelter and clothing for all, and this was being followed by successive governments. I added that while there were pockets in the country where people did not have a house of their own, every resident of Kashmir had a house, food and clothing. I reiterated that there was no major problem of unemployment in J&K as the tourism, handicrafts and horticulture sectors provided jobs and that not a single resident of the state slept on an empty stomach.

The visiting dignitary said he had not been aware of these achievements and that India's neighbouring countries had been propagating a different picture of Kashmir. He added that India needed to be more efficient in spreading positivity about Kashmir to the global audience.

After the dinner was over and the dignitary had left, Rao asked me to accompany him in his car. On the way, he exclaimed that he didn't know I had known the visiting dignitary before. I said that I had met him for the first time, which surprised him because going by how the UAE leader had been talking to me, Rao had had the impression that we had known each other for long! I then narrated what the president of UAE had told me about Kashmir. On hearing this, Rao commented that we had to improve our public relations with the Gulf nations.

A few months later, he suggested that I should pay a visit to the Gulf countries and promote the true picture of J&K and India as a whole. When the process was initiated, all Arab nations except Saudi Arabia gave the green signal. Riyadh was upset over the demolition of the Babri mosque and cold-shouldered us. During my visit, I had extensive interactions with senior members of the Gulf nations' governments, including their heads of government. They were all unanimous in their criticism of our public relations and the limited interaction between the leadership of both nations. They pointed out that while Pakistan regularly sent high-level delegations to their respective countries, there were almost none from India. Get your public relations act together, they said.

I briefed PM Rao on my return and suggested that we disptach a high-level delegation, comprising mainly Muslims, to those countries. He agreed, but then nothing happened. He did not follow up on my advice.

The fact is that no Indian PM, with the exception of Indira ji, had been able to develop cordial and personal relationships with the leaders of Gulf countries. It should have been relatively easy for our PMs to do so because, unlike in the case of other democratic countries where the real power was not always vested with the head of the government, the heads of States in Gulf countries held all the power. It must be pointed out here that PM Modi has, to some extent, made an effort to develop a personal relationship with Gulf leaders.

The focus of all governments in New Delhi has generally been on ensuring official visits to Western countries and the US. There is nothing wrong with that, since it is necessary considering our economic and security-related inter-dependence issues. But we must not forget that the Gulf nations have a large Indian diaspora that is employed there. If we have good relations with the Gulf, it will lead to a better work environment for Indians living there—it would positively impact their job security, pay and social welfare benefits. Besides, we receive considerable amounts of remittances from Indians working there. In addition, more frequent visits by high-level Indian delegations would help us level the propaganda that Pakistan and anti-India nations have unleashed against us. It's never too late. We live in a dynamic world and should seize the initiative.

Sometime in 1993, I reminded the PM that general elections were due in sometime and that I would like to give more time to the party for preparations and campaigning, so I would have no time for parliamentary work. I requested him to relieve me of that responsibility. He appreciated my commitment to the party and gave the parliamentary affairs charge to Vidya Charan Shukla. He was a shrewd and experienced politician but had no personal contact with the Opposition leaders or with even Congress leaders since he had changed parties two–three times between 1988 and 1991. He had been minister in the governments of both PM V.P. Singh and Chandra Shekhar, besides being Cabinet minister with Indira ji. This was followed by a ministerial berth in Rao's government.

Within a few months of my relinquishing charge, our government faced a vote of no confidence in July 1993. Shukla failed to get the numbers on our side on account of lack of effective coordination with other parties. As a result, the cash-for-votes scam broke out. There was a huge furore in Parliament, and the government's very survival became an issue. Rao moved swiftly and reappointed me as parliamentary affairs minister to do the fire-fighting. My return to the old portfolio was greeted with much applause in Parliament, both from the Opposition and like-minded party benches, with some senior leaders later telling me that they had cautioned the PM against the decision to shift me out.

After the dismissal of the BJP governments in four states following the Babri episode, Rao had appointed four Union ministers as chairmen of coordination committees for those four states going to polls. I was the chairman of Madhya Pradesh, with PCC president Digvijaya Singh and Shyama Charan Shukla (LoP) as members. A year later, when elections were held, we won two states and lost the other two.

Immediately after the results, the CWC met under Rao's presidentship at his residence to analyse our defeat. In those days, the CWC used to introspect and analyse defeats promptly in an open and transparent manner, where members had the freedom to freely express their opinions without the apprehension of being branded as dissidents or disgruntled elements. The conclusions arrived at were also pursued in a time-bound manner.

This was unlike what is witnessed today, when, even in the eventuality of one defeat after the other, both at the national and the state levels, the Congress fails to seriously introspect or take stock of the situation and act on the inferences drawn. Unfortunately, during the past few years, asking for holding such meetings of introspection is taken as indiscipline and challenging the authority of leadership, which has brought the Congress party to the level it is today.

The main agenda of our meeting that day was to discuss why the Dalit and Muslim voters had moved away from the Congress and gone to regional satraps such as Mayawati, Mulayam Singh Yadav and Lalu Prasad Yadav as well as V.P. Singh's outfit and ways to get back their support.

I was the first speaker in the CWC; I spoke for more than an hour and spilled my heart out. I said that we had really done nothing for the Dalits. The rights that they enjoyed were courtesy of the Constitution of India, and credit for that goes to the then PM Nehru and other important Constituent Assembly members and the chairman of the Drafting Committee, B.R. Ambedkar. The Dalits looked for both roti (sustenance) and *swabhiman* (self-respect). While the first was provided for under the provisions of the Constitution, the second had to come from the people. But we had failed to give them that self-respect. We continued to discriminate against them in day-to-day public life, I added, much to the consternation of the listeners.

I cited an example. While I was MoS for home affairs during Rajiv's tenure, I had visited one of the Northeastern states. Its DG Police met me late in the night with a request that he be transferred from the state. He said that being a Dalit, he faced constant insults and embarrassment even from his subordinates. The superintendent of police, who was from an upper-caste family, ignored his directives. Even an inspector from the upper caste, working as his protective service officer, deliberately humiliated him.

He narrated that once during a road tour in the DG Police's car, the protective service officer asked the driver to stop so that he could relieve himself. He did so close to the car, in the presence of the DG Police. The DG Police said with anguish that the man would not have dared to behave in such an insolent manner in the presence of even a superintendent-level officer if he was from an upper caste. I am sure that the narration of the incident must have shocked the CWC members too. This was the ground reality, which people mostly fail to understand even today.

I then took up the issue of Muslims not voting for us in the two states in the assembly elections. I pointed out that the Muslims constituted some 15 per cent of the country's population but had only 1 per cent (in 1993) representation in government jobs. The other 99 per cent jobs in the services were shared by the balance 85 per cent of the population, which included the Dalits (who had reservations). Was this fair, I wondered. Had we, as a party that had ruled the country for the longest of time, done justice to the Muslims? No. Yet we demanded votes from them and expressed anger that they had moved away from the Congress.

I went on and said that before asking the Muslims to support the Congress, why don't we ask the balance 85 per cent of the population, who have cornered 99 per cent of government jobs and businesses, as to why they don't support the Congress fully. Even the support of 50 per cent of them would be enough for the Congress to form the government. My remarks were prominently mentioned in the Mumbai-based daily *Urdu Times* the following day.

The CWC members were squirming in their seats uncomfortably, but I was not done yet. Rather rhetorically, I said that the likes of C.K. Jaffer Sharief and me (both ministers in the Cabinet) could proclaim from the ramparts of the Red Fort that they were proud Indian Muslims, but what about the rest of the Muslim population, which was constantly discriminated against? Their economic condition was worse than that of the SCs, with a few exceptions.

I gave the example of Dr Zaffar Khan, attached to me as officer on special duty, who belonged to Rampur in UP. He had done his MSc, MPhil and PhD, and yet could not secure government employment. His elder brother, Dr Dildar Ahmed Khan, was my professor of zoology when I was doing post-graduation in Kashmir University. Zaffar had applied in dozens of institutions, where the basic qualification for selection was prescribed as MSc. But unfortunately, he was not selected for any job in any institution and was told that he was overqualified! Owing to his unemployed status, it became difficult for him to get his four elder sisters married, despite the fact that all four sisters were post-graduates. Unfortunately, none of them got employment. Eventually, he and his sisters remained unmarried for life. If this was not a case of discrimination on religious grounds, what was, I demanded to know.

I turned to my Hindu colleagues, who were ministers too, and wondered how many of them had Muslim personal staff. As a Muslim, I told them that my staff was 90 per cent Hindu. In spite of being from a Muslim-majority state, if I could have so many non-Muslims, why could they not have at least a couple of Muslim staff?

Rao heard me out patiently and with deep concentration. After I had completed my address, several other members of the CWC who were slated to speak withdrew their names, saying that I had already given a detailed overview and that there was nothing left for them to add. I had perhaps been a little harsh on my colleagues, though I had only stated the facts and the ground reality. I readily apologized for having hurt their sentiments.

But Rao said that I had raised very relevant points on the subject and announced the formation of a group of CWC members, headed by Home Minister Chavan, to study the matter and recommend a suitable course of action for uplifting minorities. Although Chavan was not a member of the CWC, Rao said that being a senior party leader, Chavan could head the group, which comprised others such as K. Karunakaran, Arjun Singh, Ahmed Patel, Jitendra Prasada, Rajesh Pilot, perhaps one or two other leaders and me. Rao also directed the group to submit its report within 15 days and deferred the CWC meeting to be held after 15 days.

I could not attend the first meeting of the group since I was travelling outside Delhi. However, for the second and final meeting before the deadline of the fortnight expired, Chavan telephoned me to be present without fail, which I did. At the beginning of the deliberation, the group presented a list of recommendations to win back the confidence of the minorities and the SCs. Most of them harked back to programmes that had been announced in earlier years and partially implemented. There was nothing new in them. Since those schemes had no financial support in the Budget, I rejected those recommendations outright and suggested the setting up of a minority finance corporation (known today as National Minorities Development and Finance Corporation) on the lines of similar bodies that existed for the SCs and the OBCs.

I also suggested that the government could establish an initial corpus of ₹500 crore to kick-start the functioning of the corporation. The idea gained favour with the CWC members. However, Arjun Singh remarked that the PM would not approve the idea. I retorted that if Rao shot down the suggestion, I would expose his 'anti-minority mindset'. During those days, there was an open war going on between Rao and Singh.

Led by Chavan, 15 days after the CWC meeting, we met at the PM's residence and briefed him on the deliberations of the group. We presented him a note that contained all the recommendations. He had one look at it from top to bottom and remarked that there was nothing new in the list—they were *ghisey-pitey* (old, hackneyed), except for one suggestion made by me: that of setting of the minority finance corporation. He immediately gave his approval and told us that the proposal could be sent to the Ministry of Finance for implementation.

I looked at Singh, who was sitting open-mouthed. He had obviously not expected the PM to give the go-ahead. Rao appreciated my way of working and said, 'He speaks harshly in the CWC and the Cabinet but defends the government and party decisions in public, unlike some others.' He was hinting at Singh!

Sadly, my robust suggestion could not gain the traction we hoped for because the bureaucracy in the finance ministry played truant. First, as against our recommendation, the corpus was reduced from ₹500 crore to ₹200 crore. Then, it said that 50 per cent of the amount should come from the states, and only then would the central government release the rest. Once the corporation was created—it was later renamed after Maulana Abul Kalam Azad—several states expressed their inability to contribute their 50 per cent share, citing various reasons. The end result was that the corporation never really delivered the desired results for such a huge population.

Notwithstanding the final outcome of my suggestion, this incident reiterated the fact that PM Rao never took offence at the harsh words or outbursts that I indulged in. I respected him for his tolerance and erudition. He was also gentle, gracious and always appreciative of my organizational skills and dedication.

9

RESILIENCE AMID POLITICAL TURBULENCE

Throughout my term as a minister in the Rao dispensation from 1991 to 1996, the PM had issued standing instructions for me regarding J&K, which was under central rule those days. The instruction was that I was to visit the state every time lives were lost due to terror attacks or any other eventuality, console the victims and/or their families and announce the requisite government monetary compensation. However, I was not supposed to interfere in law-and-order situation or the handling of security agencies.

On the morning of 7 January 1993, when I was getting ready to leave for the airport to catch a flight to Srinagar on account of one such grave terrorist-related incident, Rao called up on the RAX and asked me to meet him immediately. After I explained that I was bound for Kashmir in an hour or so, he said, 'Arrey bhai, your good friend Madhavrao Scindia has resigned, and he refuses to reconsider his decision.'

Madhavrao was the minister of civil aviation and tourism. An aircraft that the state-run airline had acquired on lease had met with an accident while landing at Delhi airport early that morning. While no lives had been lost, a few people were injured. Madhavrao had rushed to the spot, where he encountered a bunch of angry people who accused him of wrongdoing in the agreement for the plane's lease. Agitated by the accusation, Madhavrao had gone straight to the PM and put in his papers, saying that his ego could not digest this outrageously false accusation. Rao tried to persuade him against taking this knee-jerk step but was unsuccessful. Nobody resigns on such specious grounds, he told the minister. However, sensing Madhavrao's determination, he had phoned me. He said that he was forwarding the resignation letter with his acceptance to the president, and that I should hold the charge of the civil aviation and tourism ministry.

Being Madhavrao's close friend, I wriggled out of the situation by suggesting that Rao hold back the resignation until I returned that evening from Kashmir and convinced Madhavrao to recall the resignation. On my return to Delhi that evening, I went straight to Madhavrao's residence from the airport and had an hour-long discussion with him. However, he obstinately held to his position, promising only that he might consider returning to the ministry after a year or so. 'How dare people say I took money for the deal!' he fumed. Madhavrao was an honest and a straightforward politician.

Thereafter, Rao appointed me as the minister for civil aviation and tourism. However, I continued to hold the parliamentary affairs portfolio as well until 1996, except for a brief period.

When I took charge of the ministry, the pilots of Indian Airlines had been on a 45-day strike. They had a plethora of demands. Soon after taking over, I got in touch with the leaders of the striking pilots' union. I happened to know many of them well since Rajiv's time. They would visit him often, and since I was with Rajiv on several occasions when they came calling, I had developed friendships with quite a few of them. That came in handy as I went about resolving the issues that had led to the strike. The protesting pilots were happy to deal with someone they knew and trusted. The problem was solved within two–three days after my taking over. My success was not lost on PM Rao.

In the backdrop of the strike by pilots, I had come to realize that we could face similar problems in the future too, since people in Indian Airlines knew that they were operating as a monopoly and could twist our arms. I believed that more private airlines would give us the desired leverage to deal with such situations and avoid inconvenience to passengers who suffered as a result of the strikes. Keeping these factors in mind, I took my proposal of the 'open skies' policy, by which private operators too could fly internationally and domestically, to the Cabinet. This was approved. Thereafter, various technical experts, including those from the Directorate General of Civil Aviation, were involved because several matters, including the safety aspect, were to be considered.

Once the new policy was announced, many private players evinced keen interest. It was in line with the new wave of economic liberalization that was sweeping the country. Private players were happy and so was the public. After all, this move provided a real choice between airlines to passengers and led to a huge increase in capacity. The open skies policy ensured that only the fittest survived. East West Airlines was an early starter but it could not survive for long. Jet Airways was one of the pioneers in the private sector. Sahara Airlines also started off on a solid footing, having the biggest aircraft in the private arena. Over the years, only the most robust have remained while others have faded away.

I had also taken some other novel steps such as improvement of in-flight services and itinerary and on-time performance. It was during my period that cigarettes and drinks were banned on domestic flights. I also helped thousands of students and patients going abroad for studies and treatment, providing them free tickets against vacant seats available in Air India. Another important decision taken in my tenure was to introduce Indian Airlines flights to the UAE. As a result, we began to get revenues that were earlier going to foreign airlines. As civil aviation minister, I ensured that the ministry got its own civil aviation building near Safdarjung airport, which was named after Rajiv Gandhi. It had an inbuilt air-conditioning and heating system. We also managed to construct several small airports with government money. One other important decision I took as the civil aviation minister was to merge the loss-making National Airports Authority with the profit-making International Airports Authority of India, with the new entity called the Airports Authority of India.

Touching New Highs

The 1990s were challenging times for the entire country, including the civil aviation and tourism sectors. There was unrest in many parts of the country following the demolition of the Babri mosque and the resultant violence in Mumbai and elsewhere, bomb blasts in Mumbai, huge killings in militancy-affected Kashmir and Punjab, earthquake in Latur and communal riots in several parts, including New Delhi. Several countries had issued advisories to their citizens to avoid travelling to India. The then government-owned Air India, which was running profitably, took a big hit along with other airlines as the inflow of foreign tourists dipped alarmingly. As the minister in charge, I had the unenviable task of combating the situation.

Rather than simply wait for things to improve, I decided to face the challenge head-on. I went on a hurricane tour of Europe and the Gulf countries to woo tourists, trying to assuage their apprehensions. In Europe, I covered six–seven countries in a week. Similar was the case in the Gulf. Accompanied by my officials from both civil aviation and tourism ministries and armed with promotional material (which included short films on Indian tourist destinations), I had several interactions with trade bodies, my ministerial counterparts and the media there to persuade them to come to India. I was trying to hard sell India when there was all-round scepticism. It was not an easy task but I was determined to make a breakthrough.

Realizing the need for focus, I concentrated on the promotion of Rajasthan, Ladakh and Kerala. I pointed out to audiences that Ladakh was not affected by militancy and that they should not be under the impression that Ladakh, being in proximity to Kashmir, was in the grip of terrorism. Through a short film and my interactions, I informed them that they could visit Ladakh from Delhi without going anywhere near Kashmir. Of course, I did not forget to tell them about the beauty of Ladakh, its unique culture and traditions and the hospitality of the local people. I proudly told them that let alone militancy, there were not even petty crimes, such as chain-snatching and theft, in Ladakh. Ladakh's airport, too, had undergone massive improvements during my tenure. I am happy to say my persuasion worked, and the flow of tourists to Ladakh increased even in those trying days.

I made another sales pitch. Since Kashmir in the far north was facing huge unrest, I said, there was 'another Kashmir' in the far south—Kerala, with its sea and enchanting backwaters! Here, too, I was equipped with well-made short films on the beauty of the state. I showed audiences in Europe and the Gulf (where a large number of Indians from Kerala lived) the international-quality facilities that existed in the state, such as starred hotels, etc. But there was a problem: How could a foreign tourist fly there directly since Kerala did not have a fully operational international airport?

The airports in Calicut (now Kozhikode) and Trivandrum (now Thiruvananthapuram) in the state served as domestic airports, but they could be revamped into international ones. Calicut had a young and dynamic district collector, Amitabh Kant, who would rise to become secretary, Government of India, followed by a tenure as the CEO of NITI Aayog. When it was decided that the runway at Kozhikode airport would have to be lengthened to allow for international flights to land and take-off, he was given the responsibility to supervise the execution in a time-bound manner. Within a year, the runway had been developed for international flights, and the first Indian Airlines flight took off for a Gulf country from Kozhikode airport, much to the delight of the locals. The airport at Thiruvananthapuram, too, was developed for international travel.

But we realized that even two airports were not enough to handle the tourist traffic that we had envisaged for Kerala. The idea of a greenfield airport at Cochin (now Kochi) was, therefore, floated enthusiastically by Kerala CM K. Karunakaran. I fully backed it as civil aviation minister. I discussed the matter with the CM and extended my ministry's full cooperation. Cochin International Airport became the country's first greenfield airport built under public-private partnership.

Even as work on the three international airports was progressing, my ministry began to prepare for the forthcoming tourist season. I was determined to make Kerala a much sought-after international tourist destination. It was during that period that I attended an annual global conference of tourism ministers in Berlin. The conference was much like other international gatherings but with one difference. Tourism ministers representing their respective nations were asked on the spot and without any time to prepare to explain how their country was different from the rest from a tourism perspective. When my turn came, I said India was the only country where one could experience the four S's—sun, sand, sea and snow—in one single day. This remark would become quite famous and be quoted often by others in the days to come.

I was not exaggerating. India has sunshine throughout the year. You can get snow in the Himalayan states (we even had an ongoing project for the development of a ski resort in Uttarakhand, and it was fast-tracked as one of the major attractions for the snow-loving tourists); sea in states such as Kerala, Goa and a few others and sand in the deserts of Rajasthan. On my return to India, I decided to personally test the claim that I had made in Berlin. I first went to Jaisalmer and inaugurated a desert festival. The same day, I flew to snow-bound areas of Uttarakhand (then part of the state of UP) and inaugurated another event there in the presence of Governor Motilal Vora. From there, the same day, I landed in Mumbai, and after short journey by sea from the Gateway of India, reached the Elephanta Caves, which is a major tourist attraction. I experienced sun, sand, sea and snow, all in one day!

One important initiative that I took was to operate direct flights from different locations of the country to Saudi Arabia for Haj pilgrims. Earlier, there were two points, Mumbai and Delhi, from where the Haj flights would take off and land. The first Haj flight, besides Delhi and Mumbai, began from Bengaluru, when H.D. Deve Gowda was the CM of Karnataka. His minister Roshan Baig, one of the most dynamic and capable ministers in Deve Gowda's Cabinet and later on in the Congress government, was also the chairman of the Karnataka State Haj Committee. He was happy with my decision, but the problem was that the airport did not have facilities for customs and immigration clearances. Not to be deterred, Baig set up a temporary infrastructure on one of the city's open grounds with all the facilities of customs and immigration. Later, of course, facilities came up at the airport. Subsequently, Haj flights were introduced at other airports too. My decision provided great relief to thousands of Haj pilgrims across the country, saving them from the inconvenience of going all the way to Mumbai and Delhi; it also saved them money.

Another decision that may appear insignificant but had a big impact nationally and internationally was to upgrade the Leh air terminal.

Leh was the hub of domestic and foreign tourists in both summer and winter. But many tourists avoided coming from October to April because the temperature dipped to -20°C in winter, and there were no heating arrangements at the airport. There had been instances of children dying in the severe cold while waiting for aircrafts that were delayed. Within the first four months of taking charge and before the next winter could set in, I made sure that the entire airport terminal was centrally heated.

There were several occasions when I had to take a tough stand for the overall interest of the nation. Sometime in January 1994, I was getting ready to leave for office when Rao called. He had just met the visiting Singapore PM Goh Chok Tong at the Rashtrapati Bhavan. The Singapore leader had raised the issue of concessions from the Indian government regarding the increase in number of their flights and seats to and from India as well as in the number of points they could land at. Rao had not committed himself and, instead, suggested that the visiting dignitary should discuss the matter with me, as I was the country's minister of civil aviation.

Rao had also remarked that I was a tough minister to handle, particularly when it came to giving concessions to outsiders that compromised India's interests. I went straight to Rashtrapati Bhavan and found a team of our senior bureaucrats as well as the Singapore PM's team. I was immediately granted a one-on-one meeting with the Singaporean PM.

He said he was looking for additional airline seats and more points to land in India to take and bring passengers, far more than what we had already offered to them under a bilateral agreement. I pointed out to the visiting PM that the number of seats already allotted to Singapore's airlines was in consonance with what India had been given by his country. In fact, I added, Singapore had a better deal already: While India's airlines had been given just one point of arrival and departure in Singapore, it being a city-state, we had given three points to Singapore in India. Given the status, I said, it was not possible for India to offer further concessions.

He then suggested that we offer them additional seats for the neighbouring countries through Singapore Airlines, which I promptly declined, pointing out to him that India already had bilateral civil aviation agreements with those countries and that we were negotiating directly with them and not through a third country.

The Singapore PM was upset and made his displeasure known, but I stuck to my ground. The meeting ended on a rather sour note. I felt bad that the discussion had not ended cordially, given that Singapore was a friendly country. However, the position I had taken was in our overall national interest and in the interest of our national carrier, Air India. Immediately after that, I met Rao and briefed him on the talks. He supported the stand I had taken.

Meanwhile, our Ministry of External Affairs (MEA) was not too happy with the way things had panned out. My position was that if the MEA wanted to please Singapore, it could find other ways of doing so; it was unjust to impose an unfair deal on Air India. Had I agreed to the Singapore leader's suggestion, our airline would have slipped into losses; it was then making a net profit of ₹365 crore per year and had a reputation of being one of the best airlines globally. I told Rao that he was free to take away the civil aviation portfolio from me, but as a minister, I would not allow the airline to go into the red. He dismissed the remark with a wave of his hand. He was happy with the performance of Air India.

In September 1994, a clutch of agreements was to be signed between Singapore and India, relating to various sectors, including tourism. As tourism minister, I was supposed to visit Singapore along with the PM. A week before the proposed visit, Rao called a meeting of the ministers and secretaries concerned to fine-tune the agenda of the proposed Singapore visit. Besides the PM and a few Cabinet ministers, the Cabinet secretary, principal secretary to the PM, foreign secretary and other secretaries of the Government of India attended the meeting at the PM's residence. Bureaucrat after bureaucrat boasted about the variety of concessions India had offered in order to boost relations with Singapore. Once they had made the pitch, it was the turn of the ministers. But before any ministers could speak, I sought Rao's permission to make an observation.

On receiving his nod, I said that I had no objections to the concessions India was granting, but what was it that India was getting in return. Since when had the PM become Haatim Tai? I was referring to the famous sixth-century poet-prince of Arabia known for his generous nature. Given that general elections were around the corner, I wondered if the Rao government was keen to sell his foreign visit to Indian voters or the Singaporean voters. 'Are you going to contest elections in Singapore or in India?' I asked.

There was a moment of stunned silence. Being an intelligent person, Rao got the point. He told the secretaries that I was right and asked them why such one-sided negotiations had taken place. They were told to amend the agreements. The secretaries explained that it was too late to do that since both sides had agreed to the deals and the foreign delegation that had come to finalize them had already left. I then announced in protest that I would not be part of the Indian delegation and would instead depute my MoS, Sukhbans Kaur Bhinder, for the trip. Rao did not press the point. It was my way of lodging a protest against the one-sided generosity.

Criss-crossing Four Continents for My People

There were other official tours I embarked on, including a two-week trip to several countries in Africa and South America in the summer of 1994. I had a hectic schedule, hopping from one continent to another, one country to the next. Everything was proceeding as planned and I was happy at the way things had so far turned out. But my happiness was to be short-lived.

As soon as I landed in Brazil from South Africa as scheduled, I was told by our embassy officials at the airport that the PMO had been frantically enquiring about me and that PM Rao wanted to speak with me urgently. Those were not the days of mobile phones, and I got through to the PM on the landline with some difficulty. He asked me to cut short my tour and return home immediately. He informed me that a group of 800–1,000 Hindus—men, women and children—had fled their homes in the Kahal Jugesar village in the Gandoh tehsil of Bhadarwah and had arrived in the neighbouring Chamba region of Himachal Pradesh. They had left in fear after militants had set fire to homes and property in the area and the locals had reported that those militants had remained camped there.

The PM said that the migrants had flatly refused to return to their homes despite assurances by the government of their safety; the Centre had proposed that Union Home Minister Chavan and MoS for Home Affairs Rajesh Pilot personally oversee the arrangements and make certain that they would be secure. The migrants had demanded my presence, saying that they would return only if I were to come and offer them that guarantee.

The situation had also led to a political crisis. The BJP, at the national level, had threatened to conduct a march of 50,000 people from Jammu to Delhi to press for an early return of the migrants. The PM said the matter had to be resolved before it got out of hand.

I had no option but to comply with the PM's directive. There were still some more countries for me to cover, but I had to cancel all those commitments and return home. Since finding a direct flight to Delhi from Brazil was a problem in those days, I had to travel to South Africa first and from there to London. After a wait of several hours at each of these airports, I got a connecting flight to Delhi. My luggage containing my clothes and other essentials had been booked as check-in baggage and I had no access to it. Worse, I had been travelling across continents with different time zones and thus I was completely exhausted—I had lost all measure of day and night. I used the toothbrush offered in the flight to clean up; there was no question of either a shave or a shower.

I was received by my officials at the Delhi airport in the wee hours of the morning. A bag containing my clothes had been picked up from my residence and I changed quickly before boarding another flight to Jammu. At Jammu, a Pawan Hans helicopter took me to Tissa in Himachal Pradesh. At Tissa, I was received by my cousin, Mohammed Sharif Naaz, and Bhim Singh of the Jammu and Kashmir National Panthers Party.

So far so good. But then I was told that we were to proceed up a steep hill, covering nearly 18 km, to reach the place where the migrants had camped in caves. There were ponies to take us up. Bhim Singh had come with a heavy load of video equipment; he loved making films. I was apprehensive that he would film me riding a pony and circulate it across the country; he was a good friend but sometimes mischievous too! Although he promised me not to do so, I did not want to take chances, so I decided to walk up the slope, while he took a pony ride. I was in my early 40s and quite fit. The first 8 km were easy enough but after that the slope got steeper—almost a 90-degree upward climb. Huffing and puffing I proceeded, and finally, after some hours, reached the top. It was a lovely place, with several caves and lush green meadows all around.

The people were excited and relieved to see me. I knew many of them personally. Among those who had made the trip were pregnant women who had given birth in the caves. I held some of the new-born babies in my arms, and a feeling of happiness swept inside me. I spent few hours with the people and requested them to return to their homes. They outlined four conditions: one, that army personnel should be deployed in their village for their safety; two, a government high school should be opened in the area; three, a primary health centre (PHC) be set up there and four, free ration for six months be provided to the migrant families, as they had not been able to tend to their crops. I was happy that they had given a thought to health and education even in that time of crisis and promised them that all their demands would be met even before their return. I sought a week's time to get the needful done. They wanted to know who would escort them back to Jammu, and I said that my cousin and Bhim Singh would take care of that—they would coordinate with the authorities and ensure that a large number of security personnel would accompany them to their homes, while I would keep track of the developments.

From Tissa, I returned to Jammu and met the governor. He immediately agreed to set up a high school and PHC and issued orders for the same. Two demands met, I reached Delhi and got in touch with Buta Singh, former Union home minister. I requested him for food grains for the 800–1,000 migrants to last at least six months. Within days, he had arranged for 100 trucks laden with food grains—it was enough ration for a year! For their security, I contacted the PM, and the authorities concerned got in touch with the Chief of Army Staff. Soon, a contingent of army personnel was posted at Kahal Jugesar. Incidentally, the army continues to have a presence in the area to this day!

I continued to monitor the developments closely and heaved a sigh of relief once the migrants returned to their homes. Later, when I became CM, I visited the place on several occasions. More healthcare centres were established and a higher secondary school came up too. I also ensured, during my tenure, that a road was constructed to connect Kahal Jugesar with the main road in Gandoh tehsil. It is a matter of great satisfaction for me that since 1994, not a single case of militancy has been reported in that area, and it has emerged as the safest place in the entire region.

Locking Horns over PM's 'Guru'

My portfolio did give me several opportunities to fly high, but that did not mean that I wasn't dealing with many a political hot potato that few wanted to touch. Sometime in 1994–95, during one of the Cabinet meetings held at the PM's official residence, after everyone had settled down and the Cabinet secretary had opened the folder to read out the agenda for the meeting, I butted in, seeking Rao's permission to speak before we discussed the agenda of the Cabinet. I raised the issue of the controversial godman Chandraswami.

During those days, Chandraswami, whose real name was Nemi Chand Jain, was a much talked-about and sought-after 'spiritual guru' in political circles. He was known to be a wheeler-dealer. He was said to have provided spiritual guidance to the likes of the Sultan of Brunei, the Sheikh of Bahrain, British PM Margaret Thatcher, actor Elizabeth Taylor and arms dealer Adnan Khashoggi, besides many other celebrities, according to the media.

He was, however, very close to PM Rao, and we all knew that. He could get an audience with Rao in a jiffy. He would drive right up to the doors of the PM's official residence in his swanky vehicle, while even Cabinet ministers had to leave their official cars at the main entrance gate and be escorted in a security-cleared vehicle of the PMO to the PM's bungalow. They were so intimate that Rao sometimes would leave in the middle of Cabinet and CWC meetings to meet Chandraswami in an adjacent room.

Anyway, at that Cabinet meeting, I posed a question: 'I want to know who the PM is: Rao or Chandraswami?' Pin-drop silence descended in the room at my audacity.

Rao looked at me strangely with half-open eyes and asked, 'What do you mean? What has happened?'

I informed him that a friend of mine who visited the supposed godman often had said that Chandraswami wished to see me. The friend also told me that he had seen several Union ministers, who were present at the Cabinet meeting, in regular attendance at the godman's durbar—nearly all, barring a few like Manmohan Singh, P. Chidambaram and me. The ministers present at the meeting did not deny this, which only confirmed my statement. I must mention that I have no ill-will against godmen, whether Hindu or Muslim. I just don't believe in godmen who use spirituality to do business and politics together. I believe in God. One can either be a businessman or be a godman: One cannot be both.

Someone had apparently told Chandraswami that the government proposed to purchase aircrafts and that I, as the civil aviation minister, was in charge of the process. That had made him even more eager to meet me. This, too, was told to me by my friend. I had asked my friend to inform the godman that there was no such proposal of purchasing the aircrafts, and that I, after this news, would definitely not meet Chandraswami because he was nobody to interfere in the internal matters of the government.

When the information was relayed, the godman lashed out, threatening to get my portfolio changed. Having heard this message from the godman, I wanted to use the first opportunity to clear the air with the PM. Fortunately, the Cabinet meeting was slated to be held two–three days after the incident, and so I raised the matter.

'Please tell me, sir,' I addressed Rao. 'Is he the PM to decide on my portfolio or are you the PM? Also, why do these ministers make a beeline to the doorstep of this so-called godman?'

Rao maintained his trademark impassive look without making eye contact with me. He accepted my intervention sportingly and did not admonish me or take it to his heart. He said softly to his Cabinet colleagues, addressing none in particular, 'Why do you people go to him? You should not do so.'

I thought that after my outburst, Rao would find ways to clip my wings by way of revenge. I was holding three portfolios and thought that he would divest me of some. But nothing of that sort happened. I continued to enjoy his confidence as before.

In my view, a good leader is one who does not blindly follow the flock but has the courage to speak his mind. I also spoke my mind when Indira ji and Rajiv had led the party. I have never liked spineless people, especially political leaders. My issue with the Congress party leadership was exactly on this point at the time of my resignation in August 2022. Why did the leadership expect us to be 'yes-men' or *angootha chaap* (rubber stamps), particularly when contrary opinions were needed to strengthen the party and democracy? Leaders who are always looking for endorsements are insecure. True leaders should have the courage to accept a differing opinion and even respect it.

Rao was one such leader. He was not only an excellent PM but also had the capacity to absorb strong words against him. He would often seek my feedback on the performance of his ministers and act on them most of the time. My feedback as parliamentary affairs minister was objective, and personal likes and dislikes never came in the way of my analyses, nor did factors such as caste or religion. This is why Rao respected and trusted me in spite of my harsh outbursts. It was, therefore, with immense sadness that I was forced to demand his ouster from the position of Congress president.

Rao Makes Way for Kesri

After Rao took over as elected AICC president in 1992, while the various state units had their chiefs, it was expected that other office bearers of state units, too, would be appointed. This way, the PCCs could strengthen the organization at various levels across the country and also prepare the party for the general elections scheduled in 1996. Without office bearers, state party heads could not really function effectively. We were confident, based on the inputs that we had been receiving, that the voters were happy with the performance of the Rao government. However, it was up to the pradesh-, district- and block-level Congress units to take the message of the government's achievements to the people.

Even as a minister, I had remained in touch with our state organizations and would keep enquiring about the working of the party at the state and district levels. While the feedback I received about the government was extremely favourable, the functioning of the organization was non-existent. Hence, I kept pressing Rao from time to time on the need to appoint PCCs and DCCs.

Having failed to convince him, I then organized a group of CWC members consisting of K. Karunakaran, Rajesh Pilot, Madhavrao Scindia and K. Vijaya Bhaskara Reddy, besides Rao's political secretary, Jitendra Prasada, and me. Sharad Pawar would also be part of it from time to time and raise issues of the organization in the CWC and the need to move fast in appointing PCC office bearers. But none of this had any effect on Rao.

Later, we raised the issue again in the CWC, and Rao finally realized the urgency. But he said that he could not find time to devote attention to the matter. We then suggested that he appoint a working president, someone familiar with organizational matters, someone among the general secretaries or ministers who was ready to give up his/her ministry and take up the responsibility of organization. He promptly agreed and asked Madhavrao and me to prepare a list of probable candidates for the working president's post and also recommend the names of PCC office bearers for various states in consultation with all national and state leaders. He further suggested that we feed those names into his home computer. He would go through the names and clear them.

It took Madhavrao and me about a week to consult PCC presidents and other leaders regarding the state committees before we submitted the names to Rao. A week later, we were back in Rao's house. We sat before his computer and managed to enter the names into it with assistance from the staff provided by him. We had covered at least half of the PCCs, which was a good start. Rao was proficient in the use of technology. While Rajiv, another technology-savvy politician and the first one to use computers, used to type with one finger, all of Rao's 10 fingers danced across the buttons like a butterfly.

Six months elapsed after that, but there was still no sign of the declaration of those PCC committees or the appointment of a working president. We approached Rao again, and he was back to the old excuse of not having had the time to go through the names. We told him that time was of essence—months were flying by, elections were fast approaching and we needed to get our house in order. We suggested that he at least appoint a vice president, if not a working president, to help him in the task. He asked us for some names, which we suggested.

Six more months went by and there was no action. Our group went to him and registered a protest emphatically. Now Rao claimed that the names we had fed into his computer had been erased by some error and asked Madhavrao and me to re-feed the information. Madhavrao, now clearly frustrated, flatly refused and so I got hold of Prasada to help me out. This time, we added a few more names and fed them into Rao's computer. Weeks and months went by and no name emerged from Rao's computer, while the general elections were coming closer.

Lok Sabha elections were announced on 19 March 1996, but neither was a working president or vice president appointed, nor were state PCC committees constituted. Elections were held between 27 April and 7 May. No political party managed to get a majority—the BJP won 161 seats. We managed to win a paltry 140 seats, largely as a result of our failure to spruce up the party organization. The good work done by the Rao government, with excellent ministers like Manmohan Singh and others, had been in vain.

President Shankar Dayal Sharma then invited Vajpayee to form the government. He was given two weeks from the date of swearing in—16 May—to prove his majority. His inability to secure the required support meant that the new PM had to resign after 13 days in office. Nobody wanted another general election so soon, but we were not prepared to form the government since we also did not have the numbers. Therefore, immediately after Vajpayee's resignation, the CWC met to discuss the issue of government formation. We decided that we would support a government formed by the Janata Dal from outside. I was asked to inform the Janata Dal about the decision taken at the CWC meeting. I got in touch with Ram Vilas Paswan and I.K. Gujral over phone. They were in a vehicle with Deve Gowda, going somewhere. I conveyed the CWC's decision and suggested that their party choose a leader who could take oath as PM with outside support of the Congress. The leaders of the Janata Dal decided on Deve Gowda as the head of a coalition, who was sworn in as the PM on 1 June.

A few days later, a CWC meeting was summoned to discuss the loss in the general elections and the way forward. As president of the party, Rao would preside over it. Our group met at Karunakaran's residence the previous night to chalk out a plan of action. We were despondent; there was no doubt in our minds about who was responsible for the debacle.

We decided to move a resolution seeking Rao's ouster as party president. The question then arose: Who would bell the cat? After much deliberation, it was decided that I would initiate the proceedings and others would lend support. Thus, the next morning, as everyone settled down at the CWC meeting, I rose and said that before the deliberations could begin, I wished to make a brief statement. Rao nodded, and I continued in Hindi, at which point Karunakaran remarked, 'Mr Azad, We are also here… English, please.' I switched to English.

'Mr President, no doubt, you were one of the best PMs we have had. Under your leadership, India achieved many milestones in the last five years. You headed the first minority government in independent India without any coalition. But let me say that you were also the worst party president that the Congress ever had. You had no interest, aptitude or time for organizational work. This is the reason why we lost the elections.'

I continued as Rao listened impassively. 'Let me recall that on at least half a dozen occasions, my colleagues and I had approached you both in person and in the CWC with the request to appoint office bearers to the state party units, but you did nothing. You also ignored our suggestion to appoint either a working president or a vice president at the national level who could undertake the task since you had no time. You kept buying time, and eventually we were defeated by the voters. Hence, we hold you responsible for the party's defeat, and request you to resign here and now.'

Our group had known what was coming, but the other members of the CWC were taken aback by my bluntness. Rao slumped in his cushion on the ground and looked around. Not one member spoke in his defence. I continued, 'Since we are in the fiftieth year of our independence, and senior leader Sitaram Kesri is the only CWC member who still dons a Gandhi cap, I propose his name to be the new president of the Indian National Congress,' I concluded.

This last bit of my suggestion took even our group members by surprise. Had I not named a successor, the party would have been embroiled in a succession war, which would have been embarrassing for the party in those challenging times. Moreover, in that eventuality, Rao would have got an opportunity to continue. I pre-empted that possibility. Besides, nobody could oppose Kesri's candidature—in addition to being a tall OBC leader, he was also a veteran Gandhian Congressman.

It did not give me any joy to demand Rao's resignation. In my heart of hearts, I was feeling very bad about it since I shared cordial ties with him. He had included me in the Cabinet and given me a free hand to perform, which I had reciprocated by virtue of my performance, hard work and dedication. He had always sought my opinion on critical issues and acted on many of them. I had enormous respect and regard for him. Throughout his tenure as party chief and PM, I had kept away from the factions that were opposed to him, but party interests came before personal emotions, and I had to undertake this unpleasant job to ensure that the party does not sink—an organization to which I had given my sweat and blood since my youth.

To this day, I cannot forgive myself for using the harsh language that I did against Rao. Perhaps my colleagues and I could have said the very same things without resorting to such words. The others in the group who had wanted him to step down were senior to me, and when they gave me the unenviable task of seeking his resignation, I had no option but to comply. But Rao was a perfect gentleman and never bore a grudge against me. I remember telling him that if he were to face the courts over the Jain Hawala case, I would, even if others did not, be by his side and be present in the court—and I kept my word. I was the only leader to accompany him to court even though he was no longer the party president.

Kesri got the party presidentship on a platter. Later on, he would turn out to be very different from what I had believed him to be at the time of proposing his name.

10

THE KESRI ERA: CONFRONTATION AND COMRADESHIP

Sitaram Kesri was a man of simple tastes and lifestyle. At his home, I never saw him seated on a chair, except when he was in the lawns outside. Inside the residence, he would make himself comfortable on the cushions arranged on the floor, and his visitors had to do the same. He was always dressed in khadi and wore a Gandhi cap. He maintained this simplicity throughout his life. My association with him had begun back in 1975. He was close to Indira ji and Sanjay, and so was I. Kesri was also Tariq Anwar's guardian, who was a close family friend and colleague of mine. Thus, all of us shared a great compatibility, both in personal and public life.

One of the first decisions that Kesri took after assuming charge as party president was to select the office bearers of the AICC and some state presidents to various state Congress units. This was wise. He may have got the party chief's post out of the blue but he had to hit the ground running.

Remembering the *Achhe Din*

Elections for the Punjab Assembly were due in 1997, and the feedback Kesri had been receiving from the state's leaders and workers was disheartening. Apparently, CM Harcharan Singh Brar had failed to propel the party rank and file to meet the challenge ahead.

Kesri discussed the issue with me and asked me to resolve it. 'You know Punjab well. Do what you think is necessary,' he said. He was aware of the bold measures I had taken to revive the party back in the second half of the 1980s—resigning from government, taking over as party in charge of the state and turning things around at a time when militancy in Punjab was at its peak and a large number of our local leaders and thousands of innocent civilians were killed. Sadly, a decade later, the state unit leaders and workers had become dormant. To add to this grim situation, national leaders hailing from Punjab had stopped visiting the state.

Chief Minister Brar was a knowledgeable, soft-spoken and decent person with a refined taste. He was rich and had a fascination for horses and horse racing. He used to treat me well, and I would address his wife Gurbinder Kaur, who was also a politician, as 'aunty'. Brar had years of experience as a public representative, having being elected to the Assembly five times since 1960, besides being governor of Odisha and Haryana. But he was also seen as a leader who was disconnected from the masses—the reasons of which I would soon learn in his own words. Brar had taken over at a particularly challenging time, following the assassination of his predecessor Beant Singh in 1995. He was expected to not only deal firmly with the law-and-order situation but also simultaneously provide a healing touch to the people of the state and conduct developmental work. Unfortunately, he had failed to do both.

Having been appointed general secretary in charge of Punjab by Kesri, I lost no time in informing the party's leaders in the state, including the CM, that I would launch my mass contact programme from Dera Baba Nanak, the same place that I had chosen exactly a decade ago in 1987. I flew from Delhi to Amritsar, from where I had planned to undertake a road journey to Dera Baba Nanak along with all state and district leaders. On arriving in Amritsar early in the morning, I was told by the ministers, PCC president and other senior leaders who had come to the airport to receive me that Brar too had arrived from Chandigarh and was stationed in the city's sprawling state guest house, waiting for me to join him for breakfast.

We had breakfast at a huge dining table and were joined by other ministers and leaders. After breakfast, I told the CM that we should proceed to Dera Baba Nanak, but, to my astonishment, he politely declined and excused himself. He explained that the road was in a state of disrepair and he could not bear the dust and grime the journey would throw up. He added that he would be returning to Chandigarh. I assumed that he must have come to Amritsar by a helicopter, but I had another blow awaiting me. Brar said that he was afraid of travelling by helicopter and had, therefore, made the journey by road, and that's how he intended to return.

On hearing this, I was shocked and politely told Brar that if that was so, we would have to make some other arrangements. I wondered how a CM who feared travelling in a helicopter, was allergic to heat and dust and was unable to rub shoulders with the masses could campaign in the vast expanse of the largely rural Punjab. How could he possibly garner support for the party during the election drive over the next six months? No wonder the party had been losing ground! It was time for a change of guard, I said to myself. I went ahead with my trip to Dera Baba Nanak while Brar returned to Chandigarh.

Back in Delhi in the evening, I reported the matter to Kesri and emphasized that we needed to replace Brar if we were to have a fighting chance at the hustings. The party president endorsed my suggestion. I added that we had to act in the next two days, since only six months were left for assembly elections. On receiving the green signal from him, I returned to Punjab. By then, talk of a chief ministerial change had begun to circulate. A meeting of the party's legislators was summoned at the PCC headquarters in Chandigarh. Rajinder Kaur Bhattal was unanimously elected as the Congress Legislative Party (CLP) leader and was sworn in as the CM, replacing Brar. Brar must have been secretly relieved as he could now indulge in his hobbies, including horse racing.

Bhattal assumed charge on 21 November 1996, becoming the first and so far only woman CM of Punjab. She had the reputation of being a feisty politician—aggressive and leading from the front. Unlike Brar, she was a grassroots leader and enormously popular. As vice president of the party, she had been among the few leaders who were active during the years of militancy when Beant Singh was the PCC president. Later, she would serve as president of the Punjab PCC and leader of the CLP in the Assembly. Her parents were freedom fighters; Bhattal's mother was in jail with her husband, mother and elder daughter when Bhattal was in her womb. Bhattal's mother was given parole to deliver the child (Bhattal).

Within a few hours of her taking over as CM, her government announced a flurry of populist, mostly pro-poor and pro-farmer decisions that included free power supply to small farmers to operate their tube wells.

Until Bhattal took over as CM, the SAD, which was the main Opposition party, was having a great time exploiting Brar's poor performance. All it had to keep doing was to remind voters of his failures and inactions in the run-up to the assembly elections. However, with Bhattal replacing him, the SAD suddenly lost momentum and got worried. It could not turn its wrath on the new CM for various reasons: one, she was a woman; two, her parents had been freedom fighters; three, her government's populist decisions had seized the voters' imagination; four, she was fully prepared to hit back hard at her rivals and five, her brave role during the militancy years, helping me and Beant Singh in restoring normalcy in Punjab, had endeared her to the masses.

Time was running out for the SAD and it had to do something. Barely had I landed in Delhi after Bhattal's oath-taking ceremony that the SAD chief Parkash Singh Badal, too, arrived. He met the chief election commissioner M.S. Gill and persuaded him to conduct the state assembly elections six months ahead of schedule. Gill had served Badal as his principal secretary earlier, and the two shared a good rapport. Badal had cleverly used an amendment to the Constitution that the Congress government had brought when it was in power during Rao's tenure, which gave the right to the Election Commission of India to advance elections by six months from its scheduled date.

The advancement of elections came as a rude shock to us. We had planned to go to the people based on the good work that the Bhattal government had chalked out for the coming months. But now, those months were snatched away from us. Instead, the failures of the Brar dispensation were again brought to the centre stage. Not surprisingly, we lost. The Akali–BJP alliance returned to the Assembly with a thumping majority of 93 seats: the Akalis won 75 seats and the BJP won 18 seats. The Congress, which had swept the 1992 polls with 87 seats, was now reduced to just 14 seats. But I was happy that Kesri had at least shown decisiveness over a change of guard in the state, without resorting to 'ifs' and 'buts'.

Meanwhile, at the national level, the Congress party, as the Opposition, continued to conduct public outreach programmes across the country. To commemorate the fiftieth anniversary of India's independence in 1997, a celebration committee of the CWC was constituted, with the AICC president as the chairman; I was the convener. Being the convener, the entire responsibility to organize programmes across the country fell on my shoulders. For this, I used the services of my old colleague since my IYC days, D.P. Ray. He did a great deal of research, digging out the birth and death anniversaries of prominent freedom fighters, over 365 days.

I am beholden to him, and so should the Congress party be, for his contribution to what was the biggest-ever exercise of its kind. It was a huge responsibility, which we both undertook to chalk out year-long programmes, particularly without any allocation of funds for organizing those functions; only my travelling expenses were taken care of by the party. The rest was done with the help of friends and well-wishers and by the active participation of dedicated party workers. It was a unique way that the Congress had chosen to both get in touch with the masses and, at the same time, pay tribute to our freedom fighters.

I feel proud that I, with the help of Ray, could celebrate and observe the birth and death anniversaries of more than 500 freedom fighters that year, including Gandhi, Nehru, Sardar Vallabhbhai Patel, Maulana Abul Kalam Azad, Bhagat Singh, Sukhdev, Rajguru, Ashfaqulla Khan, Bal Gangadhar Tilak, Chandrashekhar Azad, Rani Laxmibai, G.K. Gokhale, Subhas Chandra Bose and many more legends. Senior party leaders, including me, attended some of those programmes, while state-level leaders participated in the others. At an event in Champaran, Bihar, we invited Sonia ji too.

We also celebrated the birth anniversary of Bahadur Shah Zafar—first and foremost a poet and the last Mughal emperor and titular head of the group that had carried out the First War of Independence in

1857, often considered as the country's first freedom struggle. A similar exercise could have been done even today while we are celebrating the seventy-fifth year of our independence as a means of connecting with the people. Zafar's event was organized at the Red Fort lawns because it was there that the last Mughal emperor had been arrested by the British. There were 20,000–25,000 people in the lawns of the fort for the event. Zafar may have been a weak ruler but he was a great poet. Who can forget these evocative lines:

लगता नहीं है दिल मेरा उजड़े दयार में
किसकी बनी है आलम-ए-नापायेदार में
[...]
कितना है बदनसीब 'ज़फ़र' दफ़्न के लिए
दो गज ज़मीन भी न मिली कू-ए-यार में
(My heart wanders ill at ease in this ravaged reign
Who has found fruition in transient terrain
[...]
Say how ill-starred is 'zafar', that he could not obtain

E'en two yards, to be interred, in his beloved's lane)[8]

We held a musical programme to commemorate his birth anniversary in a unique way and had invited legendary ghazal singer Jagjit Singh (whose committed fan I am to this day), singer Talat Aziz and my family friend and noted lyricist, Javed Akhtar. Jagjit Singh sang until the early hours of the morning. His greatness was that he refused to let me pay even for his airfare and stay, saying that he could not accept money for offering his tribute to a great poet and freedom fighter.

These were some of the achhe din (good days) with Kesri at the helm. Little did I know that it was to be the lull before a storm.

Kesri Resorts to Skullduggery

Meanwhile, party elections were due for the post of Congress president and chiefs of the CWC, PCCs, DCCs and Block Congress Committees (BCCs). An AICC plenary session was planned in Kolkata in 1997.

[8]Translation from bit.ly/41sMCZf. Accessed on 21 February 2023.

However, the party membership drive had been completed before that. During the membership drive, complaints of bogus members being added to the list by some party leaders at various levels are often made, and those have to be addressed, for which state-level chairmen are appointed. In case the complainants are dissatisfied with the state chairman's decision, they can appeal to the chairman of the national grievances committee.

I was holding charge of the national chairman of grievances committee, besides being the national general secretary of the organization. While appointing me as national committee chairman, Kesri had remarked that he had full faith in my integrity and fairness, which is why he had entrusted me with that onerous responsibility.

Once the membership drive was over, complaints of bogus members started pouring in from different parts of the country, but barring two cases, most of them were not of a serious nature. The two major complaints came from Haryana and UP. Haryana party chief Bhupinder Singh Hooda and former PCC President Chaudhary Birender Singh were close associates. Bhajan Lal, a hands-on leader, was the CM (1991–96). Birender and Bhupinder Hooda, too, had risen from the party ranks—they had been student activists and Youth Congress leaders too. Both were born Congressmen and sincere members of the party. On the other hand, Lal was seen as an outsider, since he had joined the Congress party only in the early 1980s. He was in the Janata Party from 1979 to 1982 as CM. When Indira ji came back to power in January 1980, he immediately defected along with the majority of MLAs and joined the Congress party.

The complaint by Birender and Bhupinder was that Lal had added lakhs of bogus members to his list. The most popular way of doing it was to pick a name from the voters' list and pay the membership fees from one's own pocket. To ascertain the facts, I dispatched a team of two–three AICC members to Chandigarh. They brought back all the membership copies to the AICC headquarters.

I asked for the bags that contained the membership forms and emptied them before the media—Zee TV was the only private channel then. I discovered that in every bag, the first few layers on the top had the names of current members, while the rest of the two-third membership forms were from 1972! I rejected the bogus membership books of Lal, who could do nothing about it. The game had been exposed on television, and he ended up cutting a sorry figure.

In UP, there was a complaint against PCC president Jitendra Prasada. It was alleged that he had accepted forms of his supporters that were filed after the deadline had expired and had not taken into account the valid ones of his opponents. Since the beginning, Prasada and I were good friends. It had been on my recommendation that he had been made Rajiv's political secretary when Rajiv was the AICC president and LoP in 1990. Rajiv, taking note of my failing health, had suggested the name of senior UP leader Rajendra Kumari Bajpai to assist me in the work assigned to me by Rajiv. She was a motherly figure and an elderly woman. How could she assist me and Rajiv, I wondered. I told Rajiv that I would instead end up assisting her! We had needed a much younger leader and, hence, I had suggested Prasada's name as Rajiv's political secretary. On the day Prasada was appointed, Rajiv had told him that he has been recommended by me to help both Rajiv and me.

To investigate the complaint against Prasada, I sent my assistant to the PCC office in Lucknow and asked for the entire record of membership receipts and registers. Fortunately, the PCC president was out of station, which made it easier for my representative to collect the records and bring it to the AICC headquarters in Delhi. I then rejected those forms that had been submitted beyond the deadline, and at the same time, revived the memberships of those that had been received on time but had been shown in the register as having arrived beyond the deadline. Prasada must have been miffed, but he could do little. I did not allow personal relationships to come in the way of party interests. I was willing to pay a political price and face the consequences but was not ready to accept wrongdoings.

Meanwhile, Bhajan Lal and Jitendra Prasada had approached Kesri to pressure me to restore their bogus memberships. Rajni Ranjan Sahu, a Rajya Sabha MP of Bihar and Kesri's close associate, was the pradesh returning officer for the party elections for UP. Being an honest gentleman, he would visit my AICC office room daily, with a message from Kesri that the party president desired that I should

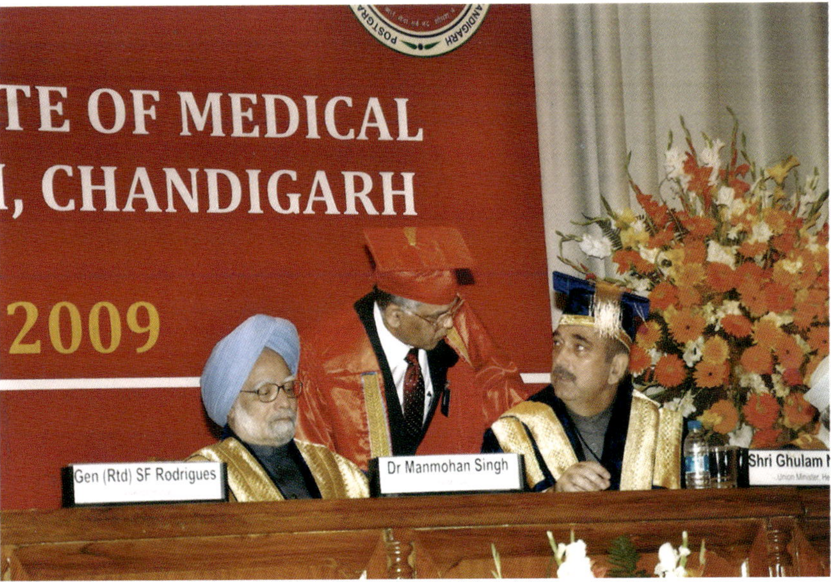

Top: Welcoming Bill Gates, co-founder and chairman of Microsoft, to a meeting with the Union health ministry in New Delhi in July 2009.

Bottom: Attending the 30th Convocation of Post Graduate Institute of Medical Education & Research (PGIMER) in Chandigarh in November 2009 as Union minister of health and family welfare along with PM Dr Manmohan Singh and governor of Punjab, S.F. Rodrigues.

Top: *Do Boond Zindagi Ke*—President Pratibha Devisingh Patil administers polio drops to a child in New Delhi in January 2010. Dinesh Trivedi, minister of state (MoS) for health and family welfare, is next to me.

Bottom: Sharing the stage with Sonia Gandhi, chairperson of the National Advisory Council, and Prithviraj Chavan, CM of Maharashtra, at the national launch of Rashtriya Bal Swasthya Karyakram by the ministry of health and family welfare in Thane district, Maharashtra, in February 2013.

Top: Addressing a convocation of the All India Institute of Medical Sciences (AIIMS) in September 2013 as Union health minister.

Bottom: Sharing a light moment with Queen Silvia, the queen of Sweden, during an official visit, as Leader of Opposition (LoP), Rajya Sabha, to the Scandinavian country in May–June 2015 as part of a delegation of parliamentarians led by President Pranab Mukherjee (seated first from right).

Top: With Gen Next, Rahul and Priyanka Gandhi Vadra.

Bottom: President Ram Nath Kovind and his family welcome me and Shameem to a dinner hosted by them at Rashtrapati Bhavan in July 2018.

Recognition for my work: Receiving the Padma Bhushan, India's third-highest civilian award, from President Ram Nath Kovind at the Rashtrapati Bhavan in March 2022.

Courtesy: RB-Photo

Leaders from all political parties graced the Eid and Diwali Milan get-togethers hosted at my residence. A few glimpses:

Top: President Dr Shankar Dayal Sharma, an erudite fatherly figure.

Bottom: Vice President Bhairon Singh Shekhawat—Different ideology, yet secular at heart.

Top: PM P.V. Narasimha Rao and Home Minister S.B. Chavan, who shared a great personal rapport and friendship since their student days, at my Akbar Road residence.

Bottom: A leader and a statesman—PM Atal Bihari Vajpayee.

Prime Minister Dr Manmohan Singh: Great moments with one of the world's greatest economists and a wonderful human being.

Top: Confrontation and comradeship—Sitaram Kesri, president of the Congress party.

Bottom: Madhavrao Scindia, charismatic Congress leader and scion of the Gwalior royal family.

Top: The woman who transformed Delhi—CM Sheila Dikshit.

Bottom: Jaipal Reddy, Union minister and senior Congress leader.

Top: Friendship beyond ideology—With PM Narendra Modi.

Bottom: Politicians on a different pitch—Interacting with Arun Jaitley, LoP, Lok Sabha, as the minister of parliamentary affairs and urban development at a cricket match during United Progressive Alliance (UPA)-I in 2004–05.

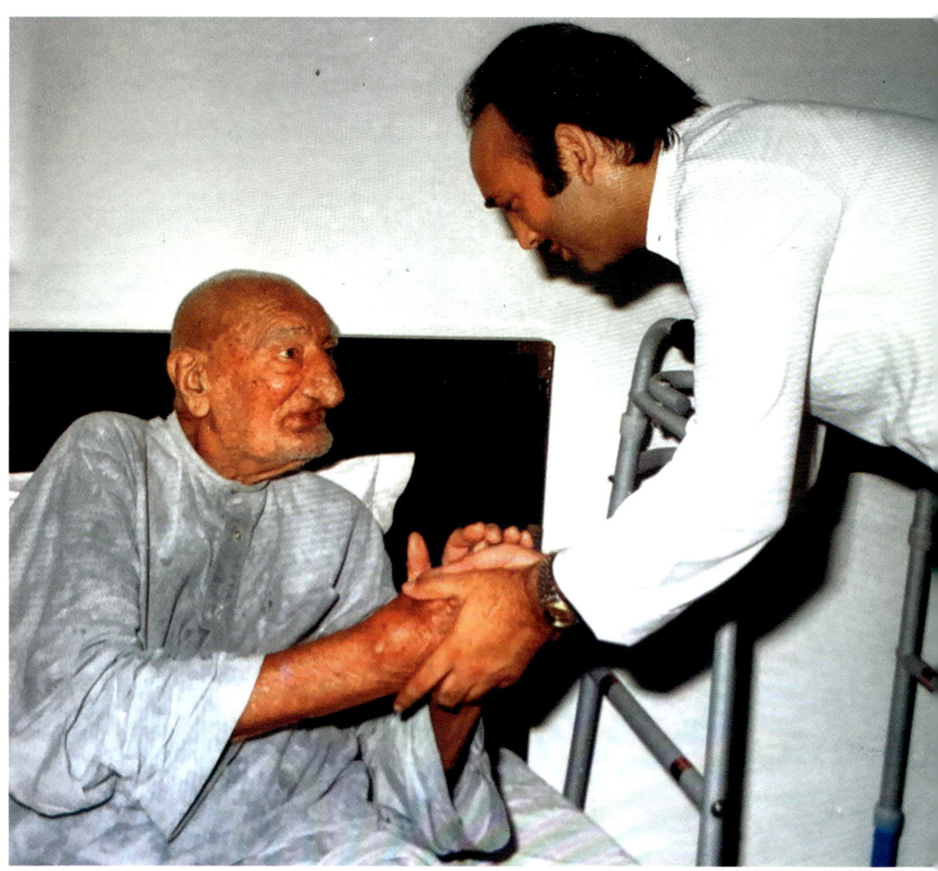

Powerhouse Pathan—Meeting Khan Abdul Ghaffar Khan in New Delhi in the early 1980s.

Friendship across the Himalayas—In conversation with King of Bhutan Jigme Singye Wangchuck as the MoS for home affairs in New Delhi in the late 1980s.

Top: Shameem and I pose with His Majesty King Hussein bin Talal, the king of Jordan, his wife Queen Noor and their daughter during the royal family's visit to India in 1986.

Bottom: Shameem and King Hussein bin Talal.

Top: A new chapter in Sino-Indian ties—Shameem and I on our first visit to China. To my left is Jiang Zemin, then general secretary of the Chinese Communist Party and later president of the People's Republic of China.

Bottom: Shameem is welcomed by Jiang Zemin.

Great equation with a charismatic international leader—Yasser Arafat, chairman of the Palestine Liberation Organization, is all smiles as Shameem and I look on.

Meeting Madiba—The president of South Africa, Nelson Mandela, hosts me at his residence in 1994.

Straight out of a spy novel—A memorable meeting with mercurial Libyan ruler Muammar Gaddafi in his tent in Libya in October 2005.

New highs in bilateral relations: Meeting US President Barack Obama at the official dinner at Rashtrapati Bhavan in New Delhi in November 2010.

In conversation with Sheikh Dr Abdul Rahman bin Abdul Aziz Al-Sudais, the Imam of the Holy Mosque in Makkah Al Mukarramah, during a dinner hosted by me in New Delhi in March 2011.

Ushering in the New Year with the president of Iran Mahmoud Ahmadinejad in Tehran in March 2011 during Navroz celebrations, which I attended on behalf of PM Dr Manmohan Singh.

Celebrating historical ties—Meeting Sheikh Hasina, PM of Bangladesh, at her residence in Dhaka.

Inspired by a life steeped in spiritualism—Shameem meets His Holiness the Dalai Lama in 2012.

Shameem meets Mother Teresa at the Missionaries of Charity in Kolkata.

restore the bogus memberships of Lal and Prasada. I would politely reject that request.

One evening, while I was in my AICC office, Kesri entered my room. I rose from my seat and requested him to be seated on a sofa and called for tea. I said that he should have called for me into his room instead of taking the trouble of coming to my office. He waved away my formality and replied that we were all colleagues—this attitude is today only a dream in the Congress party's functioning.

After talking for around 10 minutes on general issues, Kesri came to the point. He asked me to restore the memberships that I had declared as bogus and invalid. I was shocked because I had not expected such a directive from him. I did not know that he had begun to nurture a strange ambition. He wanted to emerge victorious with the highest number of votes in the history of any election to the Congress presidentship. For that, he would need the maximum number of his men from UP to be made AICC and PCC members through Prasada, since that state had the highest number of AICC/PCC members in comparison to other states, based on the population.

Sharing his dream with me, he said that if I helped him in the task, his choice of PCC members would be elected, and in lieu, I would be made the party's vice president. I was stunned, hurt and angry, I shouted, '*Laanat hai us din par jis din maine aap ko Gandhiwadi samjh kar aap ka naam president ke liye CWC mein propose kiya tha* (I curse that day when I, thinking that you are a Gandhian, had proposed your name for AICC presidentship in the CWC meeting). I believed that being a Gandhian, you would uphold personal and professional integrity, but you want to use wrongful means to win by a record margin, even bigger than those achieved by the likes of Nehru, Patel, Maulana Azad and Indira ji. Where is the need for such skullduggery when your victory is assured anyway?'

He was taken aback by my retort, but I was not done yet. I continued, 'You have dared to bribe me with the allurement of a higher party post.' Kesri was alarmed that people outside in the corridor would hear the commotion. He tried to pacify me and left the room. Looking back, I think I should not have lost my cool and behaved so insolently with an elderly person like Kesri, with whom

I shared mutual affection and respect and who had always treated me with warmth. However, I am happy I stuck to my position and did not succumb to his plans. But it did start an internal war between his supporters and mine.

War and Peace

A few days later, I had to visit Ahmedabad for a party event. On my flight back to Delhi, the aircraft got caught in a severe dust storm and began to rapidly lose height. Passengers were tossed around and I thought the end had come; it was as if I was seeing death from close quarters. I was not afraid of death, but morbid thoughts came to my mind. I felt terrified about how I would look if the aircraft crashed and caught fire; my family members and friends would see my charred body. The person seated next to me was the governor of Kerala, who suffered major cuts on his arm. I, too, was flung around, worsening the spondylitis and slipped disc that had troubled me for years. However, the pilots did a great job, and we finally landed safely in Delhi. More than 50 passengers and flight crew suffered injuries during the flight. Back home, my condition turned worse; doctors advised complete bed rest for a few days.

The date of nomination for the election of the AICC president was announced. Kesri was the candidate for presidentship; I was bedridden at home. I invited the media and issued an appeal to all the AICC and PCC members to vote according to their conscience. I did not ask them to vote for Kesri. Since our confrontation, we had not been in touch, nor were we on talking terms. We had stopped visiting each other's homes as well. When Kesri was elected as the party president, I did not even congratulate him. I realize that it was petty of me, but I was still seething with anger.

A few months after Kesri's election as party president, the AICC plenary session was held at a stadium on the outskirts of Kolkata, approximately 20 km away from the main city, on 8–10 August 1997. Arrangements for stay had been made at the location of the session site for CWC members and AICC office bearers, including Kesri. But I had no desire to be anywhere around the party president, so

I asked the then state Congress chief, Somen Mitra, to book a hotel room for me in the city. Somen was close to me since our IYC days when I was the national president and he was the president of West Bengal Youth Congress.

On the first day of the AICC session, I was seated next to Kesri on the dais. We did not speak with each other. During the proceedings of the session, Kesri had to go to his room to meet some party men, so he passed me a slip of paper with a request to preside over in his absence. I complied.

While concluding the proceedings of the first day, Kesri said in his speech that elections for the CWC would be held the following day even as the session continued. He pointedly asked the AICC members not to vote for those who were 'staying in hotels'. The barb was clearly directed at me because I was the only one staying in a hotel. Upset and infuriated after his speech, I decided not to contest for the CWC. I felt that if my party chief had such a low opinion of me and openly campaigned against me, it was better for me to keep away from the contest.

Later that evening, nomination forms were made available to those who wished to contest the elections. The form of a candidate had to be signed by the candidate and the nomination papers needed to be supported by 10 AICC members.

Some of my friends and supporters like Imran Kidwai, who is a senior Congress leader and close family friend, enquired if I had filled the nomination form. On hearing that I had no desire to contest, they refused to accept my decision and made me sign the nomination form that they filled for me and added the signatures and names of 10 AICC members as supporters. After the required formalities were complete, they submitted my form to the presiding officer. I went back to my hotel in the city, determined not to return to the venue the next day. I was sure that after Kesri's appeal and on his direction, his supporters were working to defeat me. I had no desire to be embarrassed by being at the place of my defeat. I asked the hotel staff for video cassettes of half a dozen Hindi films. The next day, when the election for CWC members was going on, I watched at least three films in my room, ate, relaxed and slept.

Somewhere around 6.30 in the evening, I received a call from Kidwai. He congratulated me and said that I had been elected to the CWC. Even as I struggled to absorb the good news, he added that Kesri wanted to speak to me. Kesri came on the line. After I said 'Namaste', he boomed, 'You won and I lost. Congratulations!' I was speechless and deeply touched. Here was a man against whom I had spoken out so fiercely and he, too, had campaigned against me openly, and yet he was congratulating me and graciously accepting his failure.

Kesri asked me to return to Delhi with him in his private aircraft that night, but I politely declined and told him that I was scheduled to attend a lunch meeting organized by the state's PCC chief the next day.

Later that night, around 10.30 p.m., my wife called from Delhi. She said that Kesri had arrived at our home straight from the airport to congratulate her. '*Bahu* (daughter-in-law; he always addressed my wife that way), *beta* (son) has won and uncle has lost!' He used to call me 'beta' and I would call him uncle. He would often come to have chicken soup at our place. That night when he had arrived straight from the airport, he had demanded his favourite dish, which my wife quickly prepared. A hot bowl of soup had broken the ice between Kesri and me.

From the party election point of view, this AICC session in Kolkata was of great political significance because since then, it has been almost a quarter of a century that no elections for the CWC, PCCs, DCCs and BCCs have been held. Another significant aspect was that it was Sonia ji's first AICC session and she was greeted with huge applause.

Both Kesri and Rao, whom I had taken head on, never sought revenge against me. Kesri could have sacked me from the general secretary's post over my stand against him. I could have done little, except maybe call a press conference and lambast them. Imagine if today a general secretary or a senior CWC member even offered suggestions to his party president to strengthen the organization by holding elections to the CWC, PCCs, DCCs and BCCs: They would be dubbed as traitors and agents of a rival party. In addition, there would demands for disciplinary action against them.

However, I believe that those were different times, with a different kind of leaders who possessed the commitment, dignity and tolerance to accommodate the suggestions of party colleagues. They respected dissent when it was in the party's interest. They absorbed even the harshest words of their colleagues.

Ballots and Break-Ups

In the aftermath of the AICC session, there were dramatic developments outside the Congress party, in the country's larger political space. Problems began to manifest between PM Deve Gowda and the Congress party after a few months, when he came under the influence of ill-placed advice by some of his colleagues. The first advice they gave him was that he should start an extensive tour in North India and project himself as a farmers' leader and an alternative to the Congress in the Hindi belt. The idea was to replace the Congress in the region. The Janata Dal was a known name in North India, and Deve Gowda, who was already an established name in the southern part of the country, thought he could get a toehold in the North too, using his party's leverage. We in the Congress party felt outraged that Deve Gowda, who depended on Congress's support, was seeking to undermine us in our stronghold. The second advice that was given to him was that his government should initiate various cases against Congress leaders. The idea was to put the Congress on the defensive and pre-empt any chance of withdrawal of support.

Both these suggestions backfired on the PM. Senior leaders met Kesri and told him that things would go awry for us if Deve Gowda was allowed to continue in office, since he was determined to cut the very branch that supported him. It was decided to tell the Janata Dal that Deve Gowda's continuance was untenable and that he should be replaced. Thus, I.K. Gujral, a well-respected, learned, experienced gentleman and a leader of stature, became the PM in 1997.

Kesri and the entire Congress party shared good relations with Gujral, and one of the reasons for that was that he had been an old Congressman and was even a Union minister in Indira ji's Cabinet. But Gujral's government was unstable from the beginning because there were groups within the group. It had some mass leaders with ambitions of their own, while Gujral was not a grassroots leader. Within some months, in March 1998, his government fell, and we faced another general election.

11

RETURN OF THE GANDHI PARIVAR

Once elections for the Lok Sabha were announced in November–December 1997, Kesri chaired the national campaign committee formed to fight the electoral battle, while I was made the convener. The party chief campaigned only in a few places, and I had to shoulder the entire responsibility of nationwide canvassing and overseeing the campaigns of other leaders. I was then a Rajya Sabha member and the general secretary in charge of a few states and the organization too. Several senior leaders of the party who were contesting the polls were tied up in their respective constituencies and were not available.

I suggested to Kesri that we should involve Sonia ji in some regions of the country for campaigning. He was receptive but added that I would have to take up the matter with her. He did not share that sort of relationship with Sonia ji that I did since Rajiv joined politics. I went to her with the offer. She did not commit herself, saying that she would give it a thought. I left, promising to meet her again. The next day when I met her, she had queries regarding her travel, accommodation, personnel accompanying her, etc. I assured her that I would personally organize her stay, travel arrangements by a chartered flight and public meetings. I also mentioned the names of two women MPs who would accompany her on the trips. She agreed, and I conveyed her consent to the party president. I excused myself from accompanying her, explaining that as general secretary and convenor of the national campaign committee, I would be busy campaigning across the country.

I then got a professional photographer the following day to take dozens of photographs of her in various poses, including waving her hands and doing a namaste, etc. Large cut-outs were made and posters designed, prominently featuring her photographs. Sonia ji was now ready for her first-ever political campaign.

Language was not a problem for her. She was good at English and, contrary to general perception, was conversant in Hindi; she could both read and write it. It was decided that she would begin her maiden election rally from South India. She spoke at various places in the South. She addressed the gatherings in English. The last public meeting was at the Ramlila Maidan in Delhi. She addressed the gathering in Hindi. She found a connection with the people instantly and attracted large crowds wherever she went.

However, the election results were not in our favour. The BJP, led by Vajpayee, emerged as the single-largest party with 182 seats. The Congress failed to get a majority on its own, winning 141 seats—just one seat more than the tally in the previous election. A CWC meeting was called to introspect on the loss. Many senior leaders, including me, believed that the main reason for the poor performances was Kesri's lacklustre leadership. In the past, leaders such as Nehru, Indira ji and Rajiv had not only provided effective leadership to the country and the organization but also been our star election campaigners. Kesri, on the other hand, failed to give us that leadership and was a poor campaigner too.

He would have to relinquish his post so that the party could choose a younger and more effective president. Our sentiments were conveyed to him during the CWC meeting, and he left the meeting deeply disappointed. He had read the writing on the wall. A resolution was drafted, seeking a change in the leadership. I was assigned the task to read out the resolution. Thus, yet again, the unpleasant job of presenting it to the CWC fell on me. The unpleasantness was even more acute since we shared a good relationship from the time he was PCC chief of Bihar and I was the J&K Youth Congress president during mid-1970s.

The adoption of the resolution asking Kesri to quit led to a situation that was different from the one when Rao had been asked to resign. It must be remembered that when Rao was the PM and party president, a section of the senior leaders, including me, had suggested that he appoint a working president or a vice president who could devote time to the party's affairs. We had mentioned the names of half a dozen leaders. While Rao did nothing in that direction, the leaders in the running had been nurturing a desire to take over the presidentship. At the same time, while the proposed names floated in the air, nobody was really that keen to take over the job because, having lost the 1996 and the 1998 Lok Sabha elections, there was little hope that a change in guard would make any actual difference to the party's fortunes.

That said, we had no dearth of competent leaders who could replace Kesri—Arjun Singh, Sharad Pawar, Madhavrao Scindia, Rajesh Pilot and Jitendra Prasada, among others. No doubt, I was senior to some of them and had a far greater outreach across the country by virtue of holding positions consistently at the national level, both in the youth Congress and the parent organization. However, one thing was always clear in the minds of the Congress leaders—that a person belonging to a minority religion could not head the organization. Even my colleagues and friends in the party would tell me that I would have been the best person to head the organization had I not been a Muslim. Unfortunately, this mindset had developed after Independence and it continues till date. That is why even 75 years after Independence, no leader from the Muslim community has become president of the Congress party. On the other hand, during the period of 62 years since the Congress party was born in 1885 till 1947, the party had had as many as 16 presidents from the minority community—which included eight Muslims, five Christians and three Parsis.

However, at this point in time, we needed someone who was acceptable to both the rank and file and to all our senior leaders and factions. We needed someone who could bring cohesiveness in the party and energize it after two successive Lok Sabha defeats.

Convincing Sonia: 'It's Now or Never'

Sonia ji's name was proposed as Kesri's replacement, and there was unanimity on the choice amongst the party's senior leaders. In the limited campaigning that she had done, she had struck a chord with the people. As part of the Nehru–Gandhi family, she commanded respect and admiration within the Congress party. The challenge was to convince her to enter active politics. At the CWC meeting, it was decided that Pawar and Antony would immediately go to her residence, which was a stone's throw away from the party's Akbar Road office, where the CWC was meeting, and get her consent. They left, promising to be back soon. The CWC members waited at the party headquarters for them to return, hopefully, with good news.

We had thought that Antony and Pawar would return in five to 10 minutes or 15 at the most, but half an hour passed, then one and there was still no sign of them. The members then asked me to go to her residence and check on the progress. When I reached there, I found Sonia ji and the two leaders, each seated separately on three different sofas, not even talking to one another. It was clear that the conversation had been over, probably in the first few minutes that they had met. I looked at them questioningly. Pawar and Antony said that 'madam' was unwilling.

I then asked Sonia ji what the problem was. She said that she wanted time to think. I asked her how much time she needed. She said, 'Six months.' We could not wait for six months since the CWC meeting was on and we had to decide immediately, I pointed out.

'First, tell me madam, are you willing to join politics?' I asked.

She answered in the affirmative but stuck to the six-month time period. 'Six months is a long time in politics,' I told her. I added, 'There is a vacancy now and that the vacancy might not exist six months later. It is possible that some competent person would become the party chief and may not be amenable to relinquishing the post for you six months down the line. You have to decide. It's now or never. Timing is of great essence in politics,' with that, I concluded my brief sales pitch.

Sonia ji was lost in thought. After about five minutes, she looked up and said she was ready to take on the mantle. We were relieved and happy. The CWC, thereafter, lost no time in passing another resolution, electing her as the president, of course in her absence. Sonia ji then took over as the Congress party president.

In the beginning, she provided good leadership to our party. She was a great listener and would always seek the advice of senior leaders on important issues. It helped her to get acquainted with the ground realities. She also met people besides Congress leaders. Whenever she visited states and received representations from the people and party workers, she would pass them on to party general secretaries and others concerned and followed up on the progress. She was both soft and tough, depending on the demand of the situation. Her memory was sharp—she would remember people and their names for a long time after having met them. She also had a capacity to take people along. She had maintained personal relations with leaders and their families—people with whom she had close ties.

My first assignment under Sonia ji's leadership was to oversee the 1998 Rajasthan Assembly Elections, without changing the general secretary in charge of the state. She asked me to spend as much time as I could in Rajasthan. I lost no time in rushing there. I held at least 200 public meetings, covering nearly 150 assembly constituencies. The party's rank and file was enthusiastic as it had a new national leader from the Nehru–Gandhi family, and so it worked harder than before. I had no problems in reaching out to the people, as I had been general secretary in charge of the state on two earlier occasions during Rajiv's time. The outcome was that we won and formed the government; Ashok Gehlot became the CM for the first time.

Teamwork in Karnataka

Immediately after government formation in Rajasthan, I was made the AICC general secretary and given the responsibility of Karnataka, where assembly elections were due the following year in 1999. I used the time to tour the state extensively. Here, I adopted the Punjab model of mass contacts. I drew a road map of the entire state, planning out various phases of campaigning that would cover nearly every major village, block, district and constituency. The difference was that while I had initial difficulty in getting leaders and workers to come on board in Punjab due to the militancy there, this was not the case in Karnataka.

I prepared a list of leaders who would accompany me for a year-long campaign. This list included former Union ministers C.K. Jaffer Sharief, Janardhana Poojary, B. Shankaranand and Margaret Alva; former CMs Veerappa Moily, S. Bangarappa, Dharam Singh; PCC chief SM Krishna; CLP leader Mallikarjun Kharge and many more.

Thus, I had 40–50 leaders who shared the dais with me throughout the campaign. Having been general secretary in charge of Karnataka twice, I not only had a good relationship with each one of the leaders but was also aware of their temperaments. I asked the PCC to make D.K. Shivakumar the general secretary and a dynamic young leader in charge of boarding and lodging during the entire campaign. We hired a 52-seater air-conditioned bus for one year so that the entire group could travel together across the state. No separate cars were allowed for anybody.

This attempt at unity was necessary because the entire party was divided into many groups, each led by either a former CM or former Union minister. However, each of these leaders had their own support bases in their respective areas, and they represented nearly all castes and communities, all regions and religions. But this factionalism soon vanished once the yatra began, owing primarily to the wholehearted support I received from all these senior leaders. Wherever we went, supporters of these leaders flocked to our meetings, resulting in large crowds. We had at least five meetings every day in each assembly constituency, and our campaigning was aggressive since we had to dislodge the Janata Dal government that was in power in the state; the BJP-led National Democratic Alliance (NDA) was ruling at the Centre. My strategy was unique; it had not been tried before except by me in Punjab from 1987 to 1990. It also symbolized that all factions of the party were together in the resolve to win.

We completed the first phase in three months, taking only a couple of days' break in between. During this entire period, we would stay at the Panchayat, block, tehsil or district headquarters for the night and sometimes even in the villages with our local workers at their residences, particularly whenever hotel accommodation for all was not available. During these overnight stays, I would interact with the locals and ask them for the names of people who could make good candidates for the assembly elections. I would select a couple of the best out of them and sound them out accordingly. I would say that they would get the ticket provided they worked wholeheartedly for the entire year. This motivated the candidates to begin work on a vigorous scale. In all the three phases of the campaign, I would keep track of these candidates.

Even though this was the third time that I was in charge of Karnataka, it was a great learning experience since I got to know the entire state down to the village level. This time I was more involved in programme implementation and micro-management, since I had conceived and drawn the programme with the help of local leaders. I was strict in the implementation of the programme, even though it caused me considerable personal discomfort. During this one-year period, I came to Delhi only twice or thrice for two–three days each and to Bengaluru not more than three–four times. I spent the rest of the time along with other party leaders in the field, attending to and personally monitoring the campaigning activities of the party. The net result of all these efforts was that I already had a list of candidates when the assembly elections were announced in July 1999 along with the Lok Sabha elections.

Hoodwinking the BJP in Bellary

I wasn't done with the state just yet. There was to be one more *nataka* in Karnataka when the Vajpayee government failed to muster the support during the vote of confidence on 17 April 1999, as a result of which Lok Sabha elections were announced on 4 May. Thus, the Karnataka Assembly Elections came to be held along with the Lok Sabha elections. The Congress Central Elections Committee met, and ticket distribution took place for the entire country. It was decided that Sonia ji would contest from Raebareli. Then an idea occurred to me, and I took it to her. I wanted her to contest from one of the parliamentary seats in Karnataka. I argued that her victory from

Raebareli was a foregone conclusion and would be no big deal; it was a family bastion. In order to emerge as a national leader, she must also contest from a southern state. I told her that I had the Bellary constituency in Karnataka in mind, and the sitting MP, K.C. Kondaiah, had volunteered to leave the seat for her. It would be an additional feather in her cap, I added. Meanwhile, Kondaiah also met her and repeated the offer.

She was initially reluctant but was eventually persuaded. I told her that she need not even campaign in the constituency; I would take care of it and she would only have to file the nomination papers and make just one appearance. After that, I requested her to keep the matter a secret. I had earlier asked the sitting MP from Bellary to also not reveal the matter to anyone. Thus, nobody else was aware of what I was planning.

One reason for the secrecy was to take the BJP at the national level and the Janata Dal in the state by surprise. One of their fiery leaders, George Fernandes, had already announced that he would contest against her if she stood from anywhere in Karnataka—there had already been a media buzz that Sonia ji would seek election from a southern state apart from Raebareli. I did not want that to happen—not because I was worried that she would lose; I was confident of her victory. But Fernandes, though an honest and upright man, could not control his acerbic tongue! He had a reputation of using rough language, and there was no telling what he would say against her during the campaigning. After all, he had been inimical to the Gandhi family since his trade union days. I was wary of the campaign getting bitter and did not want to stoop to low levels to counter it.

Meanwhile, taking initiative, our Andhra Pradesh CLP leader, Y.S. Rajasekhara Reddy, had invited Sonia ji to contest from his state's Kadapa constituency in the Rayalaseema region. This came in handy for us to maintain the facade. We announced that Sonia ji had accepted the invite. A day before the nominations closed, we took a flight to Hyderabad instead of going to Bengaluru. I accompanied Sonia ji along with Vincent George. For all apparent, she was to file her nomination from Kadapa. Even Rajasekhara did not know about the game plan while he went about making preparations for her nomination from

Kadapa constituency! For good measure, after landing at Hyderabad airport for a night stay, I told the waiting mediapersons that Sonia ji had decided to contest from Kadapa, Andhra Pradesh, not from Bellary as enquired by them. I further added that we would have gone to Bengaluru for the night stay instead of coming to Hyderabad, if she had to contest from Bellary. On hearing the announcement post my press briefing at Hyderabad airport, the BJP decided on the candidature of the well-known film star Vijayashanti from Kadapa against Sonia ji.

Early the next morning, we took a special flight to Bellary, which thankfully had an airstrip. Sonia ji's security detail was with her. When the plane touched ground, her security personnel exclaimed that it was not Kadapa. I replied, much to their amazement, that indeed it was not; it was Bellary!

Preparations had been silently made in Bellary at the returning officer's office with the help of the MP who had vacated the seat. Sonia ji filed her nomination papers, with the local police making massive security arrangements with Kondaiah's help. The news spread like wildfire; the BJP and Janata Dal CM of Karnataka were taken aback. Poor Fernandes was somewhere in the Northeast, and it was impossible for him to dash back to Bellary in time. The BJP dispatched Sushma Swaraj to Bellary by a special flight as a contestant, and she filed her papers a few minutes before nominations closed that evening; it was also the last day for filing the nominations.

We had outwitted Fernandes and the NDA government at the Centre and the Janata Dal government in the state. But Swaraj was no pushover. She was an excellent orator, in both English and Hindi, and I had tremendous respect for her. She would always call me bhaijaan, while I always addressed her as behenji. Within a week of campaigning, she had picked up Kannada and begun to speak it fluently. She began to campaign furiously across the constituency. Sonia ji, on the other hand, made just a one-day appearance in the constituency, addressing three public meetings in three assembly constituencies.

Thereafter, it was left to me to take the campaign forward. I was pitted against not just Swaraj but the entire top brass of the BJP and its allies. PM Vajpayee visited the constituency twice. Even the BJP's national president, the elderly Kushabhau Thakre, who had kept away from campaigning, came to canvas for Swaraj. Andhra Pradesh CM N. Chandrababu Naidu, then a BJP ally, deputed three of his ministers to oversee the campaigning. Another dozen Union ministers would come and go, thus making the contest difficult. I believe that the BJP should not have taken the contest so seriously. The party made it a prestige issue, and that added further stature to Sonia ji.

With all our senior leaders of the state, including the PCC president and CLP leader, proceeding to their respective constituencies to contest the assembly elections once they were announced, I was left alone to campaign. And so, I had a punishing routine during the entire campaign period. I barely slept during the last few weeks of electioneering. I would leave the small hotel I was put up in at the crack of dawn and canvas across the length and breadth of Karnataka. During the day, I would campaign by a small aircraft and a helicopter at my disposal and return to Bellary for the night. In the Bellary Lok Sabha constituency, I would go from village to village during the night, addressing people without a public address system, and return to the hotel at 4.00 a.m. I would then have my dinner and breakfast as one, from a tiffin that would be left behind by Abdul Wahab, a local party leader. After having some cold food and tea, I would go to bed with my shoes on so that I did not oversleep—I had to leave for campaigning to other parts of the state after only a few hours of sleep.

The hard work paid off. Sonia ji won hands down, and it embarrassed the BJP to no end. The Congress party also got a majority in the Karnataka Assembly, and S.M. Krishna became the CM. I was delighted that our performance in Karnataka was great both in the Lok Sabha and the Assembly. We won 132 seats in the 224-member Assembly as against 34 sitting MLAs. Similarly, in the Lok Sabha, we got 18 seats as against nine in 1998 and five in the 1996 Lok Sabha elections out of a total of 28 seats from the state. However, the Vajpayee-led NDA returned to power at the Centre and went on to complete its full term in office.

Two days after the election results, I met Sonia ji. Since she had been elected from both Bellary and Raebareli, I suggested that she keep Bellary and give up the latter in favour of her daughter Priyanka Gandhi Vadra because, during those days, she was involved in looking after the constituency. Rahul was not in politics nor did I have any idea that Sonia ji was keen to bring him into it, so his name was not in the reckoning then. This decision of retaining Bellary, I added, would strengthen the Congress's presence in southern India. I told her that I would handle the developmental work in her constituency. But Sonia ji didn't say anything. I believed that my suggestion had registered positively in her mind. But a few days later, she resigned from the Bellary seat and retained Raebareli. I am unaware of her reasons.

Inroads into the South

After the victory in Karnataka, the Congress party had to face assembly elections in two other southern states—Tamil Nadu and Kerala—and the UT of Pondicherry (now Puducherry) in 2001. Sonia ji asked me to take charge of those states as the general secretary. One thing was common among the three as far as the party was concerned: The Congress was in a complete mess.

In Tamil Nadu, we faced a double handicap. The Congress party had split, with senior leader G.K. Moopanar walking away with national leaders, such as P. Chidambaram and Jayanthi Natarajan and a host of state-level prominent functionaries, to form the Tamil Maanila Congress (Moopanar) (TMC [M]) in March 1996. We were reduced to a small unit in the state. As if that was not enough, for the first time ever, we had no alliance with either of the two major regional parties, the DMK and the All India Anna Dravida Munnetra Kazhagam (AIADMK). The DMK was in power then. From all angles, it was a lose–lose situation, and I had to do something to win it. Sonia ji had given me a free hand to deal with the situation like in Karnataka earlier and hardly interfered in the decisions that I took. This could have been because she was totally new not just to politics but also organizational matters and had practically no knowledge of the politics in the southern part of the country.

I went to Chennai and sought an appointment with AIADMK leader J. Jayalalithaa. I had known her since the time she was a Rajya Sabha MP from 1984 to 1989. I met her at her Poes Garden residence and offered an alliance between the AIADMK and the Congress for the forthcoming assembly elections. She was dismissive, saying that after the split, the Congress was finished in Tamil Nadu. What was the point in aligning with a losing party, she wondered. I told her that I would get back to her soon after thinking over her remarks.

Some days later, I met Moopanar. I shared excellent relations with him. My association with him went back to the late 1970s, when I was general secretary of the IYC and he was the PCC president; he subsequently became the AICC general secretary. The party office at 24, Akbar Road had originally been allotted to him. He had shifted to Western Courts, and his residence became our party's headquarters after the Congress split in January 1978. After he became the Tamil Nadu PCC president a second time and was relieved from the post of AICC general secretary in 1988, I, as general secretary of the AICC, had organized a big send-off for him at the party headquarters in Delhi. Such was the camaraderie we shared that when militancy was at its peak in J&K in the 1990s, I would jokingly tell him to arrange a residence for me in Chennai, as I might have to shift there for good. He disarmed me by offering his residence, saying that he would go elsewhere! Even after he split with the Congress, I would unfailingly meet him for lunch or dinner whenever I was in Chennai.

I briefed Moopanar on my discussions with Jayalalithaa. I told him that since she was not keen on aligning with the Congress, he should seek a tie-up with the AIADMK. He said it was pointless, since he shared a hostile relationship with her. I thought it over and an idea struck me. I suggested that if his party and the Congress could form an alliance, I could once again approach Jayalalithaa for a broader, three-way alliance. It was possible that she would then agree. Two-to-three days of intense discussions later, Moopanar gave the go-ahead.

Backed by his assurance, I met the AIADMK chief again. This time she was receptive because she realized the potential of a Congress–TMC alliance. But she said that she would give her consent formally and publicly only after the Congress and the TMC jointly addressed a press conference and committed themselves to the partnership.

Things had begun to work in the right direction, and I was finally seeing a real possibility for the Congress's success in the elections.

Moopanar and I discussed the matter in detail, spread over days. I suggested that he merge his party with the Congress—after all, both of us shared the same ideology. He said he would have to talk the issue over with his senior colleagues. Days later, when we met again, he said that a merger would not be possible. However, his party was ready for an alliance with the Congress. It was decided that we would, as one group, contest the election and campaign jointly for each other's candidates.

We both announced the formal alliance at a press conference at his residence. Soon after the press meet, I received a call from Jayalalithaa's residence, asking me to go over immediately and meet the AIADMK chief. She served tea and insisted that I have it after I demurred. Then she declared that her party would partner us in the elections.

Until that time, Sonia ji was blissfully unaware of what I was up to in Tamil Nadu. Once the alliances were stitched, I informed her of the development. Needless to say, she was pleased. Our alliance won the state elections with a handsome margin, and Jayalalithaa became the CM.

Meanwhile, in Puducherry, the Congress, unlike in Tamil Nadu, was united till the announcement of elections. However, both the DMK and the AIADMK had flatly refused to tie up with us, and there was no scope to change their minds. After failing to persuade the leadership of both the parties, I was reconciled to a lonely battle. Compounding matters was a unique problem: Our own Congress sitting CM, P. Shanmugam, had declined to contest elections and campaign for the party, claiming that the party stood no chance without any alliance and that it would be futile for him to waste time in contesting or campaigning!

Dismayed but undeterred, I set about meeting the challenge. I told MP V. Narayanasamy that we had to give all that we had with the limited resources at our command. We geared up, addressed several meetings with our party's local leaders and held rallies in different parts of Puducherry, explaining the virtues of the Congress. Shanmugam sat at home and announced his retirement from politics. To everyone's surprise, we won, and N. Rangaswamy became the CM. Looking back, I believe that our victory in Puducherry was a bigger feat than our triumph in Tamil Nadu because we had no allies in the former.

Similarly, Kerala was another big challenge, being a politically important state for the Congress. The party was hopelessly divided into two major factions—one led by the state's strongman K. Karunakaran and the other by A.K. Antony. It was a leadership tussle between the groups led by two tall leaders that dated back to 1978, when the Congress had split. Karunakaran had stood by Indira ji, while Antony had gone over to the other side. Although Antony returned to the Congress's fold later along with his supporters, the bitterness between the two remained. The reason for this bitterness was the same as in other states. Whenever a merger of two groups happens, more people get added in the share of the pie. Some lose out in the race, which results in their bitterness. Those who are deprived of positions would nurture ambitions, and when those ambitions do not fructify, there is heartburn. Leaders of the groups cannot ignore the grievances of their supporters, thus adding to the factionalism. While Karunakaran is no more and Antony's politics has remained centred in Delhi until very recently, their respective groups still continue to squabble in Kerala to this day, although the situation is not as bad as it was in 2001.

Fortunately, I had wonderful relations with both. Karunakaran was part of that 'core' group of which I was a member, which had demanded and got Rao's resignation as party president. Earlier, both of us were in the CWC and members of the parliamentary board during Rajiv's time. We had continued to share a great rapport since then. Antony was a soft-spoken and reasonable person, and I had an equally good relationship with him since both of us had a Youth Congress background, though he was senior to me.

I persuaded the two leaders to bury the hatchet and work united for the party's victory in the assembly polls, even if temporarily. However, there was another problem. Our ally, the Indian Union Muslim League (IUML), was rumoured to be talking to the Left Democratic Front (LDF) for an alliance. Had that tie-up taken place, the Congress party would have been in deep trouble as it would have had an adverse impact on our Muslim votes. The IUML chief, Sayed Mohammed Ali Shihab Thangal, who was also a respected religious figure, was close to me. During his rare trips to Delhi, he would visit my residence, treat my wife like his daughter and invite us over to his place in Malappuram, about a one-and-a-half-hour journey from Kozhikode.

A few days later, while I was in Bengaluru with Sonia ji at some party event, I received a call from a worker in Kerala. He said that that the LDF–IUML alliance would be announced the following day, which happened to be Eid. I told Sonia ji that I would have to rush to Kozhikode and would not be able to accompany her to Delhi.

I boarded the first available flight, landed at Kozhikode and straightaway left for Thangal's residence, reaching at night. He was enormously surprised but also pleased to see me. I told him that since I was in Bengaluru, I had decided to drop by and celebrate Eid, which was the following day, with him. I also told him that I would be staying at his residence. He hugged me warmly, but I had put him in a fix. I was told that on Eid, a senior LDF leader was supposed to visit his house and announce the tie-up between LDF and the IUML.

During dinner, we had a long discussion on the political scenario in Kerala, and I broached the subject of alliance. His response was that the Congress leaders were fighting amongst themselves and that it would be meaningless to align with a party that was faction-ridden. I assured him that I would resolve the issue of infighting. I also played the emotional card, reminding him of our family relations, and said that it would be very awkward for me as his guest while he was firming up an alliance with our rivals in the state. Moreover, it would put him in bad light too—that he was hosting me and siding with my opponent's party at the same time.

The following day, I accompanied him for the Eid namaz at a nearby Eidgah. The media, too, was there, and reporters asked me about my visit. I told them that I had come to wish Thangal on Eid and was staying at his residence. We were 'together' and we would be contesting the elections as allies. Thangal concurred and the alliance was finalized.

The icing on the cake was that I managed another tie-up with senior leader K.R. Gouri Amma's outfit, Janathipathy Samrakshana Samithi (Democratic Protection Committee). She was one of the founders of the communist movement in Kerala and a former minister in the state government. Later, she had left the party and formed her own outfit, which had quite a good influence in some pockets of the region. She was a widely respected figure, and the alliance with her boosted our electoral prospects.

Eventually, our alliance United Democratic Front won with an unprecedented 99 of the 140 seats—a record that remains unbroken to this day in the history of the alliance.

12

DIRTY BUSINESS OF POLITICS

I was back in Delhi after my southern sojourn, happy with the Congress' success. But politics in India is an endless cycle of elections. Assembly polls in the politically crucial state of UP and neighbouring Uttarakhand were around the corner in January–February 2002. I was made general secretary in charge of these two states in mid-2001. Over the next six months, I immersed myself in strategizing and campaigning.

Being a realist, I knew that the Congress had little prospects of winning in UP. The state had two strong regional parties, the Samajwadi Party (SP) and the Bahujan Samaj Party (BSP), commanding large chunks of dedicated vote banks. Besides, the BJP was a strong presence. My aim was modest: to increase our number of seats and the vote share.

As far as Uttarakhand was concerned, I believed that as it was a newly carved-out state, none of the regional parties had much presence there. My optimism was derived from the feedback I had received during my earlier visits to the state. If we used the right strategy and tactics, we could form the government there. But I ran into an unexpected problem. Senior leader N.D. Tiwari refused to cooperate. Neither did he come for any programme nor did he campaign during elections. He seemed simply disinterested. Perhaps he was not confident of the Congress party emerging strong enough to form the government. He visited the state only once, along with Sonia ji, when I had invited her to campaign for one day. I had to plead with him, saying that it would look odd for a senior person such as him to remain absent when the party president was visiting Uttarakhand. Fortunately, other senior leaders like state PCC president Harish Rawat and Indira Hridayesh, the only MLC in the state that time, were fully on board and worked hard throughout, standing shoulder to shoulder with me.

With an aim to prepare a sound foundation for the campaign, I started a six-month Parivartan Yatra in both states, UP and Uttarakhand, simultaneously. The yatra was designed to seize the voters' attention. I took the help of my other colleagues to join me in the programmes during this period. I devoted one half of a week to UP and the other half to Uttarakhand, with no break in between. I barely visited Delhi, constantly shuttling between the two election-bound states.

I had to face tougher moments while campaigning in UP. This was because the yatra had started from the month of June, followed by hot, sultry months of July and August, during which I had to stay in various poorly maintained government dak bungalows for the night. There were hardly any hotels in the state in those days, except in Lucknow and Varanasi.

Unlike in Karnataka and Andhra Pradesh, in UP, I faced the problem of power cuts. One day, after a day-long campaign, when I was put up in a government guest house in Agra for the night, the power supply failed at midnight and the power did not come back throughout the night. There was no power backup system, and I had to do without even a fan in the months of June–July. One can imagine the torture I went through. I spent the entire night in the lawns of the guest house, warding off mosquitoes and counting the stars, literally. I had never before waited so eagerly for morning to arrive!

On another occasion, sometime in August–September, after I had concluded a day-long yatra in Azamgarh and Mau districts, prominent leaders of the district, including Sudha Rai, former MP and wife of former minister (late) Kalpnath Rai, had accompanied me during my visit to various villages in the districts. We returned to the Mau district headquarters for the night's stay. Dinner was supposed to be at a worker's residence in the city, and I was to stay in the city dak bungalow. Upon reaching the city around midnight, we found that there was no power. Hence, I decided to skip dinner.

Now, the problem was that there was no hotel or guest house with power backup in Mau. It was suggested that I put up at another guest house some 20 km away from the city. That guest house had come up during PM Chandra Shekhar's tenure for his use. There was nothing around—no buildings, no residences—for as far as the eye could see. There was no security either. One could only see fields from all the sides; the place looked not only isolated but scary too. The guest house chowkidar was woken up with some difficulty around 1.30 a.m., and he guided me to the so-called VVIP room. The local leaders accompanying me wished me goodnight and left for their respective homes. The chowkidar, after making me comfortable in the room, retired to his hut, which was close by.

The room was clean, fitted with two air-conditioners, a ceiling fan and a table fan. This was an unexpected luxury in the middle of nowhere. I dreamt of a sound sleep after having a well-deserved shower. I went to the washroom, ran the water over my body and then generously applied soap all over. Just then, there was an Agra rerun; the power supply failed. I could see nothing. I sat on the floor of the washroom, all soaped up, and waited for the power supply to resume. I couldn't even open my eyes because of soap lather on the face. Fifteen minutes went by, and I began to grope for the shower knob in the dark but failed the task. Then I tried to locate the towel and the door but in vain! It was pitch dark.

After many attempts, I found the doorknob and hobbled tentatively towards the bed. I pulled the bed sheet and wiped my eyes and body, and made my way gingerly towards a small balcony attached to the room, wrapped in that same bed sheet, which now served as a lungi. I found a couple of chairs, sat on one and used the other to rest my legs. But then began the assault by mega-sized mosquitoes, apparently residents of the crop fields that surrounded the guest house from all sides. I was awake in agony the entire night, and the following morning, I was back on the road. Within a few weeks of my campaign, I became used to working in the heat and company of mosquitoes for the next few months till the arrival of the biting cold of December and January, followed by assembly elections in early 2002.

The election results were along expected lines in UP. We won 25 seats but, most importantly, the Congress came second in 76 assembly constituencies. Had the Congress worked harder in a more sustained manner over the next five years, when I was sent to J&K as PCC president immediately after the elections, I am quite sure it could have bagged close to 100 seats in the next election in 2007.

It was a different story in Uttarakhand. My optimism was vindicated. From just one seat (Karan Chand Singh) that we had earlier, we got 36 seats and commanded a majority. We also managed to get some independents on our side to form the government. I had gone personally to the house of a few independent MLAs, requesting them to either join us formally or support us; it was nice of them to oblige.

Tiwari's Tantrums

I believed that government formation in Uttarakhand would be an easy task. Back in Delhi after the impressive results, I met Sonia ji in the evening and discussed government formation. I told her that Rawat was the best choice for the CM's post. He deserved the elevation, having put in his heart and soul into the campaign that I had chalked out. Besides, he was the PCC chief and a known face across the state. My plan was to fly to Uttarakhand the following morning after getting her approval and initiate the process of electing the leader and government formation with Rawat as its head.

Sonia ji did not object to my suggestion but said that before going to Uttarakhand, I should meet Tiwari and get him on board. I stated that there was no need to consult him; his contribution to the party's victory was zero. In fact, he had proved to be an impediment. However, for some reason, she insisted, saying that he could later issue statements that would embarrass the party and the new government there. He might grumble that the party had not considered it fit to seek the advice of a veteran like him. I reluctantly agreed. That very night, around 10.00 p.m., I went over to Tiwari's Delhi residence.

Tiwari was fast asleep, so I told his aide that he needed to be woken up since the matter was urgent. After a while, I was ushered into his bedroom on the first floor, where I found him in sleeping clothes.

He enquired about the chief ministerial candidate and government formation, and I said that Rawat would head the government. Besides being PCC president, Rawat had contributed enormously to the party's success in the election. Tiwari didn't say anything, and I took his silence for concurrence and returned home.

I telephoned Sonia ji to brief her about my meeting with Tiwari. To my utter amazement, she informed me that Tiwari had called her, soon after I must have left his residence, and had sought an appointment with her for the following morning. She asked me to defer my visit to Uttarakhand.

Tiwari met her the next morning around 10.00 a.m. and left after about 45 minutes. Thereafter, I called upon Sonia ji at her 10, Janpath residence. She dropped a bombshell: 'Tiwari wants to be the chief minister,' she said, adding, 'in fact, he has insisted on it.' I was aghast. 'He had done nothing to deserve the post,' I said. Moreover, I had already sounded out Rawat about the possibility of him becoming the CM. But Sonia ji had made up her mind in Tiwari's favour, so I had no option but to accept the decision. It is possible that Sonia ji thought that Tiwari, being a senior person and of advanced age, should be given an opportunity which he might not get later. On the other hand, Rawat was young and would get several chances. Besides, Uttarakhand had been newly formed and needed an experienced administrator to take it on the path of development.

I called up Rawat and explained the situation to him and requested him to accept it. Like a loyal soldier of the party, he did. However, his supporters, about 13 of them, did not turn up for the CLP meeting. It took two-three days for me to persuade them before we could finally elect Tiwari as the CLP leader. I felt really sorry for Rawat.

Yet another miracle was in store. After becoming the CM, Tiwari was suddenly energized. He initiated a number of developmental works, became a hands-on leader and demonstrated great administrative abilities. His performance was in stark contrast to his tenure in UP as CM in the late 1980s, where he had done precious little and had contributed to the Congress party's decline and defeat in the undivided state. Still, that does not mean he deserved to be the CM of Uttarakhand at that stage.

Victory against All Odds

Success breeds enemies. This is especially true of politics. Having turned around the party's fortunes in five states back-to-back, I had won many admirers. However, there was also a clique within the party at the national level that did not appreciate the rise in my stature and my continued victory in state after state, of which I was in charge as the general secretary. Some of the senior leaders who had failed to revive the party in the states they handled began plotting to downplay my achievement. Their efforts apparently bore fruit. One fine day in March 2002, when I was just done with UP and Uttarakhand elections, Sonia ji informed me that I had been appointed as the PCC chief of J&K. Assembly elections were due there in six months' time and, for all apparent purposes, I was being sent there to perform another turnaround. But my adversaries believed that I was being sent into exile.

Some of my well-wishers told me that sending me to my home state was a ploy to get rid of me physically, as militancy was still at its peak there. I dismissed those claims as rubbish; none of my critics, and least of all Sonia ji, would have wanted me dead. I must say that she was extremely happy with my extraordinary performance, and I too had great regard for her. However, some leaders definitely wanted me out of Delhi. As the J&K PCC chief, I would have to relocate there, leaving the space free in Delhi for them to play their games. I packed my bags and left for my home state for the next six months.

The Congress party was in a shambles there. Over 90 per cent of the state's Congress leaders and workers had gone away with Mufti who had succeeded in splitting the party on three occasions: the first was the vertical split orchestrated by him after his appointment as the PCC president in the aftermath of the Indira–Sheikh Accord of 1975; the second was in 1987 when he joined V.P. Singh's Jan Morcha for a brief while, following which he rejoined the Congress in 1996 and the third was in 1999 when he floated a new party, the PDP. This, in sum, was the state of affairs of the Congress in J&K—with virtually no presence in the Kashmir Valley—of which I was made PCC president.

Militancy was rampant. For the first week or so of my stay, I did not even have state security. Ved Ram Nagar (may Almighty give this noble soul a place in heaven), a Congressman from Ghaziabad with a modest milk business, was highly impressed by my dedication and, hence, was concerned about my safety and security when I was asked to go to Kashmir as PCC president. He loaned his security personnel to me, for which I shall remain eternally grateful to him. Ved Ramji, in fact, used to give us milk free of cost in 1977–80, when I was general secretary and staying with Ramchandra Rath, the then IYC president, in his South Avenue flat.

With the intervention of the governor, state security was extended to me a few days later. I plunged headlong into campaigning without bothering about my safety and security. During campaigning, my fellow workers declared me as the party's chief ministerial face! This was needed, as both the PDP and the NC had obvious chief ministerial candidates. The Congress high command did not intervene in whatever I did or said since they had no hope of getting any seat from the state. The general belief in the party at the national level was that I would end up getting two–three seats at best.

Usually, when a new PCC chief takes charge, the first step taken is the reconstitution of the state party unit as well as the district and block units. The process takes four–five months. But I had barely six months left before elections and, therefore, did not have the luxury of reconstituting the various units. I, therefore, decided to plunge headlong into campaigning—if the organization was in a shambles, so be it!

Campaigning in J&K is not easy. One can either use road transport or walk. Added to the challenge was the fact that the Congress party did not have enough candidates since Mufti, after splitting from the party thrice, had taken nearly the entire flock with him. I required two–three dozen serious candidates. Given the situation, I decided to back several independent candidates with a good public image and, post-elections, they extended support to me.

In sum, my challenges in J&K were threefold: to prove that the Congress exists; find suitable candidates and introduce myself (although from J&K, I had spent the past many years in national politics and represented the Lok Sabha from Maharashtra). Of course, being a 'new face', I was also a subject of attraction—many people had heard of me but not seen me. And now, I was presenting myself as the chief ministerial candidate!

Elections were held in the month of September and October in four phases. The results surprised everyone, including Sonia ji. We got the second-highest number of seats—20. The ruling NC won 28 seats and Mufti's PDP got 16 seats. Another 13 seats were won by independents—I had supported some of them in constituencies where I could not find suitable candidates. The Panthers Party got four seats; Mohammed Yousuf Tarigami of Communist Party of India (Marxist) (CPI [M]) had two MLAs and the BSP had one. My political opponents had dispatched me to exile and had thought that I would become a Bahadur Shah Zafar; instead, by the grace of God and with the support of the voters, I emerged victorious!

Meanwhile, Farooq Abdullah declared publicly that he would not stake claim to form the government since he did not have the majority. I met the governor and requested him to invite the Congress party to form the government. I told him that I had the support of 15 independent MLAs, four MLAs of the Panthers Party, two MLAs of CPI (M) and one MLA of the BSP, besides 20 Congress MLAs. However, he rightly pointed out that he could not go by Farooq's statement to the media. Since the NC was the single-largest party, he would have to ask Farooq first.

However, he left a window of opportunity open for me by saying that he would extend an invitation to me provided I gave him a letter of support from all my MLAs, other supporting parties and independents. Then I could legitimately stake claim, being the leader of the largest grouping, which was close to the majority mark of members required to form the government.

I immediately got cracking. All 42 MLAs met and formally elected me as the leader and supported me in government formation. Meanwhile, the majority of independent legislators became 'associate members' of the Congress party. It is worth mentioning here that not a single leader of the Congress helped me in mustering the support of MLAs from other parties or showed any interest in doing so. To get a simple majority, I needed 44. However, there was a provision in the J&K Constitution by which the government could nominate two female members with voting rights to the House. I could later use it to secure a simple majority.

Mufti's Backdoor Entry

With the letter of support of 42 MLAs in my hand, I telephoned the governor, and he invited me the following day to discuss the date of oath-taking. I informed Sonia ji about the developments over telephone. She was happy to hear that I was now taking charge of government formation.

A few hours before the meeting with the governor, around 8.00 a.m., I was in the balcony of my room of Hotel Broadway in Srinagar, having tea with Ashok Bhan, a friend, Congressman and lawyer of the Supreme Court, when a thought occurred to me. Perhaps it was driven by emotion. I told Bhan that I should ask Mufti's party to join the government. I had a long family association with him, which I had maintained even after his split with the Congress. Though I did not need his backing to form the government, I believed that with him on board, the government would be even more stable and could perform better. Besides, he had been a Congressman, and his MLAs could be co-opted in the government.

I telephoned Mufti and informed him that I would be meeting the governor at 11.00 a.m. I suggested that his party could be part of the government and asked him to give me names of five–six MLAs of his party who could be accommodated as ministers. He said that it was a good idea and immediately invited me for breakfast, saying that I could go to the Raj Bhavan after having breakfast with him; I readily agreed. I had breakfast with him at his residence and repeated my offer.

He heard me out and said that he wanted three–four days to think it over. He suggested that I better defer my meeting with the governor until then. I should have seen through his game plan then and gone ahead with the oath-taking; after all, his party could have joined the government later. But I trusted him implicitly and did not spot his deviousness. How was I to know that he would throw our personal relations to the wind and misuse my generosity! I met the governor and briefed him about my talks with Mufti that morning, also informing him that I would get back to him after three–four days.

I returned to Delhi and narrated the whole story to Sonia ji. It was decided that Dr Manmohan Singh, then the LoP in the Rajya Sabha, and I would fly to Srinagar and meet the PDP leader to firm up his party's inclusion in the government. The following day, Dr Singh and I went to Srinagar and had lunch with Mufti, during which he confirmed his party's participation in the government.

Thereafter, Sonia ji invited Mufti to Delhi for the final announcement of the alliance. I, too, was present at the meeting. Mufti thanked the Congress president and me for agreeing to his party's participation in the government. But when he was asked for names from his party who could be part of my government, he suddenly got up in an agitated state and exclaimed, 'I thought that I had been invited to be the chief minister!' Sonia ji and I were aghast and said that no such indication or assurance had been given from our side at any point of time. Mufti nearly shouted back that he had been called to Delhi to be insulted. 'Why was I called? I could have been informed over the telephone.' It was clear that he wanted to hijack the government.

When matters seemed to be going out of hand, I intervened and requested Sonia ji that an arrangement could be worked out by which I would be CM for the first three years and Mufti could take over for the next three years (then the J&K government's term was of six years). This way, everyone would be happy.

However, Mufti, having got a toehold, now wanted full entry through the door. He insisted on being the CM for the first three years. Sonia ji was in no mood to relent. Again, I requested her that in the larger interest of the state, we should agree to his demand. That is how Mufti, whose party had come third in the elections, with just 16 MLAs, became the CM, while I, despite having the support of 42 MLAs, had to return to national politics.

Congress workers and leaders in J&K were deeply annoyed that I had handed over the government on a platter to the PDP despite our party having more than twice their numbers to form the government. But over a period of time, I did manage to placate them with my constant interactions with the rank and file of the party.

Looking back, I think I should not have been so generous to offer that alliance. It was also a blunder to invite Mufti to discuss the offer in Delhi—an advantage he seized to his benefit. Mufti was playing a game with us. By asking for chief ministership for the first three years, he had kept open the possibility of backing out of the deal when my turn came to take over the mantle. Little did I know that he would nearly succeed in that endeavour. Does it surprise anybody to say that politics is a dirty business?

13

SONIA SHINING

The year 2003 brought with it another challenge in the south of the country: undivided Andhra Pradesh. After having won Rajasthan, Karnataka, Puducherry, Uttarakhand and J&K on our own, and Tamil Nadu and Kerala with the support of allies, I was given charge of Andhra Pradesh.

The state was not a new electoral battleground for me. I had dealt with the affairs of the state during the tenures of Indira ji, Rajiv and Rao. I knew the prominent and mid-level leaders not just of the Congress, but those of the rival parties too. I shared a good rapport with both N. Chandrababu Naidu and Y.S. Rajasekhara Reddy, who served as CMs of Andhra Pradesh, and K. Chandrasekhar Rao. All the three had been office bearers of the State Youth Congress while I was first national general secretary in charge of southern India and, later on, president of IYC. I also knew senior leaders like Dr M. Channa Reddy, N. Bhaskara Rao, Janardhana Reddy, Vijay Bhaskar Reddy, K. Rosaiah and P. Shiv Shankar and many more.

Way back in August 1981, Chandrababu had come over to Delhi to extend me an invitation for his wedding with the daughter of N.T. Rama Rao (NTR), then a screen icon and later on CM, which was scheduled for the month of September in Chennai. I spent three days in Chennai attending various wedding ceremonies. It was also the year when the great film artist Nargis Dutt, who was nominated to the Rajya Sabha from the artistes' quota, passed away due to medical complications. One day, Chandrababu visited me with a request from his father-in-law for NTR to be nominated to the Rajya Sabha from the artistes' quota, following the vacancy created by Nargis's death. I promised to take up the matter with Indira ji.

I met Indira ji the following day and conveyed NTR's request. Chandrababu was then a junior Congress minister in the state government of Andhra Pradesh. She promised to let me know after discussing with her two senior colleagues from Andhra Pradesh—P.V. Narasimha Rao and Shiv Shankar, who were Union Cabinet ministers. A few days later, she informed me that these leaders were not receptive to the idea and had argued that a person with Congress ideology should fill up the vacancy. She asked me to convey the government's inability to nominate NTR. I did the needful.

Within six–seven months of our refusal, in 1982, NTR launched his famous statewide yatra on Chaitanya Ratham, his specially designed chariot, signalling his intent to enter politics and take on the Congress government and the party. NTR had an imposing personality. He was a reigning superstar. He took the state by storm and succeeded in dislodging the Congress government. He proved to be a remarkable politician, leveraging his image as a film star and reaching out to all sections of society, regardless of caste, religion or region. He would not mind even offering namaz with Muslims on Eid, which added to his popularity among the minorities.

Months later, Chandrababu met me and said that with his father-in-law in politics having formed the Telugu Desam Party (TDP), it was untenable for him to continue in the Congress. I understood his dilemma and we parted ways politically. Such was our rapport that he took me into confidence; he could have simply gone ahead and joined the TDP without informing me beforehand. Chandrababu is a gentleman and had been a man of few words initially. Later, he turned out to be an outstanding politician and did extremely good work in the information technology sector in particular, for which he gained international recognition. He also developed friendly relations with many heads of governments and States.

The Andhra Turnaround

By 2003, Chandrababu had earned the distinction of being the longest serving CM of Andhra Pradesh. He was at the peak of his popularity when I took charge of the state as Congress's national general secretary. For the party, this was a difficult period. The BJP, under the leadership of Vajpayee, was in power at the Centre. The TDP–BJP alliance had 36 out of 42 Lok Sabha MPs from Andhra Pradesh while the Congress had just five. Similarly, in the Assembly, the TDP had 180 MLAs, while the coalition partner BJP had 12 and Congress party had only 91 MLAs. Hence, the Congress had to fight against both the central and the state governments simultaneously.

Undeterred by the pessimistic prediction of my party colleagues in New Delhi, I announced a date for my visit to the state to kick-start the Congress's campaign. However, as luck would have it, I was struck severely by dengue in the beginning of 2003 that tied me to bed. I was under constant care of doctors; senior party leaders Ahmed Patel and Motilal Vora visited me every alternate day to enquire about my well-being, particularly when my platelet count had started falling. As a result, I could not go to Andhra Pradesh on the dates announced. I gave another date for my arrival in Hyderabad but could not make it again since the fever had worsened.

Having missed two dates, I came under attack from a section of the Telugu media, which was supportive of the TDP and Chandrababu anyway. The newspapers ridiculed me, claiming that I had foreseen the Congress's defeat and had chickened out by making excuses of deteriorating health. One of the largest circulated newspapers of South India, *Eenadu*, had a cartoon on its front page, depicting me as a guru seeking a Congress government as guru dakshina from my disciple Chandrababu, which he declined.

The prolonged sickness and media criticism upset me deeply. I was still on my sickbed and was showing no signs of a speedy recovery. Still, I went ahead and announced another fresh date, 20 days from then, and declared rather dramatically that I would reach the designated place dead or alive. The plan was to proceed from Delhi to Hyderabad and then to Rajahmundry by overnight train to address the first major public meeting. Unfortunately, even 20 days later, I was still in a bad shape. However, despite the doctors' strict directive that I should have continued to rest for at least 15 days more, I took a flight to Hyderabad. The bad cold and fever worsened during the air journey; somehow, I boarded the train immediately after landing at Hyderabad, accompanied by a friend and senior Congress leader and MP, T. Subbarami Reddy.

Owing to the air conditioning in the train, my health further worsened en route. I still had a runny nose and my cough did not subside. Neither could I sleep the whole night, nor did I allow Subbarami Reddy to sleep. On reaching the destination, I did not have the strength even to come out of the train, let alone stand. Senior leaders who had arrived to receive me at the station helped me get into the car. I went straight to the meeting place, where almost one lakh people and all Congress leaders from across the state had gathered to kick-start the campaign. I addressed the gathering while being seated on a chair for the first time in my life.

Eager to make a mark, I spoke with greater fervour than usual. My bravado, however, made things worse for me: By the time I finished my one-hour address, I was running a fever of almost 104 degrees and getting delirious. It was decided by the leaders present—Rajasekhara and the PCC president—that I should be taken to Vijayawada by road, from where a flight would transport me to Hyderabad and then to Delhi at the earliest. I proceeded to Vijayawada accompanied by MLA Vasant Kumar. Along the way, my condition further deteriorated and I had to stay at a party MLA's residence. By chance, his brother was a doctor who gave me some medicines. It was only the next day that I boarded a flight from Vijayawada to Hyderabad, and from there I returned to Delhi. Back home, I collapsed on my bed and remained there for several days. The media in Andhra Pradesh that had been following me closely was now convinced that I was indeed sick and that I should have not travelled in such a condition. It stopped taking pot-shots at me; rather, it appreciated my dedication towards the party.

I may have been physically exhausted but I was mentally and politically alert. Even as I recuperated, I began to finalize the outlines of my campaign for the next one year till elections. I decided to adopt the same model of campaign that I had used to good effect in Karnataka a few years ago: taking a busload of the top leadership of the Congress party representing various sections along with me on the campaign trail of the entire state in a phased manner.

However, this journey was beset with challenges. Caste factor was, and continues even today, to play a big role in the electoral politics of Andhra Pradesh. The Kapu caste was considered backward in Telangana while it was forward in the Andhra Pradesh area. Then there were the Reddys, the SCs and OBCs, besides a good number of minorities spread across both regions. Finding the right balance was of great essence. Rajasekhara, being a Reddy, was acceptable in both the regions. I was now looking for a good Kapu leader. I was told that Dasari Narayana Rao, a Congressman and a very famous director, producer, screenwriter, actor and lyricist, was available to work for the party during elections. When I checked this with Rajasekhara, he opposed the idea of involving him in the campaign. But I did not stop here. On making further enquiries, I was told that the two did not get along well, since Rajasekhara preferred not to have another leader of prominence steal the show from him. Narayana Rao also attracted crowds and got as many cheers as Rajasekhara did during public meetings; the difference between the two was that Rajasekhara was highly political, unlike Narayana Rao.

Having been satisfied, I appointed Narayana Rao as the chairman of the state campaign committee. Rajasekhara was the LoP in the Assembly and, hence, didn't require any party post. Rajasekhara and Narayan Rao both would get equal respect and attention in Andhra. D. Srinivas, a backward Kapu in Telangana, was the PCC president. Besides, the SCs and Muslims were fully supportive of the Congress party.

The other challenge was that our leadership in the state was hopelessly faction ridden. Before I took over as general secretary, Rajasekhara and his group had begun a padyatra in his region, ignoring other state leaders. As a result, some senior leaders from the Andhra region and Telangana had simply stayed at home and others remained confined to the party office. I asked Rajasekhara to stop his yatra altogether, which he did readily. I then got hold of all senior leaders, former CMs, former Union ministers, former PCC presidents, former CLP leaders, former Speakers, Deputy Speakers, chairmen of councils etc., and began travelling with them in one air-conditioned 52-seater bus, stopping along the way to address five–six meetings in each assembly constituency. All along, crowds surged to see their leaders together in one bus for the first time in their lives. At public rallies, all these leaders would be on the dais, along with a few local leaders, to address the massive crowds of 40,000–50,000 people. Throughout the campaign, I ensured that every leader, local and the ones selected for the trip, got an occasion to speak during the course of the day. The media covered our campaign extensively; it was a novelty for them, too, to see all the leaders from all regions at one place.

We would stay back in constituencies for the night after addressing the meetings, be it urban or rural areas. In rural areas, we would stay in different houses of our village party workers. On one such occasion, I stayed back for the night at the residence of a village sarpanch in a very remote area. There were no chairs or tables and certainly no dining table. I had to sit on the floor to eat dinner, which was not that bad. But what was bad was that there were no indoor toilets and I had to take a trip with a small tumbler full of water to the nearby fields for my ablution in the morning. The problem was that on reaching the fields, I would find them already occupied, with several people, both men and women, defecating openly, and I had to return unsuccessful. On that day, I remained hungry for the entire day, lest I feel the pressure of using the toilet.

Thereafter, on such occasions in future, I decided to change my timings and reached the field at five in the morning whenever we would stay in rural areas for the night. This time I found it relatively isolated. But then I faced another problem. After I was done, I tried to rise up but found to my horror that I could not, not because of age, but because I was used to the Western-style commode and not to squatting on the ground. Thereafter, whenever I stayed back at night in our workers' homes in villages, I carried along a wooden stick for assistance in getting up. This was a unique experience, which I had never faced in any other part of the country during my life (except once in Karnataka), but in the interest of the party and to succeed in my mission, I gladly accepted this challenge. I felt proud of going through this ordeal.

The bus trip idea was such a big hit in the Andhra region that leaders of Telangana, despite being initially sceptical of its success, demanded that I conduct a similar exercise in their region as well, which I did as part of the second phase.

During my yatra in this region, I realized that in order to bolster our prospects of victory, I had to win over the Muslims, who doted on Chandrababu for a number of reasons, including the fact that he had helped them in building mosques, graveyard boundaries etc., besides helping them politically. One day, while travelling in the region accompanied by senior Congress leader Mohammed Ali Shabbir, in one of the press conferences, I announced that if the Congress came to power, it would give 5 per cent reservation to the Muslim minorities in the state in government educational institutions and employment, on the lines of what existed in Kerala, Tamil Nadu and Karnataka. That clicked across the state, particularly in the Telangana and Rayalaseema regions, and Muslim voters switched over to the Congress overnight.

The entire campaign was designed in a phased manner, with each phase covering three months. After every phase, there was a gap of three–four days when leaders would go to their respective homes and I would return to Delhi. I would barely get two days in Delhi before I had to return and pick up the yatra from where I had left. As a result of the hectic three–four rounds of campaigning spread over a period of more than one year, I addressed more than 1,500 public meetings during the pre-election and election periods, besides attending a number of women, SC/ST, minorities and frontal organization conventions. After all, it was a campaign for both the Lok Sabha and assembly elections.

We registered a massive victory in both. From 95 MLAs (including allies) in 1999, we now had 230 MLAs, including allies. Rajasekhara became the CM. Similarly, in the Lok Sabha, from just five MPs from the state, we now had 37 (including allies); the TDP–BJP, which had 36, ended up with five seats. Had those 37 Lok Sabha members from Andhra Pradesh not been elected, we could not have become the single largest party with 145 seats, and would not have been able to form the government. Though we got 37 Lok Sabha seats from undivided Andhra, nationally, the Congress performed badly. We had won only 116 seats from the rest of the country, while the BJP, with 138 seats, was behind us by just seven seats.

After the results, mediapersons reminded me about the guru dakshina cartoon. I laughingly said that a good guru is one who keeps one last trick with him and does not pass it on to his disciple. The concept of taking along leaders of all castes, communities and regions in a bus for campaigning was that one trick that I had not shared with Chandrababu, I said. I was very happy that our collective hard work brought fruits; subsequently, I was happy that Rajasekhara did extremely well. I also admire Chandrababu for his dedication to the cause of the state's development. Sadly, Rajasekhara's untimely death in 2009 during his second tenure as the CM not only led to the bifurcation of the state but also ensured the party's rout in subsequent elections.

There is an important lesson for the future generations of the Congress party from my experiences in Andhra and other states before it in North and central India right from the time I became the AICC general secretary in 1987. No political party can win and form the government by merely sitting in Delhi and depending totally on tweets and issuing press notes. As general secretary in charge of southern states, from time to time, I used to draw up year-long programmes for each individual state touching villages and blocks myself along with state leaders and would come to the national capital once in five–six months for only two–three days. Which is why, by the grace of God, the Congress won all the states under my charge.

Congress's Comeback

Once the dust settled on the Andhra Pradesh elections, the question of government formation at the national level arose. Being the single largest party, a group of our senior party leaders, including me, began talks with the LDF, DMK, SP, BSP, Nationalist Congress Party, Rashtriya Janata Dal and other like-minded parties. We would tell them that Sonia ji was our choice for PM, and they had no problems with that. However, the BJP upped the ante, with Sushma Swaraj declaring that she would shave her head if Sonia ji, a person of foreign origin, became India's PM. Sonia ji was upset by the opposition to her name as the PM candidate and decided that the government could not begin its administration with such controversies. She ended the unsavoury matter by opting out of the race despite being elected as leader of the parliamentary party and declared Manmohan Singh as the Congress party's prime ministerial choice. At the meeting of senior leaders, when Sonia ji had declined, I had walked out. I have no idea why she chose to reject the overwhelming demand that she take over as the PM. It is said that she took the decision after discussions with her family members. Another meeting was called the same day at 4.00 p.m., which I did not attend. Once she had said a clear 'no' to prime ministership, I had lost interest in persuading her further.

There were several claimants to the post who had nurtured hopes of becoming PM. Pranab da must have placed hopes too. But everyone agreed that Dr Singh was a good choice: he was a gentleman; had personal integrity; did not belong to any group and was knowledgeable, accessible, modest and, above all, an economist of international repute.

The group of senior leaders then briefed the potential allies about the new development. Pranab da, Ahmed Patel and I did several rounds of discussion with other leaders. Some of these parties joined the government; others like the Left and the SP supported us from outside. That is how the UPA government came into being.

Talks then began on the formation of the ministry. Sonia ji, Dr Singh, Patel and I had series of meetings on government formation. In Sonia ji's presence, I requested Patel to join the ministry, but he politely declined, laughingly saying that I had to be part of the government without fail. 'You are the campaigner on the ground and also a good minister whereas I am just an observer from Delhi!,' he said graciously. I also proposed the name of Ambika Soni, but she too declined to be a minister as she was the political advisor to Sonia ji. She was happier in that role, enjoying more power.

When the portfolios were distributed, I got parliamentary affairs, urban development, housing and poverty alleviation. However, I realized that there was no portfolio left for Kumari Selja, so I came forward and told Dr Singh that he could divide my portfolio into two and give housing and poverty alleviation to Selja. He was very happy with my generous offer.

Although I was familiar with parliamentary affairs, the challenge for me this time was bigger. During Rajiv's time, I was the MoS, but our party had a massive majority and was not dependent on allies. Even when Rao was PM and I was Cabinet minister for parliamentary affairs, we had decent numbers, though not a majority. This time, however, we had only 145 of our own and were completely at the mercy of our partners. I had the unenviable job of managing allies, who had their own agenda that conflicted with those of the Congress at times. The LDF, for instance, had its own agenda of economic policies.

I managed the differences largely because of my personal equations with the leaders of other parties, including those in the Opposition like Advani. I would go to his residence before the start of each Parliament session and during the session period too. I can never forget the motherly love and affection that his wife Kamla Advani would shower on me and my junior colleagues. She would always insist on us having a glass of homemade lassi, if not a complete meal.

Vajpayee would often drop by at my office, and I too would meet him often as a minister both at his residence and in his office. Later, as the PM, Vajpayee directed his parliamentary affairs minister, M.L. Khurana, to meet me and understand the techniques of floor management. I gave Khurana some tips, without, of course, compromising the Congress party's political interests inside Parliament. Khurana would regularly consult me whenever he faced problems during Parliament sessions.

Such floor management is unthinkable today, which is why we often witness chaos and commotion in Parliament, which affects not only the functioning of the two Houses but also lowers the image and prestige of MPs in the public eye.

14

CHIEF MINISTER, AT LAST

In the UPA-I government, I continued with my responsibilities as minister of parliamentary affairs and urban development till November 2005. It was now time for Mufti to pass on the mantle of chief ministership to me.

But Mufti began to give indications of his reluctance to vacate the office. He lobbied with a few national parties, such as the Left and others with whom he had developed close contacts when he was in V.P. Singh's government, to gain support for his continuance. He began to spread the impression that a change in guard would lead to instability in J&K and hamper its progress. In sum, Mufti made it known that he was not going to give up the chief ministership.

The CWC met to discuss the matter. I pulled no punches when my turn to speak came. I told the members categorically that the Congress had already lost space in J&K because of our accommodative policies towards successive non-Congress CMs by supporting them from time to time. The party would have no future left there if we continued to bow to pressure from the regional outfits. I was not against arrangements with them, but they had to be on equal terms.

In the CWC, I was supported by Karan Singh and M.L. Fotedar. Of course, all other CWC members had been supporting my stand since the beginning. The CWC unanimously decided that Mufti should honour the decision taken in 2002 and quit as CM after completing his three-year term. Thus, Mufti reluctantly vacated office. I took oath as the CM of J&K on 2 November 2005, becoming the first CM from Jammu province since Independence.

The government secretariat was in the midst of the process of shifting its headquarters from Srinagar to Jammu for six months during the winter season. As a symbolic gesture, I took oath in Srinagar four–five days before government offices would open in Jammu. I used this time to work out my priorities.

The state had become infamous for a few things. The first was rampant, if relatively small-scale, corruption. The second was a complete lack of work culture. Government offices hardly worked in the secretariat; no field work took place. Infrastructure-related projects would take years to complete. Similarly, the Assembly functioned only five days a week, that too from morning until lunch, with Saturdays off. There simply was no accountability in government functioning. To make matters worse, nepotism at all levels was at its peak.

A day before the opening of government offices in Jammu, I addressed a press conference and laid down my immediate plan of action to tackle these two issues. I announced that within 15 days, the assembly session would be summoned and an amendment to the Jammu and Kashmir Prevention of Corruption Act, 1949, would be brought, enabling the state vigilance organization to attach disproportionate assets of corrupt public servants (politicians and government officials). The law would apply to everybody, from a peon to the CM.

The second decision that I announced was a change in the office timings of the government secretariat—it would be from 9.00 a.m. to 5.00 p.m. The gates of the secretariat building would be closed at 9.05 a.m. and the keys would be placed on my table. Those who arrived late would be turned back and marked as absent.

My third decision was that, in consultation with the Speaker, the Assembly would function from 10.00 a.m. to 5.00 p.m., even beyond if necessary, for six days a week instead of having the five-day-week schedule. The fourth decision was that the visiting time for general public in the government secretariat would be limited to post-lunch hours, so that the secretariat could devote and concentrate on their work without interruption. In addition, the fifth decision that I announced was that legislation would be brought to cap the number of ministers to 20 per cent of the total strength of both the Houses.

To curb nepotism, I passed an executive order that no ministers could appoint his/her blood relation as his/her private staff and that no interference of the relatives of ministers would be tolerated in the working of their departments. To set an example, I said that none of my relatives should be entertained by the officers. I further directed the chief secretary to send these decisions in writing to all the principal secretaries, commissioners, heads of departments and police officers from superintendent to DG.

CHIEF MINISTER'S SECRETARIAT

All the Hon'ble Ministers and other functionaries of the Government may be informed, in no un-certain terms, that in case any of my relatives, acquaintances approaches them for a favour, such requests must not be entertained and I should be informed promptly. I would expect the Hon'ble Ministers and the Government officers to discharge their duties conscientiously and in accordance with law.

2) You may kindly have appropriate instructions issued accordingly.

Chief Minister 14.11.2[illegible]

Chief Secretary

0191-2545702 (J)

Government of Jammu and Kashmir
General Administration Department
(Administration Section)
Civil Secretariat,
Srinagar/Jammu.

Circular No. 21-GAD of 2005
Dated- 14-11-2005.

The Hon'ble Chief Minister has been pleased to observe that:-

a. in case any of his relatives or acquaintances approaches any of the Hon'ble Ministers or Government Functionaries for favours, such requests should not be entertained and the same should be brought to his notice promptly.

b. Hon'ble Ministers and Government Officers are expected to discharge their duties conscientiously and in accordance with the law.

The above instructions are brought to the notice of all Hon'ble Ministers, Administrative Secretaries and Heads of the Departments for strict compliance.

Sd/-
(Vijay Bakaya)
Chief Secretary

NO:-GAD(Adm)329/2005-V Dated:-14-11-2005.

Copy to the:-

1. All Financial Commissioners/Principal Secretary to Chief Minister.
2. CEO, Economic Reconstruction Agency.
3. Director General of Police.
4. All Principal Secretaries and Secretaries to Government /Principal Secretary to His Excellency the Governor.
5. All Commissioners and Secretaries to Government.
6. Resident Commissioner, J&K Government, New Delhi.
7. Chief Electoral Officer.
8. Divisional Commissioner, Jammu/Kashmir.
9. All Heads of Departments.
10. All Deputy Commissioners.
11. All Managing Directors of Corporations/Boards.
12. Secretary, J&K, Public Service Commission.
13. Secretary, J&K, Services Selection Board.
14. Secretary, J&K Legislative Assembly/Council.
15. Chairman J&K Board of School Education/Registrars, Universities of Jammu/Kashmir/SKUAST Jammu/Kashmir.
16. Chairman, Board of Professional Entrance Examination.
17. Director Information/Estates.
18. General Manager, Government Press, Srinagar.
19. Private Secretaries to all Ministers/Ministers of State.
20. Principal Private Secretary to Chief Secretary.
21. Private Secretary to Principal Secretary, General Administration Department.
22. Circular file.

14/11

(Asgar Hussain)
Under Secretary to Government

My announcements created a huge stir and brought about positivity and hope across J&K, with people sensing that, at last, change was coming.

The Assembly often sat late at night, even up to 11.00 p.m. or midnight, and people would watch the proceedings and listen to the speeches with great interest. On the first day of the assembly session, I noticed that the photographers, including TV crew, were inside the Assembly Hall and would thrust their mikes at the members of the Assembly when they spoke. I requested the Speaker on the very first day of the session that this had to end. From the next day, the cameramen were confined to the media gallery in the balcony and were allowed to interact with the MLAs only outside the House.

On the Path to Development

I announced that all government infrastructure-related works, like roads, buildings, hospitals, colleges, schools, bridges, etc., would be completed in double and triple shifts, with each shift lasting eight hours. Multiple shifts created three times more employment opportunities for both skilled and unskilled workers. Further, it eliminated huge cost overruns by avoiding delays; the taxpayers' money was also saved in the process. In a number of cases, we actually saved 20–30 per cent of the funds earmarked for that particular project. It also made facilities available to the public at large well before time.

Several major projects that I personally monitored were completed well before the stipulated time under this double/triple-shift system, particularly in the state's health sector. For example, work on the new building for the Dental College in Jammu began in August 2006 and was completed in November 2007 under the double-shift system. The same system also saw a 200-bed paediatrics block in Sri Maharaja Gulab Singh Hospital in Jammu completed in a record time of two years. Between 2006 and 2008, 33 district and sub-district hospitals were established in Kathua, Kishtwar, Doda, Rajouri, Kulgam, Anantnag, Poonch, Baramulla, Bandipora, Kupwara, Sopore, Bhadarwah, Sarwal, Zainapora and Rajpora. Medical infrastructure, like the Jawahar Lal Nehru Memorial Hospital in Rainawari and the

OPD block in the government hospital in Gandhi Nagar, Jammu, was constructed in record time, and medical facilities, including emergency and OPD blocks, were upgraded quickly. I also oversaw the establishment of College of Nursing and Medical Technology in Srinagar and an oncology wing at the Government Medical College Srinagar. Besides, I also ensured the construction of two greenfield super-specialty hospitals in both Srinagar and Jammu. The Sher-i-Kashmir Institute of Medical Sciences in Srinagar was upgraded with the establishment of a regional cancer centre; a radioiodine treatment ward was set up with state-of-the-art facilities; an advanced centre for genetic diseases too came up and a 100-bed maternity hospital was added. Close to ₹100 crore were invested in the establishment and commissioning of water treatment and filtration plants in J&K.

Thirteen new degree colleges and nine Industrial Training Institutes were sanctioned across the state, and the buildings were constructed in double shifts. I also ensured that a large number of infrastructure projects relating to bridges and roads were fast-tracked so that the people could benefit from them at the earliest. The Kunzer bridge in Baramulla district, for example, was completed in a record time of seven months. Thirteen more bridges in the Kashmir Valley and four in Jammu were completed in record time under double shifts.

Among the most important projects undertaken during my chief ministership was the construction of the 84-km-long Mughal Road, the foundation stone for which was laid by Mufti when he was the CM, at an estimated cost of ₹200 crore sanctioned by the UPA government. But after I took charge, I got the entire project revised. The estimates were raised three-fold to ₹600 crore to make the road far wider than what had been conceived during Mufti's tenure. I monitored its progress by helicopter. Two years after I took charge, 70 km of the road had been ready, 35 km each from Poonch and Shopian sides.

During my tenure, optimum use of the Pradhan Mantri Gram Sadak Yojana was made, and over 71 projects under the scheme were completed. Besides, a number of road projects were sanctioned under the PM's reconstruction plan. In addition to this, many irrigation and power projects as well as water supply schemes came up. I personally monitored the construction of the first ever greenfield Haj House in Srinagar and commissioned a four-storey Yatri Niwas for Amarnath yatris. The double/triple shifts also ensured the speedy completion of the new Sri Pratap Singh Museum complex at Lal Mandi in Srinagar, which greatly increased the floor area and repaired damage from the 2005 earthquake. I was to inaugurate this museum on 30 July 2008 but had to resign a few days earlier under rather unfortunate circumstances. It is the misfortune of the state that successive governments have not been able to inaugurate the museum and shift the artefacts and antiques into the new building. They were dumped somewhere after the earthquake struck Uri.

Yet another shining example of the stupendous success achieved by the shift system was the new assembly building, which was completed in 11 months. Work on the project had begun way back in 1978 but was later abandoned due to paucity of funds after barely 10 per cent of the work was done. When I took over as the CM, I spent two–three days in the city in search of land for the new assembly complex but failed to find any suitable place. Daleep Thusu, then managing director of the Jammu and Kashmir Projects Construction Corporation Limited, suggested that I look at the abandoned construction site, which was located just opposite the state secretariat.

I visited the place and suggested redesigning the whole complex: We could have a two-storey complex, one each for the Legislative Assembly and the Legislative Council. I suggested adding other offices to it, such as one for the CM, the deputy CM, etc. I must say that Thusu did a wonderful job of redesigning it the way I had desired. Sadly, he had to suffer under various governments for his hard work later. Once the final design was ready, we started to work on it in three shifts.

Then, in the winter of 2007, I happened to read in the *Srinagar Times* a piece of news that argued that given that it was the month of January, when the cement would not have time to settle, the quality of construction in the new assembly building would be poor and could even lead to the collapse of the building. I was amazed because I had given express instructions that only non-cement work should be undertaken during the winter season, particularly in Kashmir and some snow-bound parts of Jammu.

After reading the news item at midnight, I decided to check the matter out for myself. Early next morning, around 6.00 a.m., I took the state aircraft from Jammu and reached Srinagar. I went to the construction site straight from the airport. The supervisor on duty told me that no cement work was being done. Instead, the interiors, such as doors, windows and various other woodworks were in progress. I went from room to room and was satisfied to see that no cement work had been taken up. I was equally happy to see that at 7.00 a.m. in sub-zero temperature of winter, the work of the assembly complex was going on in full swing under the triple-shift arrangement.

I called up the editor of the newspaper, who was still asleep, and gave him the facts. He was surprised that I had taken the news so seriously as to actually fly down from Jammu to Srinagar early in the morning. He complimented me for my dedication. I ensured that the assembly complex was completed without any further hitch. It was inaugurated on 7 July 2008, in less than a year.

Dreams Meet Reality

Of all these projects, my dream project, which was conceptualized, designed, monitored and created by me, was the Indira Gandhi Memorial Tulip Garden, Asia's largest tulip garden. It took 18 months to complete from the day of conception, when I visited the site, to the day of inauguration.

The genesis of this tulip garden lies in my desire to find a solution to the festering issue of militancy in the Kashmir Valley. From the accounts of various people who were arrested and interrogated by our security agencies, I learnt that while there were those who had become radicalized under the influence of Pakistani elements that were operating in the Kashmir Valley, there were also many other local youth who had taken the path of violence out of sheer frustration of dealing with abject poverty and unemployment. I believed that if my government could create and enhance employment opportunities for the youth, it would be a great help in bringing down the level of militancy in the Kashmir Valley.

Kashmir's economy depended a great deal on the income from tourism, but the tourism season only lasted from mid-May to September. I wondered: What if some more attractions could be added to expand this tourism period? Tourism could provide significant employment to the youth, whether in hotels or as roadside tea/coffee shop vendors, shikara operators and tourist guides.

It was during this period in March 2006 that a government official brought to me a file for my signature. It proposed the construction of private houses in the form of an officers' colony on a government land located on a hillock near Chashme Shahi. Needless to say, the land would be parcelled out at very concessionary rates or no rate at all. I found the proposal fishy since I had already taken huge steps to retrieve government land from illegal occupation of leaders and bureaucrats in Srinagar. I read the file carefully; in any case, I never cleared files without reading them thoroughly. It took me no time to realize that my signature would sanction an official *kabza* (encroachment) of prime government land.

The following morning, I went on an inspection of the site, accompanied only by security staff. I could not trek up the hillock, but I noticed a small nursery called Siraj Bagh at the base of the hillock. It had several flower plants, including two–three dozen tulip plants in full bloom. This gave me an idea: If tulips could grow on that land, perhaps we could explore the prospect of having a tulip garden at the site where the hillock stood, which could be levelled for the purpose.

Back in the office, I contacted the officials of the geology and mining departments and asked them to find out the composition of the hillock. Three days later, they informed me that the entire hillock was made of fertile soil, with no stones at all. The following morning, I gave orders for the flattening of the hillock. The mud generated in the process was to be dumped in the two dry nullahs on either side of the hillock.

By 2006, a considerable part of the work had been done. Nearly one lakh tulip bulbs were then imported from Holland and planted, followed by about 12 lakh more in October–November 2007. The garden, spread over an area of 800 kanals, was finally inaugurated in March 2008 by UPA chairperson Sonia ji in the presence of then defence minister, A.K. Antony. However, work on the site still continued, since I had to make a provision for 20 lakh bulbs.

Lakhs of tourists from across the country began to visit the tulip garden, leading to the tourism period in Kashmir getting extended by two-and-a-half months. Today, the tulip garden is the one of most sought-after tourist destinations in the country in general and Kashmir in particular. Recently, when I visited the garden along with my wife, I was told by the officials there that 30,000–40,000 tourists visited the place daily. En route, I noticed a long queue of tourists in vehicles. I was overwhelmed to see the employment opportunities that had been created for a large number of people. What else could have given me more happiness than this!

After the stupendous success of the tulip garden in Srinagar, I dreamt of creating a similar garden, if not bigger, in Jammu. I asked the revenue department to identify land of more than 1,000 kanals in and around Jammu city. While a site consisting of a few hundred kanals was identified in the Gandhi Nagar area, I came across a large parcel of land right next to it that had remained unused for years. Enquiries revealed that the land belonged to the irrigation department. My office approached the irrigation minister, who was a member of the PDP, to transfer that land to the floriculture department for the purpose of constructing a flower garden, but unfortunately, the minister refused to comply. This attitude of the PDP forced me to retain the irrigation portfolio in the subsequent Cabinet reshuffle. Thereafter, I immediately passed the order affecting the transfer of this irrigation land. Within a year's time, a huge flower garden was created in Gandhi Nagar in double shift, with the potential to attract tourists from the world over. Sadly, this dream was short-lived. After my departure from the CM's office the following year, the garden failed to blossom again. It is rather unfortunate that neither the successive governments nor the citizens of Jammu took any interest in its revival.

My attempts to enhance the tourist potential of Jammu city continued as I realized that of the lakhs of pilgrims visiting the holy shrine of Mata Vaishno Devi, most would head straight for Katra after alighting from the train at Jammu, and after the darshan, would head back to the railway station at Jammu to board their trains to their respective states without spending a single night in the city. I, therefore, conceived of a project to attract tourists. This involved creating a huge lake, about 5–6 km long and 1 km wide, from the base of the Bahu Fort up to Sidhra Bridge on the river Tawi.

I made a mention of this proposed project in one of the important Cabinet meetings. The PDP ministers immediately objected to this project on the pretext that the land for the proposed lake, which was under the jurisdiction of the state's irrigation department, headed by a member of the PDP, could not be spared for this purpose. In an attempt to address their concerns, I requested the PDP minister to accompany me on a visit to the project site. All the ministers accompanied me on this visit. However, regional biases run deep. And so, soon after the visit, they were all vociferously united in their opposition to the project. Owing to the lack of support, I had to shelve the project.

But I was determined not to tolerate this stepmotherly treatment towards Jammu city. In a few weeks, I started constructing an 18-hole golf course on the bank of the Tawi in Sidhra without seeking permissions from my PDP colleagues in the Cabinet. My perseverance ensured that the people of Jammu can today tee off at the city's first civil golf course—the Jammu Tawi Golf Course.

Leading by Example

Just as I had set double/triple-shift schedules for others, I too worked in a similar fashion. From morning till lunch, I would devote time to touring different parts of the state and participating in public meetings, inaugurations, laying foundation stones, etc. I would stop on the way to check on major ongoing projects on the way. If the work was progressing slowly, I would call up the engineer concerned directly from the worksite and notify them. I kept everyone on their toes. Similarly, while I was touring in a helicopter, I would tell the pilot to fly low and take a round of the construction sites to ascertain the progress of the work.

In the second half of the day, which was my 'second shift', I would work in the secretariat till 9.00 p.m. My 'third shift' would begin after dinner around 10.00 p.m., when I would settle down to study important government files, read local and national newspapers and agency reports. I would then visit the site of two–three projects in the city where the works were in progress under the third shift, up to 1.30 a.m. Coming back home, I would sleep for just four hours and be awake at 6.00 a.m.

Why did I work so hard? I had realized that if I did not take the lead and if I didn't work in triple shifts myself, I had no moral right to ask others to work in double and triple shifts. When people often asked me as to why I was working like a man in a hurry, I would reply that I just had a three-year term to deliver, so every minute was precious for me as CM.

Every six months, I would take departmental reviews, and each review would not last less than 10 hours. Similarly, district reviews were done with district-level officers at the district headquarters on yearly basis; each review lasted eight–nine hours. Nobody could fool me because I kept myself abreast of all the ongoing projects and their timelines.

I also ensured that my government did not show any bias on the basis of caste, religion or region when it came to development. Whether it was the BJP, the NC, the PDP, the Communist Party, the Panthers Party or, for that matter, even the All Parties Hurriyat Conference (APHC) or the Rashtriya Swayamsevak Sangh (RSS), if they came up with any public-related demand, such as construction of roads, water supply, schools and hospitals, the government was duty-bound to provide those facilities. In every public meeting, I would say, 'If any minister or officer in my government discriminated against anyone on the basis of region, religion and party politics, I would feel ashamed to be the head of such a government.' My views were crystal clear, and I still believe in that philosophy of justice to every citizen, irrespective of caste, creed, religion and region.

Focus on Clean Governance

I also strove to improve the deliverance on governance at local levels. To this end, eight new districts were created—four in Jammu and four in

Kashmir province—besides four new sub-divisions and 12 new tehsils. It was the first time in the state's history that eight new districts were added at a time through one Cabinet decision, thereby resolving an age-old demand of the people, particularly people of Kishtwar and Reasi.

Incidentally, all my predecessors had promised to create new districts as per the demands of the public, but none of them fulfilled their promises, whereas I did it without having made any such promises. Actually, in Sheikh sahab's time, there was a huge agitation in Kishtwar and Reasi to demand separate districts. The Kishtwar agitation continued for few months, and three students were killed in firing. The then BJP leader in the Assembly from Reasi constituency, Rishi Kumar Koushal, who was a very popular leader across the state, took a vow that he would not shave his beard till Reasi was made a district. Therefore, when I made Reasi a district and went to address a public meeting there, Kaushal, by then very old, with long hair and a long beard, came along with his family members and a barber and got his head shaved on the dais in full view of thousands of people! It showed the genuine sentiments of the people of region who had longed for the demand to be met.

As a part of my drive to tackle corruption and encourage hard-working officers, I decided to reward honest and efficient officials. I announced that the government would award the Chief Minister's Gold Medal for Honesty, Integrity and Meritorious Public Service, to be announced by the CM in his 15 August speech. The medal (30g, 24K gold), a trophy and certificate would be given by the governor in a special function at the Raj Bhavan in the presence of the entire Cabinet and senior officers. The selection of such officers was made in the most transparent manner—a committee headed by the chief secretary, with members including the DG Police, DG Vigilance, finance secretary, inspector general of CID, etc., was constituted. The panel's list was then submitted to the Cabinet for final selection and approval. Thereafter, the CM would make the announcement on 15 August.

In my war against corruption, I ensured the following:

- Amendment to the Jammu and Kashmir Prevention of Corruption Act 2006 (1949 AD), enabling the state vigilance organization to attach disproportionate assets of corrupt public servants. Properties were seized in 10 such cases.

- Registry of 177 cases by the organization involving 111 gazetted officers and 255 other officials, and out of these, completed investigations in 130 cases.
- Sending 161 cases for according sanction for prosecution.
- Sanction to prosecution issued in 143 cases under J&K Prevention of Corruption Act.

The other step I took was to declare a reward of ₹1 lakh for anyone who helped the authorities catch corrupt public servants red-handed, whether a politician or officer. Quite a few compromised officials were nabbed and jailed, and cases were filed against them due to the efforts of whistle-blowers. I was surprised that my initiative to curb corruption had been noticed by the world at large. The representatives of the European Parliament, for instance, reached Srinagar to ascertain these extraordinary steps to curb corruption from me and remarked that the steps I had taken were worthy of replication.

However, I faced an acid test in connection with my drive to root out corruption. During the assembly session, an independent MLA, Shoaib Lone, rose and claimed that the education minister had taken a bribe of ₹40,000 from him for the transfer of a teacher. The minister was a personal friend since my time in the IYC. We had had family relations since then, which continue till date. He was also the president of the state's Congress party, besides being education minister. Hence, there was a huge uproar in the Assembly. I got up and assured the members that I would make a statement once the Assembly met after lunch.

During lunchtime, I spoke to the minister concerned, who vehemently denied the allegation. I believed him, but action was needed to clear the air. I called up the governor and informed him that I would be dropping the person concerned from my Cabinet. I also called DG Vigilance to my office and asked him to conduct an enquiry by himself in this case. The DG was one of the most honest police officers in the history of the state and, hence, enjoyed an impeccable reputation. I told the DG to submit the report within four weeks, which he did. I then spoke with Sonia ji and asked her to relieve him of the PCC chief's post too, which she did, knowing that I was dealing with corruption with all the force at my command.

When the House reassembled after lunch, I informed the members with a heavy heart about the action taken and the Vigilance inquiry. For a while, there was stunned silence in the Assembly after my statement. They had not expected such a swift and rather extreme action. Some members even claimed that I had behaved in a dictatorial manner!

A few weeks later, the report was submitted by the DG Vigilance. The report said that the allegations were false and the person who had taken the money in the name of the minister was the minister's driver and not the minister. Action was taken against the driver under the anti-corruption law.

A few months later, after my tenure came to an abrupt end in 2008, I recommended to Sonia ji that the same MLA whom I had removed be inducted into the Cabinet, headed by CM Omar Abdullah, in a coalition with the Congress, since his name had been cleared by the vigilance department. She was surprised but also appreciative of my principled stand—that when there were allegations against the minister, I took a firm decision, but after having been cleared by Vigilance, he deserved another chance. Thus, he was reinstated in the Cabinet and continued in the government till our coalition lasted for the next six years.

However, whatever might have been the circumstances in which I took that unpleasant decision, I regret it and cannot forgive myself during my lifetime. The minister has always stood by me, politically, in spite of that harsh decision, and is still standing with me like a rock. May God forgive me and give him good health. But while I am saying such good things about him, there are some leaders whom I helped a lot, putting my reputation and image at stake, yet they have become my enemies. But God is great, and He knows everything.

Guidance the Gandhian Way

Another issue that was a cause for concern for me was the increasing trend of Kashmiri youth resorting to violence, taking up guns or pelting stones, misled by those who did not want a united India. I thought to myself: If Mahatma Gandhi could dislodge the mighty British Empire through non-violence, why do the youth have to resort to violence to get their demands fulfilled within the constitutional framework of India? I decided to launch a programme to promote Gandhi's ideals of truth and non-violence among the youth.

On 2 October 2006, while I was addressing a gathering, I declared that a year-long programme would be launched in colleges and schools across the state. There would be a debate competition on Gandhi's philosophy of truth and non-violence. The first prize consisted of ₹1 lakh cash, a trophy and a certificate; the second prize of ₹50,000 in cash for each of the two winners and the third prize of ₹25,000 in cash for each of the four winners. The event would be telecast live on DD.

The idea caught on like wildfire. More than 12 lakh students (both boys and girls) participated through their respective schools across the state. The demand for books on Gandhi grew exponentially across J&K and even outside. More than 40,000 students, representing different schools, had gathered at the venue for the final competition, where the awards were distributed.

Peace and Progress Derailed

It was during my chief ministership that one of the most historical political initiatives was undertaken: that of holding of roundtable conferences, starting in February 2006, to suggest confidence-building measures in the state. PM Manmohan Singh had constituted five working groups for the purpose, of which four had submitted their recommendations.

An oversight and monitoring committee was formed and tasked with the implementation of the recommendations. The PM announced a special package for J&K at a public meeting in Akhnoor, Jammu, in April 2008.

It was pursuant to the deliberations of the roundtable conferences that major outreach was extended to Kashmiri Pandits. A total of 1,024 two-room tenements were taken up for construction in Jammu district (in Nagrota, Purkhoo and Muthi) and completed. Work on a new township for Kashmiri migrants, consisting of 4,218 flats, at a cost of ₹294 crore, was taken up at Nagrota, and a corpus fund of ₹5 crore for migrants was set up. Under the central package, 6,000 jobs for Kashmiri Pandits were created—3,000 of these were filled during my tenure and the others are still being filled. It's an ongoing process. As the CM, some of my top officers, including my chief secretary, DG Police, DG Vigilance and managing directors and chief engineer in charge of several major infrastructure projects, were all Kashmiri Pandits, and they performed their duties with great dedication, honesty and integrity.

As a result of these steps, Jammu, Kashmir and Ladakh were on the path of progress. People were happy with my commitment and my government's performance. However, my rivals, particularly the PDP, were not. They saw the ground slipping from under their feet. If I was allowed to function unhindered, their chances of making a comeback would have been dim. Little did I realize that very soon, my honesty, dedication and achievements would become my enemies.

On 26 May 2008, my government had reached an agreement to transfer 99 acres of forest land to the Shri Amarnathji Shrine Board for setting up temporary shelters and facilities for Hindu pilgrims visiting the shrine from all over the country. This had resulted in a huge religion-based political controversy. The PDP members, who had been part of the Cabinet decision to introduce the Bill, resigned from the Cabinet after the Bill's passage. Violent protests broke out in the Kashmir Valley. The APHC too jumped into these protests, with its leaders muddying the waters. A week later, the PDP and the Panthers Party finally withdrew their support from my government. Sensing the situation, I had no option but to revoke the order on 1 July.

With the PDP withdrawing its support, the governor asked me to prove my majority in the Assembly. My government would have still survived without the PDP's support had the Panthers Party with its four MLAs continued to support my government. Incidentally, a few legislators from the PDP and other parties had assured me that they would defy their respective parties' whip and abstain from voting in order to help me sail through, but I was not comfortable with that idea. As CM, I had brought in a legislation by which MLAs, whether comprising two-thirds, three-fourths or even 100 per cent of the total strength of their party's legislature wing, would face disqualification if they indulged in any act that attracted the provision of the anti-defection law. Such a stringent measure did not even exist in the central law on anti-defection for MPs and MLAs in states. How could I now agree, in order to save my chair, to flouting of the very law that my government, as per my directions, had brought into the Assembly and that had been thereafter enacted in J&K? In any case, I have always been against *jod-tod* (make-and-break) politics.

Thus, I had to announce my resignation on the floor of the house on 8 July. In my speech on the floor of the House, I said that the people of the state had been happy with my government's performance and the initiatives I had taken to curb corruption, develop infrastructure, create a strong work culture, restore accountability, introduce the double/triple-shift system to complete projects ahead of time and strengthen law and order. Those who had lined their purses through corrupt means were upset with me and had worked for my ouster, I added.

Taking a swipe at the APHC, I said that some people sent their children to Dubai for studies and some did business, but they incited the children and poor Kashmiri youth to pelt stones, take up guns and become militants. Such diabolical forces were also inimical to my continuance as the CM. As a matter of fact, some political parties, both in the Jammu region and Kashmir Valley, saw in me a potential threat in the election to be held in the month of October–November that year. Hence, everybody became part of the conspiracy to bring down my government. After submitting my resignation, I returned to Delhi.

In hindsight, I think I could have mustered the required numbers to survive had I devoted enough time to the task. However, I was not in a frame of mind to do so, as Shameem had been admitted to a leading hospital in Mumbai with a medical complication that needed major surgery. Her well-being was my priority, and I was spending more time in Mumbai than in Srinagar or Jammu anyway. I never regretted the decision to prioritize my family. With the Almighty's blessings, she recovered and returned home.

In the end, my opponents who had plotted my downfall had finally succeeded. The seeds of discontent sown by them continue to yield disastrous results to this day.

15

HERE TODAY, GONE TOMORROW

Four months after my resignation and the fall of my government in J&K, fresh polls were announced to be held in seven phases. I was reluctant to contest elections for two reasons. The first was that I would be campaigning for the party across the state and would not have time for my constituency. The second was that I was unsure of support from the voters since I had antagonized Muslims through my government's decision to give land on lease to the Shri Amarnathji Shrine Board for setting up temporary infrastructure and Hindus with my Cabinet's decision to withdraw the order when Kashmir was on the boil after my earlier move. However, I was forced to change my mind due to pressure from local Congress leaders, who said they would certainly lose if I kept myself out of the fray.

Incidentally, after becoming the CM in November 2005, I had contested the by-election from Bhadarwah in March 2006. I had stated at a press conference in Jammu that I would not go to the constituency to seek votes. I had also said that all local government officials posted at Bhadarwah would be transferred out of the constituency and brought back only after the election and that any government official indulging in electoral frauds would be immediately suspended. I had said that I would request the Election Commission of India to countermand the election if any Opposition candidate alleged any sort of irregularity. My announcements were widely hailed by the media and the public.

During the election, the Opposition parties kept reminding me of my promise, and I assured them, both publicly and inside the Assembly, that I would honour it. Interestingly, there wasn't a single case of complaint, either during the elections or after the declaration of the results. I had swept the by-election, getting a whopping 93 per cent of the votes polled and winning by a margin of nearly 60,000 votes; it's a record that remains unbeaten to this date in the history of J&K elections. My constituency comprised an equal number of Hindu and Muslim voters, and they all backed me.

Later in 2008, despite the furore raised by the land transfer and its subsequent revocation, I won by a comfortable margin of about 30,000 votes and again secured the number one position in the entire state. Clearly, the voters had realized that my intentions had been noble and that people with dubious intent had made me a victim. The Congress did well too, getting 17 seats, just three seats short of its 2002 number. In hindsight, I believe I took the right decision to contest the assembly elections in 2008. Had I not done so, my critics would have claimed that I had fled the scene because I had sensed defeat.

However, within a month, I gave up my assembly seat, as I now had work to do in Delhi. The 2009 Lok Sabha General Elections were round the corner and I got busy campaigning for the party across the country.

Capital Calling

I became Rajya Sabha member in February 2009. A few days later, the Election Commission announced that elections to the Lok Sabha would be held in April and May. The Congress, riding on Dr Singh's stature, won 206 seats on its own. He had endeared himself to the people by taking a firm stand in favour of going ahead with the India–US Civil Nuclear Agreement in 2008, despite stiff opposition from the Left, which then supported our government from outside, and reservations from a section within our own party. Dr Singh had even threatened to quit if the agreement was not allowed to fructify. The UPA-I had also provided a massive ₹75,000 crore agricultural loan waiver package to the country's farmers that had made a positive impact on the voters in rural India. Besides, the UPA government had taken many pro-people and pro-poor decisions, such as the

Mahatma Gandhi National Rural Employment Guarantee Act, 2005 (MGNREGA), the credit of which goes to Sonia ji.

Following the return of the Dr Singh-led UPA-II government to power, I was inducted into the Union Cabinet on 22 May. After the swearing in, I spoke with Sonia ji over the telephone and requested that I be given the health and family welfare portfolio. Incidentally, this was only the second time in my political career that I had sought a particular ministry. The first was during Indira ji's time in 1982, when I desperately wanted to be relieved of the law and justice portfolio and requested her to give me the charge of I&B as a junior minister.

Sonia ji advised that I talk directly with Dr Singh, with whom I shared a good understanding. Earlier, in Rao's tenure, Dr Singh and I were ministerial colleagues. I telephoned the PM, and he was surprised that someone as senior as me should be asking for a 'lightweight' portfolio. He had probably expected me to seek a 'major' ministry and remarked that I was too senior to take the health ministry. I said that I wanted to bring in a number of changes in the health sector, which could have a far-reaching impact for decades to come. I reminded him that as the CM of J&K, I had asked him for additional funds for health-related infrastructure, which he had been good enough to sanction.

My reasoning was rooted in the observations I had made during my stint as CM, when I had kept the health portfolio with myself. India has a well-structured, multi-tiered public health infrastructure, comprising community health centres, district hospitals, PHCs and sub-centres spread across rural and semi-urban areas. Tertiary medical care is provided in multi-specialty AIIMS-like hospitals and medical colleges. Improvements in health indicators can be attributed, in part, to this network of health infrastructure. However, there was low penetration of healthcare services in rural areas due to the fact that a majority of secondary and tertiary healthcare facilities were restricted mostly to cities and towns, far away from rural areas, where 75 per cent of our population lives.

I realized that the health sector needed major policy work and huge reforms that could only happen at the central level through the Medical Council of India (MCI). I wanted to do something comprehensive to improve the situation for both present and future

Shameem, our daughter Sofiya and I welcome melody queen Asha Bhosle to our home in New Delhi.

Top: An iftar party with Bollywood's 'Tragedy King'—Shameem, me, Dilip Kumar, his wife Saira Banu, my sister Zahida Muzaffar and my brother-in-law Muzaffar Dev (seated left to right) at a gathering at my residence in New Delhi's South Avenue Lane in 2005.

Bottom: I am all smiles as I greet actor Sanjay Khan and his wife Zarine on their visit to my residence.

The real Pathaan: Shameem and I with Bollywood superstar, Shah Rukh Khan.

Top: Shameem welcomes popular singer and composer from Bangladesh Runa Laila to our home in New Delhi.

Bottom: Howzzat! I greet cricket legend Sachin Tendulkar after he is awarded the country's highest civilian honour, the Bharat Ratna, by President Pranab Mukherjee in February 2014.

Love, marriage and companionship: Shameem and I at the reception organized by friends in Bombay in April 1980, immediately after our marriage in Srinagar.

Top: Happily, ever after—On vacation in Switzerland.

Bottom: Shameem joins me on a visit to Jordan in 1994, when I was the minister of civil aviation and tourism.

Shameem and I offer prayers in the holy city of Mecca, Saudi Arabia, during the five-day Haj pilgrimage.

Adventure outside the CM's office: Shameem and I ride a snowmobile in the lofty snow-capped mountains of Gulmarg.

President Dr APJ Abdul Kalam confers the Padma Shri on Shameem in 2005.

With our son Saddam.

Saddam with his daughter Ava.

With our daughter Sofiya.

Moments to cherish—With our daughter-in-law Gauri and granddaughter Ava.

Top: Teeing off in Srinagar as CM, away from the political course.

Bottom: The photographer's eye—Indulging in my passion for photography as a minister in the UPA government.

Beyond paperwork and meetings: Finding my place in the world on the African continent in 2013.

The magic of my green fingers: In my garden at home in New Delhi in 2021.

generations to come and, thus, I asked to be made the country's minister for health and family welfare.

Medical Education Requires Urgent Cure

As CM, when I had visited the Government Medical College in Jammu, I was told that the infrastructure had improved manifold over a period of time as per the demands of the ever-increasing number of patients. However, the intake of the number of seats for the MBBS course had remained the same over the last 50 years since the days of the college's inception. This had, over time, resulted in a shortage of qualified doctors. Faculty members informed me that the MCI, which functioned under the Union health ministry, decided on the intake of seats, depending on the level of infrastructure and the strength of the faculty available in the medical college. If there was a shortfall in the parameters of those two areas, the MCI refused permission to increase the number of seats. Clearly, this huge shortage of doctors and specialists was the most important issue that the country faced.

After taking over the health ministry, I kept thinking about ways to increase the number of MBBS seats and specialists, thereby making India's public health system more effective and robust. I immediately initiated several rounds of discussions with MCI officials, impressing upon them the need to revamp the rules and regulations, of course without compromising the overall quality. They were receptive, particularly then MCI chairman, Dr Ketan Desai, who was very cooperative and progressive in his thinking and approach, though I did feel that some members were reluctant to make changes. The MCI was dissolved in May 2010, and post that, I found it easier to pursue my agenda.

I initiated path-breaking amendments to the regulations to increase the maximum intake of students at the MBBS level from 150 to 250 across the country. This meant that with all other considerations being met, a college could induct a maximum of 250 students for its MBBS course every year. Since the enhanced number would also have to be matched by an increase in the faculty and infrastructure, the cap on age limit of the faculty—one of the greatest impediments faced by medical education institutions—was increased from 58 to 70. These moves had a cascading positive effect. One, the number of doctors increased. Two, the additional intake of faculty resulted in greater employment. Three, with private medical colleges taking advantage of the rise in cap and securing the employment of retired faculty members, the poaching of faculty by the private sector from government colleges stopped immediately.

I wrote to all CMs, spoke with them on several occasions and requested them to take advantage of the changed rules. Most of them, regardless of their party affiliations, agreed and increased the numbers of seats and the faculty by meeting the new age limit.

Similarly, there was a huge shortage of specialists. I also learnt that the teacher–student ratio for MD/MS courses across the country had been stipulated by the MCI at 1:1, that is, one professor could teach just one MD/MS student at one time. A shortfall in the faculty and specialists, thus, had a direct bearing on the number of students who would have completed their MD/MS course. That, in turn, meant fewer MD and MS doctors. The regulations were tweaked at my behest, and the ratio was changed to 1:2 for all MD/MS disciplines and 1:3 in the subjects of anaesthesiology, forensic medicine, radiotherapy, medical oncology and surgical oncology. These happened to be the areas that needed a greater number of specialized doctors to cater to the rising demands of patients. In all, with these changes, from 2010 till I left the ministry in 2014, an additional 18,412 MBBS seats and 10,358 postgraduate seats were created every year.

However, some medical colleges, hobbled as they were by long-existing constraints, had trouble meeting the new stipulations. I passed an executive order stating that medical colleges that had not increased their seats in the past two decades could double the intake of MBBS seats straightaway; this initial order applied to private colleges as well.

But this decision led to an unforeseen situation—I began to receive calls, especially from southern states, that private colleges had begun to collect donations to give additional seats. On hearing this, even health ministers of a few states had begun to indulge in bribery to allot the seats. I immediately amended the order, which stated that this particular rule applied only to government medical colleges.

Some people with vested interests, who were adversely affected by this decision, appealed against it in the Supreme Court. Fortunately, the apex court not only appreciated my historic decision, but also upheld the government's position.

When there is an expansion in the number of doctors and other medical facilities, it is necessary that the support staff, chiefly comprising nurses, expands accordingly too. For the first time, my ministry sanctioned 269 auxiliary nursing and midwifery colleges (ANMs), which would increase the capacity of ANMs' and general nursing and midwifery colleges' (GNMs) staff by an additional 20,000 trained personnel.

In addition to increasing the number of medical seats, I was also keen to improve the quality of students that enrolled in the undergraduate and postgraduate medical course. To this end, a single entrance examination, the National Eligibility cum Entrance Test (NEET) was introduced from the academic year 2012–13.

With a view to encourage medical students to serve time in rural and remote parts of the country, both to provide those regions with quality medical care and acquaint the students with the grim healthcare situation that prevailed in those regions, it was announced that additional marks would be awarded in the postgraduate entrance examinations at the rate of 10 per cent for each year of service that the students provided in those rural areas, subject to a maximum of 30 per cent. Fifty per cent of seats in postgraduate diploma courses were reserved for medical officers in government employment who had served for at least three years in the remote/difficult/rural regions. Besides, one year of rural posting for MBBS pass-outs was made compulsory from the academic year 2015–16.

Breaking the Tyranny of Geography

I discovered, to my surprise, that 80 per cent of the private medical colleges were located in southern and western parts of India, while the rest of the country had only 20 per cent. The anomaly had a direct impact on healthcare because medical colleges also necessarily have a hospital attached. These hospitals provide speedy treatment to patients for the simple reason that faculty members, who are also doctors, are always readily available. In contrast, services in the district government hospitals were not satisfactory since doctors would often be absent or on leave without providing a replacement.

It was evident to me that the solution was to have more medical college-hospitals in North and central India as well as in the Northeast, an area that had remained neglected thus far. On discussing the matter with my officials, I was told that for a medical college to come up, at least 25 acres of land in one tract was needed. This was a stipulation fixed way back in the 1950s. Land was available and easier to acquire in those days, but the situation had changed over the decades. I asked the officials to change the guidelines as follows:

Instead of 25 acres, only 20 acres be mandatory across the country. Only those states where there were either no or a few medical colleges were given further concession. The 20 acres (in two plots of 10 acres each) could be located within a distance of 10 km. One parcel of land could house the hospital, and the other would have the college and administrative block. In all metropolitan cities, the medical college could come up on 10 acres of land only by constructing the buildings vertically.

As a result of these new decisions, there was a rise in medical colleges across North and central India and in the Northeast. To ensure that more medical colleges come up in deficit regions the bed occupancy for newly constructed colleges in the Northeast was reduced from 60 per cent to 50 per cent at the inception, and from 80 per cent to 60 per cent on subsequent renewals. In medical colleges across the country, the bed occupancy was brought down from 70 per cent to 60 per cent at inception, and from 80 per cent 75 per cent during the third renewal. Thereafter, it remained at that level.

In addition, several medical colleges were converted into super-specialty hospitals, on the lines of AIIMS. In all, 40 such super-specialty hospitals were established during the UPA-II tenure.

In my first year as health minister, I took another major decision. Until then, only state governments and private institutions could establish medical colleges by funding them. I asked my officials why the health ministry could not fund new colleges and hand them over to the respective state governments since health is a state subject. Once they were on board, several medical colleges funded by the Government of India came up in central India and the Northeast. In all, 97 medical colleges, including six new greenfield AIIMS in Jodhpur, Rishikesh, Bhopal, Patna, Raipur and Bhubaneswar were established in record time of just two-and-a-half years during my tenure as health minister. The capacity of institutions and hospitals directly under the health ministry were further strengthened by creating more infrastructure as follows:

1. AIIMS, New Delhi
   - Teaching block: The tallest nine-storey building in AIIMS with two basements consisting of major teaching laboratories was completed in 2013. The total cost of building was around ₹100 crore.
   - Basement parking: The first basement parking of approximately 600 cars was constructed and made operational in 2011 at an estimated cost of ₹50 crore.
   - Student hostels: Four blocks of student hostel with the capacity of approximately 600 students was built and made operational at an estimated cost of ₹150 crore in 2014.
   - Surgical block: The surgical block with more than 20 operation theatres was taken-up for construction in 2013 at an estimated cost of ₹50 crore.
   - Mother-and-child block: Construction of an approximately 250-bed mother-and-child block was taken up at an approximate cost of ₹250 crore.
   - In addition to the new convergence block in 2013–14 and the renovation of patient wards, the main casualty ward of AIIMS was renovated along with 12 operation theatres to improve the sterility and functionality, and an underground passageway was built to connect AIIMS and Safdarjung Hospital.

2. AIIMS, Jhajjar
   - The outreach OPD was constructed in record time of six months, in Jhajjar, Haryana, and the OPD started its operation from November 2012.

- New cancer institute: Foundation stone of the 700-bedded greenfield National Cancer Research Institute was laid by Dr Singh, and construction was started in 2014.

3. RML, New Delhi
   - Constructed new emergency care building with 268 beds, all modern medical facilities and three emergency OTs and 65 ICU beds.
   - Upgraded School of Nursing to College of Nursing, commissioned a renal transplant unit with state-of-the-art operation theatre and post-transplant ICU facilities.
   - Diploma in Hearing Language Speech in the ENT department.
   - Constructed four storied (G+3) new building for its dharamshala with 42 rooms and an area of 2,157.569 m^2 for patients and their relatives.
   - Computerization of RML along the lines of Postgraduate Institute of Medical Education and Research (Chandigarh).
   - New infrastructure was created for advanced microbiology lab.
   - New sections like modular microbiology, immunology, virology, advanced bacteriology, etc. were introduced.
   - New equipment was put in place to strengthen for better identification of pathology for patient's care.
   - Newer tests for hepatitis A and E, along with enzyme-linked immunosorbent assay (ELISA), amoebic serology and malaria antigen tests, were started.
   - Burn, plastic surgery was upgraded for comprehensive management of burn injuries.
   - A post-graduate institute building was made at the cost of ₹60 crore.
   - A trauma centre was built at the cost of ₹60 crore.
   - Student hostel with capacity greater than 300 was constructed.

4. Safdarjung Hospital, New Delhi
   - Emergency block: The biggest emergency block in India, with 500 beds, was made functional at an estimated cost of ₹400 crore.
   - Super-specialty block: The 800-bed super-specialty hospital block was made functional at an estimated cost of ₹600 crore.

- Sports Injury Hospital: Asia's first nine-storeyed Sports Injury Centre (SIC) was established in a record time of one year in double shift. Inaugurated by Dr Singh on 26 September 2010, the SIC provides integrated surgical, rehabilitative and diagnostic services under one roof for sports-related injuries and joint disorders.

5. Lady Hardinge Medical College, New Delhi
   - Residential complex: Approximately 400 units of residential complex were made functional in 2013.
   - Redevelopment of hospital complex: An approximately 1,000-bed hospital was redeveloped at an outlay of ₹700 crore.

During the 12th Five Year Plan (2012–17) period, I presented a proposal to upgrade the existing medical colleges with an aim to increase the MBBS intake by an additional 10,000 seats. The Centre would give ₹7,500 crore and the states/UTs would contribute ₹2,500 crore towards the upgradation plan. For the Northeast and states with Special Category Status, the funding pattern would be 90:10 (Centre:state/UT). The proposal was approved by the Cabinet Committee on Economic Affairs, and work to implement it was initiated.

But it was not enough to upgrade the existing medical colleges and increase the MBBS intake. A large majority of our population, especially the less privileged, depends on district hospitals for treatment, whose performance across the country has historically been less than satisfactory. They too needed attention. I initiated a new Centrally Sponsored Scheme (CSS) in the 12th Five Year Plan period, by which 58 new medical colleges were created, with the upgradation of district hospitals in deficient states. These had an intake capacity of 100 MBBS seats each. The proposed central assistance was to the tune of ₹8,457.40 crore, and the contribution of the state/UT was pegged at ₹2,513.70 crore. This enabled me to sanction five medical colleges in J&K to overcome the acute shortage of doctors.

As Union minister for health, I was always conscious of the dangers that diseases such as diabetes, hypertension, cardiovascular failures and cancer posed to the country's population, especially in the subsequent years. Even the World Health Organization (WHO) has identified these non-communicable diseases (NCDs) as major killers in the near future. According to the WHO, NCDs kill 41 million people globally each year, which is 74 per cent of all deaths worldwide![9]

During the second half of 2010, the National Programme for Prevention and Control of Cancer, Diabetes, Cardiovascular Diseases and Stroke was launched by the health ministry. The focus was on prevention and control of NCDs through health-awareness campaigns and early diagnosis and treatment. The programme was initiated under the 12th Five Year Plan and was slated to cover all the then 640 districts in the country. In 2013–14, the project was subsumed in the National Health Mission to give it greater focus. Various steps were proposed to tackle the impending crisis, such as strengthening facilities at district hospitals and the establishment of 20 state cancer institutes and 50 tertiary cancer-care centres.

If NCDs were a challenge for India, vector-borne diseases had been tormenting the country's population for decades. I closely monitored the performance of the National Vector Borne Disease Control Programme that dealt with six of the most common and dangerous vector-borne diseases, even though the implementation of prevention and control programmes is done by state governments. We succeeded in bringing down the dengue fatality rates by 67 per cent between 2008 and 2013. The National Institute of Virology (NIV), Pune, was entrusted with the task of providing testing kits for dengue and chikungunya, and a mid-term plan for its check was circulated to all state governments.

The other scourge was Japanese encephalitis. The first indigenously developed vaccine for it via public-private partnerships was called

[9]'Noncommunicable Diseases: Key Facts', *World Health Organization*, https://bit.ly/3aLabq6. Accessed on 10 June 2022.

Jenvac; I launched it in October 2013. A mass vaccination drive was conducted targeting children in the age group of one–15 years with single-dose vaccine in endemic districts. This was followed by routine immunization with two doses of the vaccine.

Public health continued to remain a major area of focus for me. The National Centre for Disease Control rose to the occasion to combat severe acute respiratory syndrome (SARS), avian flu and the H1N1 (swine flu) pandemic. We signed a memorandum of understanding with the Centers for Disease Control and Prevention, Atlanta, USA, to establish a global disease centre in India.

Realizing that mass vaccination was the most effective shield to counter the spread of such diseases, the Central Research Institute (Kasauli), the BCG Vaccine Laboratory (Chennai) and the Pasteur Institute of India (Coonoor) were in active mode 24x7 to meet the challenges. I made sure that suspension of licences of the three institutions was revoked so that they could resume their production.

Experts had pointed out to me that we needed high-tech laboratories that met the stringent safety standards to research and develop drugs and vaccines to combat lethal infections and agents of bioterrorism as well a research facility to study the infections. Thus were established Asia's first biosafety level (BSL)-4 laboratory at NIV, Pune, and the National Institute for Research in Environmental Health, Bhopal. The NIV lab would play a critical role during the COVID-19 pandemic that hit the country in 2020.

Health for All

I have always believed that women in our country have often been neglected in terms of healthcare and hygiene. While it is true that the status of women has improved over the past decades, they still struggle to get access to even basic healthcare. In rural India, for instance, women still make do without sanitary napkins. Somehow, this had remained a taboo subject.

At Sonia ji's suggestion—which, I must say, was an excellent idea—my ministry launched a scheme for the promotion of menstrual health in the age group of 10–19 years. The focus was on adolescent girls in rural areas. The programme involved the dissemination of information on menstrual hygiene at the grassroots level and access to quality sanitary napkins at affordable prices along with safe disposal mechanisms. The scheme began with the roll-out of sanitary napkins in 17 states. Till December 2013, over 1.9 crore sanitary napkins had been distributed through the health ministry, reaching 1.9 crore adolescent girls. On another front, we introduced a scheme for the distribution of contraceptives at home by Accredited Social Health Activist (ASHA) workers in July 2011 as well as sanitary napkins in rural areas.

A name-based Mother and Child Tracking System was launched, whereby pregnant women and children up to five years could be tracked and reached, along with a feedback system for the ANMs, ASHA, etc., to ensure that all pregnant women received their antenatal care and post-natal care check-ups regularly and their children received full immunization cover. The Universal Immunisation Programme was also expanded to include hepatitis B and pentavalent vaccines. As a result of these measures, there was an accelerated decline in maternal mortality rate and infant mortality rate, bringing us closer to the Millennium Development Goals.

Other initiatives for children included the launch of the Rashtriya Bal Swasthya Karyakram or the National Programme for Child Health Screening and Early Intervention Services, aimed at a continuum of care extending over different phases of the life of a child from birth to 18 years, which included early detection and management of defects at birth, diseases, deficiencies and development delays, including disability. Thirty select health conditions prevalent in childhood were identified and their treatment was made free at all government institutions available in India with the health ministry covering those costs.

For the adolescent group, the Rashtriya Kishor Swasthya Karyakram (National Adolescent Health Programme) was launched, which marked a paradigm shift from existing clinic-based care to community-based health promotion and prevention, reaching out to adolescents where they were, that is, schools and communities. The programme focussed on six priority areas of action: reproductive and sexual health, nutrition, mental health, injuries and violence (including domestic and gender-based violence), substance misuse and NCDs.

In addition, the ministry launched a Weekly Iron and Folic Acid Supplementation Programme in 2012–13 to tackle the high prevalence of iron and folic acid deficiency, especially among young girls, leading to anaemic conditions. It was rolled out in 31 states and UTs. The National Iron Plus Initiative for supervised administration of iron-folic acid syrup to children up to the age of 10 years and women of reproductive age to combat the problem of anaemia in Indian children and women was launched in February 2013. The programme covered 13 crore adolescents.

In addition to mother-and-child care, my ministry also launched the National Programme for Health Care of the Elderly in 2010. Twelve additional regional geriatric centres were planned to be established, two National Centres of Ageing were to be established at AIIMS, New Delhi, and the Madras Medical College, Chennai.

If physical well-being was our focus, so was mental health. According to a study, in 2017, roughly 14 per cent of the country's population suffered from mental health issues, as many as 45.7 million suffered from depressive disorders and 44.9 million suffered from anxiety disorders.[10]

The ministry took several initiatives to tackle the crisis that loomed over us. More than 120 districts were covered under the District Mental Health Programme, grants worth more than ₹300 crore were released for the purpose; a mental health authority was constituted in every state and UT; an expert group was constituted to study the subject and the Mental Health Care Bill, 2013, was introduced in the Rajya Sabha in August 2013.

Home-Grown Efforts; Overseas Recognition

The Department of Health Research had come into existence to bring modern medical care technology to the common man. It encouraged innovations in the areas of diagnostics, treatment methods and prevention of diseases. It also assisted in strengthening of the Indian

[10]'The Burden of Mental Disorders across the States of India: The Global Burden of Disease Study 1990–2017', *Lancet Psychiatry*, Volume 7, Issue 2, 2020, 148–61, doi: 10.1016/S2215-0366(19)30475-4.

Council of Medical Research. The chief purpose of the department was to generate scientific knowledge and its implementation for the good of the common man.

Mainstreaming of AYUSH

The ministry also focussed on Ayurveda, Yoga & Naturopathy, Unani, Siddha and Homeopathy (AYUSH) during my tenure. A grant-in-aid of nearly ₹624 crore was made available to states and UTs to establish AYUSH facilities in PHCs. Under a CSS in 2011–12, a new component of setting up integrated AYUSH hospitals was introduced. Financial support was also extended to establish drug-testing laboratories, and AYUSH Research Councils were also set up.

There was also emphasis on collaboration with other nations. India hosted the 31st meeting of ministers of health of countries of the WHO South-East Asia Region Organisation (SEARO). I also led a high-level delegation to the South–South Cooperation. Moreover, we hosted the SAARC Technical Committee on Health and Population Activities meeting. I headed the Indian delegation at the third BRICS health ministers meeting in South Africa's Cape Town.

It would take many pages to list out all the policies and programmes that were initiated during my tenure as minister of health and family welfare that changed the face of the healthcare sector. However, the launch of the National Urban Health Mission (NUHM) as a sub-mission of the National Health Mission and the polio-free India programme brought accolades from all corners of the world.

The NUHM

This was approved by the Cabinet on 1 May 2013 and was launched on 20 January the following year. An initial provision of ₹1,000 crore was made for the programme, and it was to cover all state capitals, district headquarters, cities and towns with a population exceeding 50,000, with particular focus on slum-dwellers and other marginalized groups.

It was also during my tenure that the country achieved the milestone of completing three years without any report of a polio case. On 24 February 2012, the WHO removed India from the list of endemic countries with active polio virus transmission. It was a major achievement, considering that until 2009, India accounted for more than half of the world's active polio cases. On 11 February 2014, India marked its success in eradicating polio at an event organized by my ministry. It was graced by the then president Pranab da, Dr Singh, UPA chairperson Sonia ji, LoP in the Lok Sabha Sushma Swaraj and director general of WHO Dr Margaret Chan. Needless to add, I was happy to have achieved this milestone.

In my five-decade-long career in politics, I have managed election campaigns, devised strategies and mostly seen success. But none gave me the kind of satisfaction and joy that I derived from the work I did as CM of J&K and later as Union minister for health and family welfare. This is simply because my efforts in these capacities impacted the last man/woman in the line.

I am reminded of a quote from my idol, Mahatma Gandhi. He had said: 'Recall the face of the poorest and the weakest man whom you may have seen, and ask yourself if the step you contemplate is going to be of any use to him.' In my own small way, I believe that I have tried to live by the advice of that great soul.

16

A 'MODI-FIED' ROLE

My singular efforts in reaching the poorest and weakest in India, however, came a cropper when the results of the 2014 Lok Sabha General Elections were declared. The BJP, under Narendra Modi, created history by becoming the first party since 1984 to win a majority on its own. The all-India tally of the Congress was a meagre 44 seats. The magnitude of the loss could be gauged from the fact that the party hadn't even won 10 per cent of the total number of Lok Sabha seats required to nominate the LoP.

With the party relegated to the Opposition benches, I was given a new role—LoP in the Rajya Sabha, a position I held till my retirement from the Upper House in February 2021. It was a new experience from what I had been used to in the earlier years.

My stint as parliamentary affairs minister under three Congress PMs came in handy. I had developed excellent personal contacts with many leading Opposition leaders, and those relations helped me in my new role in many ways. But I had worked in an era in which we still had numerous stalwarts in Parliament across party lines. There existed lot of mutual respect. Attending each other's parties and visiting each other's houses was common, unlike today.

By 2014 though, much water had flown down the Ganga. The entire composition of MPs had changed in comparison to the mid-1980s and early 1990s, when academicians, literary figures and statesmen would rule the roost. Unfortunately, with the passage of time, the quality of MPs has come down. There are very few who visit the well-stocked Parliament library to collect material and improve their knowledge. Many people have entered Parliament with an aim to further their business interests or the interests of vested groups. There are a number of cases against sitting MLAs and MPs in the country. I wish they were fast-tracked, so that the guilty get punished without delay and the innocent ones are left to do their work.

Thankfully, there were some known faces. Arun Jaitley, an old political adversary but also a personal friend, was leader of the House in the Rajya Sabha. His wife, Sangeeta, is from Jammu, and his father-in-law, Girdhari Lal Dogra, a Congressman, had been Congress minister for almost 30 years in the J&K government. Jaitley was not just articulate but also well-read. He would present his views in a clear and forceful manner. It was a treat to hear him speak. The ruling party also had other good speakers, such as Piyush Goyal and Bhupendra Yadav in the Rajya Sabha. I am happy that Yadav has been made a minister; he is capable and efficient.

Prime Minister Modi would attend the Rajya Sabha proceedings when the Question Hour of his ministry was slated. However, he would not reply to any of the questions; his capable MoS in charge of the PMO did the needful, like all previous PMs. My interaction with PM Modi was mostly during the all-party meetings that he chaired before every Parliament session (thrice a year), unlike the previous PMs. It is to his credit that he would meet and address floor leaders of all political parties of both Houses of Parliament before the commencement of every Parliament session. However, unfortunately, he never spoke in Parliament about his foreign visits, unlike all his predecessors.

In these meetings, PM Modi would always assure the Opposition leaders that every issue that the Opposition parties wanted to raise would be discussed on the floor of House. He was very clear on this issue and wanted every issue be discussed threadbare to the satisfaction of the Opposition. However, despite his assurances, such discussions never happened to the extent they should have inside the House. In my opinion, the minister of parliamentary affairs and the ministers in charge of those particular subjects that were to be discussed would ensure that the discussion didn't take place.

The parliamentary affairs minister can only be successful either if he's sufficiently senior or his proximity with the PM is known to all. Otherwise, he needs to have the ability to influence the PM and the capacity to recommend to the PM the promotion/demotion of ministers based on their ministerial performance on the floor of the House. I was lucky enough that when I was MoS for parliamentary affairs with PM Rajiv Gandhi, I was more powerful than a Cabinet minister since I enjoyed the trust of the PM. He had told me on day one that any future expansion of the Cabinet would be on my recommendation, based on the performance of the individual MP/minister in the Lok Sabha. Similarly, in Rao's time as Cabinet minister, a similar authorization was given to me by the PM. This is why my opinion carried weight. I don't think any parliamentary affairs minister has had this kind of authority. During my stint as the minister in the first two years of UPA-I, no one had the power to recommend names for the ministry. Later on till 2014, it was only Sonia ji who was taken into confidence by the PM during Cabinet formation.

The other thing that PM Modi would do during Parliament sessions, which benefitted his party immensely, was that he would hold weekly meetings with all MPs of his party. I believe he would even pull up his MPs who had not performed well according to his expectations or had a poor attendance in Parliament. I wish the Congress party had also undertaken a similar exercise, which incidentally existed during the tenure of Indira ji and, to some extent, during the tenures of Rajiv and Rao. Sadly, this practice totally disappeared during the last two-and-a-half decades.

In my stint as the LoP of the Rajya Sabha, I delivered more than 100 speeches, both short and long. Of all these speeches, the one delivered on 5 August 2019 in response to the justification given by the government for the abrogation of Article 370, downgrading the status of J&K and dividing the state into two UTs, left the ruling benches groping for words.

I believe the decision of the government to abrogate Articles 370 and 35A was an impromptu one. To begin with, due parliamentary procedure was not followed. It is a prerequisite for all bills to be approved by the business advisory committee, which is presided by the chairperson of the Rajya Sabha (vice president) and comprises leaders of all major national or regional political parties, including leader of the House, parliamentary affairs minister and LoP. The business advisory committee recommends the time that should be allocated for the discussion of all bills. Further, any bill that is to be taken up for discussion has to be listed in the business of that day and should also be circulated beforehand. None of these formalities happened. The home minister was supposed to speak on another bill pertaining to 10 per cent reservation for non-reserved categories of J&K. Earlier, this had been passed for the entire country but could not be passed in J&K as Article 370 was still in force. I was supposed to be the first speaker after the home minister's speech to initiate discussion on that subject.

The moment the home minister announced the Centre's move to repeal Article 370 of the Constitution and bifurcate the state into two UTs, I threw my earphones off and went straight into the well of the House. I called up on the entire Opposition to sit in dharna. I urged the Congress party people to follow suit, and they joined, except Jairam Ramesh, who remained seated and did not protest. When Amit Shah was done with his speech, the chairperson called my name. I remained seated in the dharna for the next three–four hours. The television cameras were not focussed on us; in fact, the cameras had been taken off the Opposition benches, so they never showed that I was seated on the floor.

After about three hours, one of the Congress MPs asked me if he could visit the washroom in my LoP room. In that room, there are two big TVs, one showing live proceedings of the Lok Sabha and one of the Rajya Sabha. When he came back, he told me that my staff had asked him where I was because they could not see me on my seat. He maintained that if no one knew that I was sitting on dharna in the well of the House, what was the point of this entire exercise? Then after about four hours, I sent a slip to the chairman of the Rajya Sabha, requesting him to permit me to speak. The chairman sent his marshal to me, who told me that I would be given a chance, but I would have to speak from my seat.

When my name was called, I started speaking from my designated seat. I had no idea about the bill since it had not been circulated earlier. Though I had been very angry initially, my anger had subsided after having been seated on the floor for a few hours. In my speech that lasted for about 45 minutes, I drew the attention of the House to the fact that the government had claimed that its decision would ensure that students of J&K would now get the benefit of the Right to Education that guarantees free education to children between the ages of six and 14 years. I pointed out that free education from primary to post-graduation had existed in J&K since the 1950s. Similarly, the government claimed that in order to curb corruption, the jurisdiction of the Central Vigilance Commission would now be extended to J&K. Again, I pointed out that J&K already had a vigilance department. During my time as CM, there was DG Vigilance. Besides this, the Prevention of Corruption Act, 2006 (1949 AD), was passed during my chief ministership, enabling the state vigilance organization to attach disproportionate assets of corrupt public servants (both government servants and politicians). I pointed out that such a law did not exist anywhere else in the world.

The government had said that with its decision of abrogation of Article 370, SCs/STs would get the benefit of reservation in government employment, government educational institutions and legislature. Here, too, I punctured the government's claim by pointing out that J&K had already reservation for SCs, both in services and in legislature and for STs in services. I also spoke on the health parameters in J&K, a subject that I was familiar with. I proudly said that in most of the cases, the state had fared better than the national average.

Notwithstanding these points raised during my speech, what is more important is that no LoP in the Rajya Sabha had ever sat on the floor in the well of the House in the history of parliamentary democracy. Moreover, no top leaders of the Congress, holding a position in the Congress Parliamentary Party in the Lok Sabha, had spoken on Article 370, except for Manish Tewari and Shashi Tharoor, both members of the G23. Similarly, in the Rajya Sabha, only the three of us—Anand Sharma, Kapil Sibal and myself—spoke on this matter. Interestingly, we were all from the G23.

After my speech, an emergency CWC meeting was called at my insistence and at the request of Ahmed Patel. There were a number of CWC members who immediately supported the abrogation of Article

370. It was at my insistence that, after showing statements by people from across the country, the CWC members were reluctantly forced to pass the resolution opposing the government's decision. Unfortunately, during the last three-and-a-half years, no Congress leader inside or outside Parliament has supported restoration of Article 370. Even today, I strongly feel that Article 370 was part of the Constitution and cannot be considered to be against the interests of the country. It has helped the state and the country as a whole to bring its people closer together.

Pride without Prejudice

I would like to believe that as LoP in the Rajya Sabha, I not only effectively countered many claims of the ruling coalition but also raised several issues pertinent to the country's well-being. I never spared the government whenever any issue of public interest arose.

Throughout my speeches, I found Modi to be a great listener. Not even once did he rebut my arguments or speak against me, inside or outside Parliament. He would always remain calm, though he would taunt me by making some political references. But he never attacked me personally. This may also have been because, unlike other leaders, I would not call the PM or other members of the ruling party names or abuse them. But some other leaders would only think of pleasing the Congress leadership by abusing the BJP and its leaders without making any substantial contribution or suggestion on the floor of the House that could pin down the government. In the Congress party, some leaders feel that abusing the Opposition and calling names is the only way to fight the political rival. I have always felt that Opposition parties, whether in the Assembly, Parliament or outside, are our competitors and not our enemies. So while speaking, each political party must keep this in mind and not cross the Lakshman Rekha.

My tenure as the LoP was very eventful and memorable; it's a stint that I look back on with satisfaction and pride. Unlike most of the LoPs, I had no problem in dealing with a crisis or a difficult situation. It was particularly easy for a person like me, who has always been very friendly with the leaders of all political parties irrespective of their political ideology. I was able to oppose their ideology and way of working and functioning while keeping my personal contacts intact. I am open to similar opposition and discussion at the level of ideology as well. However, being friendly with Opposition parties did not mean that I sought any favours from them at any point in my political career.

When I was the parliamentary affairs minister in Rao's government, the Congress didn't have a majority. We didn't have an alliance with another party either, and we were running a minority government. As the minister, I ensured that we won all votes of confidence. The reason was my personal relationships with other leaders, right from Advani and Vajpayee to leaders of smaller political groups. I have gone on record on the floor of the House to take the side of the Opposition when there was a conflict between the ruling and Opposition parties. I would take the side of the Opposition if the demand made by them was just and fair. My argument was that the parliamentary affairs minister is supposed to represent both the ruling party and the Opposition parties. He has to be fair and neutral, so that parliamentary proceedings run smoothly. I have always held this opinion that if the government refuses every demand made by the Opposition, then why should the Opposition cooperate with the government when it comes to passing bills? Hence, there has to be give and take.

I continued to believe in this philosophy even during my stint as LoP. Through discussions between leaders of the House, I ensured, to some extent, that the ruling BJP government did not say no to each and every subject that we wanted to discuss on the floor of the House. Of course, the Modi-led government was a little reluctant to agree to some of the contentious issues we wanted to discuss, yet we succeeded, unlike in the Lok Sabha, in discussing matters, much against their wishes and desires.

In the winter of 2021, it was time for me to bid adieu to the Upper House of Parliament. As is the norm, one-third of the MPs retire after every two years. If they are not re-elected, they are replaced. Unlike the Lok Sabha, the Rajya Sabha is a permanent House that never gets dissolved. In lighter vein, our young leaders of the Lok Sabha insist that old leaders should retire, not realizing that the Rajya Sabha is called the House of Elders where age doesn't matter, only experience does.

On 9 February, my seven-year stint came to an end. I could not be re-elected since the J&K Assembly had been dissolved. Like my colleagues, I too was given a farewell by way of speeches, which is customary in the House of Elders. The chairperson was the first speaker. I am highly obliged to Venkaiah Naidu, who made an excellent speech and said many good words about me. I shall be beholden to him for the observations he made about me.

The second speaker was PM Modi. He praised me for my performance as LoP and for being a good human being. His speech was totally unlike his other speeches. He got very emotional, especially when narrating a particular incident. Everyone had forgotten about it, as it was from 15 years back, when I was the CM. I too had forgotten about it. He went back to 25 May 2006, when militants in Srinagar had hurled a grenade at a tourist bus carrying tourists from Gujarat. The attack took place when the government shifted to Kashmir in the first week of May, and the militants attempted to create a sense of fear and panic in me. They 'welcomed' me by killing innocent people in this horrifying incident.

On the morning of 25 May, I received information that militants had attacked a bus carrying passengers from Gujarat. Some passengers, including two children, were killed and several were injured. The bodies of the dead had been mutilated. The site of the attack—in the neighbourhood of Batpora—was close to my official residence, so I was able to rush to the site immediately and saw women and children weeping bitterly. I too was moved to tears. It was at this juncture that CM Modi called me. My staff told him that I was in no condition to speak with him since I was completely shattered.

I spoke to him a while later even as I continued to weep. He wanted the dead bodies to be sent immediately to Gujarat. I spoke to Dr Singh and requested an Air Force aircraft to transport the dead and injured. After taking the injured to the hospital, I ensured that the dead bodies were kept safely. By the evening, the aircraft arrived. We were also ready to send the bodies around that time. We knew how methodical Modi was; he and his office kept enquiring on an hourly basis about the injured passengers and the dead bodies so that his government could receive them in Gujarat.

I went to see off the mortal remains and the rest of the tourists at the airport. As I entered the aircraft, they all began weeping. I too was unable to control my emotions. Meanwhile, Modi called again. I choked and could hardly speak. Addressing the tourists, I could only ask for forgiveness. I said, 'You had come to enjoy Kashmir, and instead I am sending back dead bodies. So, please forgive me.'

The media in Gujarat reported this much more than the national media did. Modi had seen all this on TV. I think a similar emotion arose in the PM during this farewell speech. He choked and could not speak; he just saluted. It was kind of him to have remembered a 15-year-old incident and share it at the most appropriate juncture in Parliament. He went to the extent of saying that I had called him as if my own family members had been killed. That was his way of describing me as a good human being. I am thankful to him.

Prime Minister Modi's farewell speech, which was given wide coverage by the media, should have been a matter of great pride for the Congress party as well as its leadership, as a senior member of the party was feted by none less than the PM and by the leaders of other Opposition parties. Unfortunately, instead of appreciating my efforts and concern for the people of Gujarat and the tributes that the PM paid to the LoP of the Congress, the party leadership was extremely unhappy and critical. They dubbed me a BJP man. This clearly shows that they have no empathy for human tragedy and cannot think beyond petty politics. This is further reinforced by the fact that none of these Congress leaders or my opponents quoted a single good word said by almost two dozen other political leaders. If they were honest, they should have quoted those as well.

17

THE GRAND OLD PARTY: BLOOPERS AND BOMBAST

There can be nothing more distressing for a Congressman, or a former Congressman like me, than to see the Congress party spiral on a downward path. For someone like me, who devoted five decades of his life since his student days to strengthen the party's organization, the free fall is depressing, more so because there has been no serious attempt to check the decline.

The tragedy is there for all to see. The 137-year-old party that ruled the country for 55 years since Independence has today shrunk so abysmally that it governs only three states on its own. This is a sad fall for an organization that was one of modern India's oldest political entities, whose leaders led the country's freedom movement, laid the foundations for the sovereign republic of India and played a stellar role in drafting the country's Constitution. For several Congress people, it is a matter of immense pain and great concern that their 'Grand Old Party' has been marginalized and reduced to being almost a fringe player in national politics that constantly looks for the support of regional parties from Kashmir to Kanyakumari.

Many of its leaders don't seem to grasp the gravity of the situation and have their heads buried in the sand. They argue that the party had lost before and bounced back, for instance, in 1977–80, and thereafter, post the electoral setbacks in 1996, 1998 and 1999. They are right, except that in the past nine years, there has been no sign of any such bouncing back. After all, never before had the Congress faced the Lok

Sabha routs like it did in 2014 and 2019, in which the party managed to win only 44 and 52 seats, respectively. On the other hand, in 1977, the party had won 154 Lok Sabha seats, and thus started bouncing back within months after being in the Opposition. A few of us were a part of that revival. Those at the helm of party affairs today may have heard of it but they were not part of that fight and, hence, cannot understand the enormity of the crisis. Sadly, they have scant regard for those leaders who were part of that struggle.

Several reasons contributed to the party's recovery in 1977–80 after suffering reverses. The first was Indira ji's charismatic leadership. Even when out of power and hounded after losing the 1977 elections, she continued to reach out to the people without bothering about her security, boarding and lodging—she travelled by air, car, jeep and even elephant back. She kept up her connection with the grassroots. She continued to work relentlessly to win back their confidence. Sanjay faced many challenges too, but he led the IYC from the front, helping revive the unit.

The second reason was that Indira ji gave full freedom to general secretaries of the party to take decisions, keeping in view the local political situation at state levels. There was hardly any interference in the working of the general secretaries and PCC presidents and CMs from the central leadership. This indicated the level of trust that Indira ji had in her team of organizational leaders. Most importantly, Indira ji and Sanjay were available to leaders and workers for at least 14–16 hours daily, both at their offices and residence. There was hardly any need for an appointment; one could walk straight to their house and they were available to meet people. Sanjay would meet people even in his business office at Barakhambha Road. Today, even senior leaders, CWC members, MPs and PCC presidents have to wait for months to meet the leadership and one cannot even imagine the prospect of a meeting without a prior appointment.

Third, there were Congress units right down to district and block levels. There were hardly any regional parties, like the SP, BSP, NCP, TMC, RJD, BJD, TDP, Bharat Rashtra Samithi (formerly Telangana Rashtra Samithi), Aam Aadmi Party (AAP), Yuvajana Shramika Rythu Congress Party (YSRCP) and Shiv Sena, except in Tamil Nadu, where the Congress had to face two regional parties, DMK and AIADMK. Today, the Congress has more competition from regional parties than national parties. Hence, the present situation cannot be compared with the 1977–79 scenario. The Congress leaders who indulge in such a comparison lack an understanding of the Congress's historical background and are unaware of the emergence of regional political parties in the last four-and-a-half decades.

The other significant comeback the Congress had made was between 1996 and 2004. Although the party was in the Opposition at the Centre for those eight years until mid-2004, it won several assembly elections, including in Rajasthan, Karnataka, Kerala, Puducherry, Tamil Nadu (in alliance), Uttarakhand, J&K and undivided Andhra Pradesh. Incidentally, I can proudly say that I was the general secretary in charge of all these states. Subsequently, the party also tasted victory in Delhi, Himachal Pradesh and Punjab. It did well in states that had dynamic in-charges and state leadership but fared poorly where the person made in-charge by the central leadership was not equipped for the task.

In contrast, since January 2013, the Congress has lost as many as 39 assembly elections, some states once and others two consecutive times. In some of the few that it won, the party formed the government only to lose power a few months later, like Madhya Pradesh and Karnataka. There has been, thus, no sign of revival.

G23: Rebels with a Cause

Several senior leaders have brought this crisis to the notice of the party's central leadership repeatedly, both individually and collectively, from time to time. In August 2020, a few senior leaders, including me, wrote a letter to the leadership, stressing on the need to undertake a course correction. There were many more in the party at all levels who agreed with us. Some of the leaders who supported us, openly or covertly, have devoted their life to the party, particularly since 1977, when the Congress party was down.

Our aim of writing the letter was not to run down the party, any individual or the central leadership. As a Congressman who had worked at various organizational levels, I was aware of the flaws that existed and the corrective measures that were needed. Thus, our intention in penning the appeal was honest, fair and just. We had the interest of the party at heart.

However, some party leaders lashed out at us, calling us dissidents, traitors and ingrates. I would like to tell them today that some of us had given many times more than what we got in return, unlike many others who took undue advantage but did nothing for the party except by showing their presence through tweets. These regular tweets by so-called leaders cannot build the organization. Some even accused us of being agents of the BJP! One senior party leader, a lateral entrant in the party and government, wrote an opinion piece that read: 'Ultimately, it is a relevant question whether it is fair to kick the very ladder you have climbed to the top storey of life from where making speeches is easy.'[11] Another senior leader, with whom I had worked closely in the past, termed the contents and the timing of the letter as 'cruel', while a third, whose name I had strongly recommended for ministership when the UPA-I came to power, demanded action against us.

I would like to reiterate that we have not kicked the ladder that we had used to climb to the top. Rather people like me *were* the ladder that some leaders used to reach the top, and after reaching the summit, they found no need for the ladder anymore. Our aim was to strengthen that ladder, which had begun to creak under the weight of undeserving and inexperienced people. Those who were telling us that we had reached the top by using the ladder that we were kicking now forgot that others had reached the top by parachute. In addition, neither the contents nor the timing of the letter was cruel; if anything, it was timely and necessary. We did not fear any action against us because our conscience was clear.

Ironically, some of those who were vocal in criticizing us had dumped the Congress when it faced a crisis from 1977–79. While these critics opted for what they considered greener pastures, those

---

[11]'Is It Fair to Kick the Ladder You Climbed to Reach in Life: Khurshid Asks G-23', *The Times of India,* 3 March 2021, https://bit.ly/39fOBK4. Accessed on 13 June 2022.

like us had worked hard to rejuvenate the party. Others were not even in the party or in politics when we were moving from prison to prison in different parts of the country to save the party by organizing agitations against the then ruling dispensation. We were fighting court cases and political battles on the streets, travelling in second- and third-class train coaches, both in the heat and biting cold, eating barely once a day, either because of lack of time or non-availability of food and, sometimes, even lack of money. I and many others in the IYC during that time do not know how our youth passed. Parties, hotels and holidays were all alien to us, unlike the leaders of the present generation, who like to attend parties and go for holidays abroad at the slightest opportunity. I believe the BJP is happy to face this kind of 'Opposition' that hardly poses any challenge.

But what did we say in our letter that was so damning to the party? All that we sought was a full-time and effective party president, who should be visible, active and easily available.[12] We pointed out that the revival of the Congress was a 'national imperative', especially at a time when the country faced its 'gravest political, social and economic challenges since Independence'.[13]

We had asked for elections to the CWC, the party's highest decision-making body, and the Central Election Committee, which is charged with the finalization of tickets for Parliament and Assemblies and which is to be elected every five years, as well as an 'institutional leadership mechanism' to guide the party's revival. No elections had been conducted for the last 25 years either for the Central Election Committee or the CWC. If even a quarter of a century of inaction was not timely enough to raise the issue, pray, when was the right time to do so? The CWC had not been effective because it is 'nominated' rather than elected, without the backing of the party's rank and file. A similar failure to hold elections for a quarter of a century existed right from the state to the district to the block levels. We wanted decentralization of power by having transparent party elections at

---

[12]'Read the Full Text of the Letter Written by Dissenting Congress Leaders Demanding Sweeping Changes within the Congress Party', *OpIndia,* 28 August 2020, https://bit.ly/3QhtdVo. Accessed on 13 June 2022.

[13]Ibid.

state, district and block levels after every five years, as per the party's constitution. Clearly, the sound democratic system that had been introduced by the tallest leaders of the freedom movement had been disrupted.

Similarly, there used to be the CPB, the party's supreme political decision-making body, consisting of seven–eight members chosen from the CWC members, which would take political decisions on matters of national and international importance. I had the honour of being the member-secretary of the CPB from 1987 to 1992. Sadly, the board has not been in existence for the last 30 years.

It is important to understand the irony: Nominated members who have no organizational background and experience, understanding of grassroots politics or connect with the people are tasked with handing out tickets to aspirants who are supposed to be connected with the people. Many of these nominated members are retired; some are semi-retired politicians who are out of circulation. Yet they decide the fate of active party leaders who work on the ground and are key to the party's success or lack thereof.

Nominated members to these bodies did not owe their position to the rank and file of the workers and, therefore, they could not appreciate their sentiments and aspirations. Since they did not owe their position to the workers, they were not bothered about them and, thus, lost connect with the public and party workers. Had they come through elections, these nominated leaders would be compelled to go to the field and win the trust and confidence of party workers. If they could do that, only then would they become members of the AICC and be eligible to seek a place in the top-three decision-making bodies of the party. If they fail, they would lose their position. The loss of position is what the nominated leaders dread the most, which is why they are happy with the status quo. All that they have to do to continue in their posts is to keep the leadership happy by all possible means. They do not want to share the decision-making powers, which are presently concentrated in a few hands.

It is, therefore, not surprising that many of the leaders who had turned against us were beneficiaries of this present system. They were worried that if the malaise was addressed, they would lose both their jobs and clout. They don't care if the party bleeds because they have not contributed to the making of the organization and have made no sacrifices. All that they desire is to keep their hold.

But those of us who wrote that letter were concerned because we had literally given our sweat and blood for this party. There have been several occasions when I faced many personal hardships and challenges and yet continued to work for the party's welfare. Let me recall a few.

After the demolition of the Babri mosque in December 1992 and the decision of the Union Cabinet to dismiss the governments in four BJP-ruled states, PM Rao appointed four Union ministers as heads of four coordination committees for each of these states to ensure that the Congress party did well. I was made chairman of the coordination committee for Madhya Pradesh. While campaigning in Madhya Pradesh during assembly elections in 1993, when I was also the minister for civil aviation, tourism and parliamentary affairs, I was running high fever but decided not to rest. During the same period, I was to address a public meeting in the Jama Masjid area in Old Delhi, where polls were to take place as per schedule in 1993. When I reached there, I found Sanjay Khan, who had also been invited, present before a huge crowd. I was running a temperature of 104 degrees when I reached the venue from the campaign in MP.

The moment Sanjay began to speak, some miscreants in the crowd released a snake in the crowd to disrupt the rally. Even though Sanjay was a great orator and a crowd-puller, he could hardly speak owing to this disturbance. I got agitated with the miscreants' behaviour. Quickly gulping down a Crocin with water, I asked Sanjay to end his speech abruptly and sit down. Then I rose to speak, nearly delirious with fever.

I was uncharacteristically loud and aggressive; it was perhaps the effect of the fever coupled with my anger. I strongly reprimanded the miscreants and the leaders behind them and took our opponents to task. There was pin-drop silence since the audience had not expected such harshness from me. After I completed my 30-minute speech, I checked my fever with a pocket thermometer; it showed 106 degrees. I was rushed to RML straightaway. Slabs of ice were placed around me to bring down the temperature.

By morning, my temperature had come down but doctors advised me rest for a few days. But my programmes for different parts of Madhya Pradesh had already been finalized for the entire day. I ignored the advice of doctors and left for Madhya Pradesh along with a family doctor. On reaching Madhya Pradesh, I was still running temperature, but I continued to campaign throughout the day, taking medicines and injections. I remained sick for one full week but did not rest, nor did I miss any public meeting. My hard work and dedication coupled with coordinated efforts of all the leaders of the state, including Digvijaya Singh, S.C. Shukla, Arjun Singh, Kamal Nath, V.C. Shukla and many other senior leaders paid off. The Congress formed the government in the state in 1993.

I continued to remain dedicated to the party's welfare even when faced with grave challenges of a personal nature. During the J&K Assembly Elections in November–December 2014, my wife Shameem had to undergo a second major operation for a medical complication, which took almost 11 hours. She was hospitalized in Tata Memorial Hospital, Mumbai, where she had to remain for nearly a month. I was the chairman of J&K PCC campaign committee, besides being the LoP in the Rajya Sabha.

It was one of the most difficult times of my life. I had party responsibilities on one side and my duty towards my wife on the other. I had to cope with both, and I cannot state in words the agony I had to undergo. Unfortunately, unlike other states, J&K elections were held in several phases. Hence, it was a two-month-long campaign. I had to shuttle between Jammu/Srinagar and Mumbai via Delhi and back on a daily basis.

I would address five–six public meetings in J&K, travelling by helicopter, and land at the Jammu/Srinagar airport before sunset. I would then take a commercial flight to Delhi, and from Delhi, a connecting flight to Mumbai, and reach the hospital around midnight. I would attend to my wife, spending three–four hours a night at her bedside on a chair or a sofa in her room. I would wake up at 4.00 a.m. in the morning to take the 6.00 a.m. flight for Delhi and then a connecting flight to Jammu or Srinagar airport and plunge into day-long campaigning.

This was my routine for nearly first 20 days. I would snatch barely two–three hours of sleep a day, that too either on a sofa or in the aircraft. Luckily, those were winter months, and I could manage without a shower and change of clothes for a few days! At times, I could not change my clothes for two–three days at a stretch.

These are the kind of sacrifices that I have made for the Congress. Therefore, it hurt when the party men levelled allegations against me. It also showed how ignorant party leaders were about my sacrifices and work for the party. That is why it was up to leaders like me to undertake the onerous responsibility of working for the party's revival. The BJP or any regional party was not going to do this for us, nor were these parties going to come in the way of the Congress party's rejuvenation. If there is anything stopping the Congress, it is the lack of will to work hard and the overdependence of the top leadership on so-called leaders who are only remotely connected with party.

We made it clear that we did not wish for any party position. Our demand was simple: Address the problem, take quick action, be accountable to the party and public and have collective leadership; else, the party shall reach a point of no return on its downward journey.

Whither Democracy

The best way to run a party is to have a collective leadership. A robust and transparent internal democratic system is the only way forward. Therefore, if the Congress has to revive itself, a revamp of its organization through fresh, genuine memberships, followed by free, fair and transparent elections at every level is essential. When I say 'genuine' membership, I mean that each and every member must fill up his/her membership form and deposit the membership fee from his/her own pocket. Normally, in majority of the cases today, one person sitting at home takes the voters list, fills up the forms and deposits the membership fee on their behalf, claiming that a lot of membership has been undertaken. This is nothing but self-deception.

By doing this, they are betraying millions of active workers who form the backbone of the party and also millions of voters who repose trust and faith in the philosophy and ideology of the Congress. Leaders who refuse to understand the gravity of the situation or those who know the reality but refuse to speak up because they lack the courage are killing the very party they belong to. They fail to realize that the party not only represents millions and millions of Indians but is also the custodian of the philosophy and ideology of stalwarts such as Gandhi, Nehru, Patel, Azad, Bose and many others who have sacrificed their lives for what this party has stood for.

Since inception, the Congress and its leaders framed a fundamental rule: There would be elections to the president of the party at the national level every year. No matter how big the leader was, this rule applied to everyone without exception, from Gandhi, Nehru, Patel and Azad to Bose and Rajendra Prasad. Some of the leaders had repeat tenures as president, but it was after a break of at least one year. This system continued for a few decades, and there were elections after every second year.

The only exception was in the period 1940–46, when Maulana Azad remained the all-India president. This was because of unforeseen circumstances. The Second World War was on and there was uncertainty across the country. As a result of the Quit India Movement, which was launched in August 1942, all senior leaders of the party, including the national president Azad, Gandhi, Nehru, Patel and other CWC members, were jailed for close to three years. There was, thus, no question of party elections during that time. Hence, Azad continued as the AICC president for a good six years.

From 1947, elections took place regularly till 1977, every two years. In 1978, Indira ji became president after the Congress split and remained in the post until her death (she was re-elected in 1983). Rajiv was president for six-and-a-half years; Rao remained president for five years. After Sitaram Kesri was voted out in under one-and-a-half years in 1998, Sonia ji took charge. She continued till October 2022, with a break of two years, during which time Rahul took over, before she handed over the baton to Mallikarjun Kharge. Nonetheless, the fact is that the Congress presidency remained with Sonia ji for nearly a quarter of a century at a stretch! This is a first in the history of the Congress.

The earlier system of regular elections had many merits. A change in guard at regular intervals led to greater regional representation at the helm of the party. If you glance at the list of Congress presidents since 1885, you will notice that every region of the country was represented over time.[14] This way, regional aspirations were fulfilled and the party gained strength in those regions.

The system also ensured that leaders from different religious affiliations reached the party's top position. From 1885 to 1947, Hindu, Muslim, Parsi and Christian leaders became party presidents. Moreover, among the Hindus, there was representation from the upper castes as well as other castes. This helped the party solidify its base among those constituents and regions.

Perhaps the most significant outcome of the regularly held elections was that it helped in the creation of new and many national-level leaders. When people led the Congress, they gained national stature and recognition and became assets for the party during elections at the national level. The party, too, was strengthened at the grassroots as a result of the emergence of leaders through the democratic process.

The lament today is that the Congress party has no leaders who have a pan-India appeal. The dearth is because the party has abandoned the system of elections to the top positions and earmarked the post for one or two individuals. This system precludes the emergence of new national leaders in the party. When leaders are selected instead of being elected, there is bound to be a crisis of leadership at all levels. The selected candidate is seen as an imposition. Besides, the candidate's merits are decided in drawing rooms instead of among the people who work on the ground.

Further, a candidate who is at the helm of affairs for years loses the zeal to work, taking everything for granted. At times, fatigue sets in. I am aware of one such DCC president who held the post for 22 years and appealed to me to get him relieved from the post! He said he was no longer interested, nor were his people interested in him. When elections don't happen and selected leaders continue for years,

---

[14]Singh, Kanishka, 'Indian National Congress: From 1885 till 2017, a Brief History of Past Presidents', *The Indian Express*, 4 December 2017, https://bit.ly/3twIRCH. Accessed on 13 June 2022.

the party begins to stagnate because fresh talent gets no opportunity to rise from the bottom to the top.

I have been neither supportive of nor impressed by the ideology of the BJP. But I have to say that it did the smart thing by copying the Congress party's old system. They change the national party presidents every two years, thus ensuring all the gains that I have listed earlier above. New leaders get a chance to emerge, new regions are represented and people from different castes and communities get an opportunity to demonstrate their leadership qualities.

Over the years, the BJP has expanded its social base across the country, and one of the reasons is the system that it follows in the change of party leadership after two years or at least frequently. While the Congress has been busy destroying its own potential leaders, the BJP has been creating new ones. The net result for the Congress, besides electoral reverses, is that good leaders have become disgruntled, have quit the party or are sitting at home.

One Man, One Post

The other reason why the Congress has slipped is that it failed to give attention to the party's affairs when it was in government at the Centre. Organizational leaders such as state party chiefs join the government, and the primacy of the party is lost. For example, as party president, Sonia ji was also the chairperson of the National Advisory Council (NAC), a Cabinet rank, during Dr Manmohan Singh's tenure as PM. There is no doubt that the NAC, under her leadership, did a very good job, initiating the right to food security, Right to Information (RTI), MGNREGA and many more programmes. However, there was a flipside too. As she was busy with the NAC, she could not devote time to the party. It would have been better if we had a full-time president or at least a working president who could have given attention to the organization during that period.

Even at the state level, the Congress has been repeating a similar mistake over the years, by having the same person as both CM and PCC chief, or as minister and PCC president, or a Lok Sabha or assembly member and PCC president or DCC president and MLA. I had consistently opposed this practice. I had pointed this out in many AICC sessions, particularly at the January 2013 session at Jaipur, and had even taken up the matter with the top leadership.

Such dual responsibilities have two disadvantages for any legislature. One, the party president finds little time for the organization. He/she is busy with either legislative work or with nurturing his/her constituency. The party work, therefore, gets paralysed. Two, those legislators who aspire to the party's top position in the state or district are blocked and become disgruntled. They either quit the party or become inactive. Other political parties that are mass-based and cadre-based have not made that mistake. They have ensured that the party remains active at all levels, whether the party is in government or in Opposition.

Yet another drawback of the Congress party has been its ineffective management of the media. The press has had a free run where Congress governments ruled. It was vocal in its criticism of Indira ji, Rajiv, Rao and Dr Singh. But somehow, even the good work that we did got downplayed, unlike today, when even the smallest achievement of the NDA government is presented as a monumental success. The path-breaking initiatives during UPA-I and UPA-II in the areas of education, food security, agriculture, rural development, health and telecommunication were overshadowed by other fringe negatives. If the Congress had a robust party organization down to the grassroots level, it could have taken the message of the government's good work to the masses, and the media criticism could have been blunted.

Self-Destruction in States

In addition to these weaknesses in general, the Congress has also made mistakes at local levels over the years, which led to its marginalization in some of the politically important states and loss of power in others. The first bricks from the fort that was the Congress were removed with the implementation of the Kamaraj Plan, thus initiating the weakening of the party. In 1963, veteran Congress leader and CM of the erstwhile state of Madras, K. Kamaraj, advised PM Nehru to seek the resignation of senior party leaders from the Union ministry and chief ministerial posts and direct them to devote time to the organization. It had a greater impact at the state levels, where many popular, mass-based CMs, including Biju Patnaik, S.K. Patil, Partap Singh Kairon and Bakshi Ghulam Mohammad, quit. Kamaraj also quit. But this exit of stalwarts cost the Congress party heavily in the states. Even in Tamil Nadu, the party lost the assembly elections in 1967 and facilitated the rise to power of the first regional party under C.K. Annadurai.

Six Union ministers, including Lal Bahadur Shastri, Jagjivan Ram and Morarji Desai, also tendered their resignations. I do not recall many of them being actually drafted for party work, though Kamaraj did become all-India president of the party. I fail to understand, to this day, what the real motive behind the Kamaraj Plan was. Of course, I was keen to know the real reason since my youth. Ultimately, one day, I mustered the courage and sought an appointment with one of India's former rashtrapati, who had been part of the Congress history. A historian in his own right, he had a photographic memory and could remember the dates and locations of each AICC session held in the past along with details of resolutions passed. It was only after a great deal of persuasion that he told me the real reason behind the Kamaraj Plan. I was shocked by his answer. However, it's a secret that I will take to the grave with me.

Unfortunately, for the party, after the Kamaraj Plan, the 'appointment' system of CMs came into being. Earlier, the party had stalwarts as CMs in various states—leaders who were tall enough on their own and did not have to depend on patronage from the party's high command. Once the CMs were made to resign as per the Kamaraj Plan, they were replaced by nominated leaders, who were more beholden to the high command than to the voters and the grassroots workers of the party in their respective states. The elections of leaders became a mere formality. The domino effect of that decision was to be felt across the country for the party for decades to come.

UP and Bihar

Over the years, the Congress has made major mistakes in handling affairs in important states like UP and Bihar. During Emergency, popular leader H.N. Bahuguna was eased out. Bahuguna was an upper-caste leader and had the support of his caste voters and, more importantly, he was acceptable to every section of the society as well, including the SCs, minorities and backward classes. N.D. Tiwari, whose acceptance levels among the masses were not that high, replaced him.

In a similar fashion, Vir Bahadur Singh was relieved of the CM's post after the party lost in the Lok Sabha by-election in Allahabad (now Prayagraj) in June 1988. Vir Bahadur was a humble, down-to-earth leader and popular among all sections of the voters by virtue of his accessibility, simplicity and hard work. Again, Tiwari, who took on the mantle reluctantly and proved to be disastrous for the party in the state, replaced him. It was not that Tiwari was less capable or experienced; he had no interest in the state and was more interested in national politics. Unfortunately, he was forced to take on that assignment in the state, much against his wishes.

Then, in the mid-1990s, the rebellion of V.P. Singh, who incidentally had no mass base, single-handedly sunk the Congress's boat. The rise of the SP and its leader Mulayam Singh Yadav as well as that of the BSP and its leader Kanshi Ram served to further dent the party's support base in UP. The Muslims, the OBCs and the SCs left the Congress and went to them, while the upper castes extended support to the BJP. The Congress never recovered after that exodus. Till the 1980s, Muslims, Dalits and Brahmins were its vote base and others would join, if not fully then partially. This was more than enough to win parliamentary and assembly elections. However, unfortunately, in the 1989 Lok Sabha Election, that combination was totally shattered.

The party did no better in Bihar, another state where it had a major presence. In the mid-1980s, the most popular and respected leader Jagannath Mishra was asked to quit his chief ministerial post. Thereafter, the party tried various leaders but failed to get back the past glory because none of the successive CMs put together could match Mishra, both in popularity and governance.

After having replaced fighter jets with handcarts in both states, it is not surprising that the leaders failed to revive the party thereafter. Once the stalwarts were marginalized, their supporters also lost interest in party work, further damaging the organization. Some of the leaders later quit the party and floated their own outfits. They may not have succeeded, but they ensured that the Congress was finished. Unfortunately, the Congress leadership has always marginalized and cut to size its own popular state leaders and supported weak leadership, and that system continues till date. Nothing summarizes our predicament better than this quote:

Khud kiye tum ne apni diwaron me surakh,
Ab koi jhaank raha hai tou shikayet kaisi?

(You have yourself made holes in your walls;
Now if someone is peeping through, why should you complain?)

The other reason why the Congress has lost UP and Bihar is because of its overdependence on regional heavyweights from other political parties. The party has had ties, formal or informal, with the regional parties at one time or the other. It has indeed become a necessity in today's fractious politics. However, having a tie-up with a regional party does not mean that you abandon the pursuit to expand and grow in that state. This has happened across the country, from J&K to Tamil Nadu. The Congress has had alliances in J&K, UP, Bihar, West Bengal, Assam, Maharashtra, Karnataka, Kerala, Gujarat, Andhra Pradesh, Tamil Nadu and Puducherry. It survived in Rajasthan, Madhya Pradesh and Chhattisgarh, since it never had an alliance there.

The party's decision to try various alliances over the years, without much success, has caused a great deal of harm. I cannot avoid taking responsibility, since I too was responsible for managing the alliances with some political parties in different parts of the country. But in retrospect, the very policy of the party to have alliance after alliance, regardless of who was at the helm of affairs, was wrong and proved fatal.

In fact, I have been blamed for one such decision, even though I had nothing to do with it. I was then Union minister of civil aviation and tourism, while another leader was the general secretary in charge of the state, and Jitendra Prasada was the PCC president. The Congress tied up with the BSP, led by Mayawati, for the UP Assembly Elections in 1993. Unfortunately, the Congress gave Mayawati 300 seats, while it contested the rest 125 seats (it was undivided UP then, with 425 seats). Our position then was not that bad, since we were in government at the Centre and had considerable support in UP. But surrendering 300-odd seats was a wrong decision, and the Congress was wiped off. The support structure in those constituencies was lost for good.

Tamil Nadu

Another glaring example of the pitfalls in subordinating the party to regional satraps is evident in Tamil Nadu. Over the decades, the Congress has continued to depend on either of the two regional outfits, the DMK and the AIADMK, to the extent that the party gave up efforts to build its cadre in the state. Local leaders never even entertained the ambition of the party doing well without the crutches of the regional parties, let alone forming the government on our own. This was never my intention when I worked to tie up with these parties at different times in the past.

Karnataka and Andhra Pradesh

The case in Karnataka has been different. Even though I adopted innovative ways to bring the state's leaders together, unfortunately, they were back to their old games soon after I left the state. The situation today is such that everybody wants to be the CM, which is not a bad thing, except for the fact that they expect it without earning it.

The other mess that the party made was in undivided Andhra Pradesh. It read too much into the noise that a handful of MPs from the Telangana region made in Parliament, especially in the Rajya Sabha, when they demanded a separate state. Leaders, including me, realized later that these MPs did not have the kind of popular support they claimed to have.

Congress leaders in Andhra, on the other hand, were ambiguous, barring CM Kiran Kumar Reddy, who made his opposition clear. When the party asked its MPs and MLAs from the Andhra region for their opinion, they said they would go by the high command's decision. However, once the bifurcation was announced, those very Andhra MPs and MLAs rose in opposition, claiming that they had not expected the Union government and the Congress party's high command to accept the division! That is why they did not oppose the division; moreover, they did not want to antagonize the people of Telangana. This was such a silly argument. The fact is that they had remained silent because they had business interests in Hyderabad and nearby places, and so did not want to antagonize the Telangana leaders by openly opposing the demand for a Telangana state.

Once the bifurcation was endorsed by the Union Cabinet, Congress leaders of Telangana should have seized the opportunity by going to the people to tell them that the party had given them a new state. There was a six-month gap between the CWC and the Cabinet decision, during which Congress leaders and ministers from Telangana stayed in Delhi instead of being among their constituents. They were furiously lobbying for the CM's post of the state to be formed. Though I was not in charge of the state, I called all the senior ministers and leaders of Telangana to my residence on two occasions and impressed upon them that instead of wasting their time, they should tour the entire state, both individually and collectively, and take credit for the creation of the new state. Unfortunately, they did not heed my advice, maybe because I was not the general secretary in charge and could not hurt them in anyway politically. K. Chandrasekhar Rao, on the other hand, took advantage of the absence of Congress leaders in the field and went from village to village pretending to be the champion of the state formation. From there on, the Congress has been going from bad to worse.

The conduct of the Congress party in a few other states over the past few years makes one wonder if it has indeed resolved to self-destruct. From a strong presence at the state level and even forming governments for long periods, the party, over time, has been reduced to a marginal player, virtually extinct.

West Bengal

In West Bengal, the Congress party had two stalwarts who had, for decades, kept the party's flag flying high in the 1970s and 1980s: A.B.A Ghani Khan Choudhury and Siddhartha Shankar Ray. The latter left the party in the 1978 split, and Choudhury was dropped as Union railway minister in mid-1980s by the then PM. Although Ray returned to the party fold later, he remained marginalized; Choudhury, too, was side-lined. Over time, the two veterans lost interest in party affairs. Other leaders were promoted in their place, but they were simply alien to both the party and the people of West Bengal.

Subsequently, a young, firebrand woman leader emerged in the state from our party—Mamata Banerjee. She had zeal, ambition and a tremendous fighting spirit. She had defeated the Left stalwart Somnath Chatterjee in the 1984 Lok Sabha General Election, but somehow, the party did not acknowledge her services in the manner it should have. She was not given the role she desired to revive the party. She quit and formed the All India Trinamool Congress (AITC or TMC) in 1998. Today, she and her party are the dominant players in West Bengal, ruling the state. The Congress has not just ceded ground but is reduced to a position that, for the first time in history, the party failed to win a single seat in the assembly elections in 2021. Not surprisingly, the BJP has occupied the space vacated by the Congress party. When the party treats veterans and hardworking, popular upcoming leaders like Mamata and many others with scant regard, it has to pay the price of becoming extinct.

There is also the burden of unfulfilled political promises, which creates a trust deficit that can ultimately lead to anti-incumbency. In the run-up to the 2004 Lok Sabha Elections, before the process of ticket distribution for West Bengal had begun, Pranab da met me and expressed a desire to contest the elections, saying that he had spent enough time in the Rajya Sabha. He had identified a constituency—Jangipur—that had a 70 per cent Muslim population. He said that he would seek a ticket from there if I promised to campaign for him for four–five days. I told him that being the general secretary in charge, my campaign schedule for undivided Andhra Pradesh had been already drawn up and I might not be able to give him time in case the dates for both Andhra Pradesh and West Bengal clashed. Luckily for him, it did not, and I campaigned in his constituency for four full days and addressed about 25 public meetings. Pranab da won, though with just around a margin of over 36,000 votes.

In the 2009 elections, he repeated the request. He was already a Union Cabinet minister. This time, I played another 'card' with the poor innocent voters. I told them that it would be a shame for me if a senior minister like Pranab da failed to win by a large margin despite my campaigning and my travel all the way from Kashmir to a Muslim-dominated constituency. I also told them that Pranab da had promised that in the next election from the constituency, a Muslim candidate from the Congress party would contest. That appeal clicked, and Pranab da won with a handsome margin of more than 128,000 votes.

Five years later, in the 2014 Lok Sabha election, I was under the impression that Pranab da would keep his word and back a Muslim candidate from the constituency. But unfortunately, that did not happen. During the campaigning, I was attending a WHO meeting in Geneva as the country's health minister. Pranab da, who was the president by then, called and told me that his son Abhijit would be contesting from that constituency. With only two days left for campaigning to end, he urged me to campaign for Abhijit. I was shocked. I told him that I would not be able to make it in time from Geneva. But he insisted, saying, 'Do it for me.'

It was difficult for me to face the people, yet, I agreed. I took the earliest flight from Geneva to London and the next flight to Delhi, and headed straight to Kolkata. From there, I took a night train to the constituency. I had already contacted some senior leaders there. I reached early in the day and held seven or eight meetings on the last day of campaigning. I apologized to the people for having failed to get a Muslim contestant. Abhijit won, but it wasn't long before the spectre of unfulfilled promises came to haunt him. Having taken the voters for granted by repeating a candidate from outside who had done precious little for the voters and the region, the Congress lost the 2019 Lok Sabha Elections to the TMC.

Odisha

In Odisha, J.B. Patnaik, a great politician and scholar, was among our tallest leaders through the 1970s and 1980s and even in the mid-1990s.

He was the PCC chief after the 1977 debacle. In the elections, which were held under his leadership in 1980, the Congress got a resounding success and he became the CM. In 1985, the assembly elections were held under his leadership, and the Congress again successfully formed the government with him as the CM.

However, unfortunately, in December 1989, when assembly elections were to be held within the next three months, he was replaced by Hemananda Biswal without any concrete reason. Biswal was a comparatively unknown leader in the state and a very weak CM. As a result, the Congress lost the election in March 1990 and the BJD, led by freedom fighter and the tallest Opposition leader Biju Patnaik, formed the government.

After realizing this huge mistake, the Congress again requested J.B. Patnaik to take active part in the party and, subsequently, he was made the PCC president. Thus, again the 1995 elections were contested under his able presidentship, and the Congress formed the government with J.B. Patnaik as CM. But, unfortunately, like in 1989, he was again replaced by Dr Giridhar Gamang in February 1999, after completing three years and 11 months in office.

Within the next 13 months before the elections, the Congress changed two CMs one after another: Gamang and Biswal. That was the end of the Congress era, since he was replaced by the fourth CM of BJD, Naveen Patnaik. It has been almost two-and-a-half decades since the BJD occupied the space ceded by the Congress, which has been virtually wiped out.

Some eight months after Gamang took charge, Odisha was devastated by a supercyclone in October 1999. The new CM simply abdicated his responsibility and disappeared from the scene. His ministers and other MLAs too followed suit, receding to their respective constituencies instead of supervising relief and rehabilitation work across the state. With the government virtually non-existent, the administration also came to a grinding halt. There was complete chaos in the state.

This period also happened to be a time of personal challenges for me. My father had been suffering from medical complications in his digestive system and had come to Delhi for treatment. The doctors gave me shocking news—that he had developed stage four cancer and had, at the most, three weeks to live. They suggested that we take him back to Jammu, where he could spend his last days in the midst of his family and loved ones. Arrangements were made, and I prepared to accompany him back to Jammu the next morning.

The evening before I was to leave for Jammu, party president Sonia ji telephoned me to inform me that the then AICC general secretary in charge of Odisha, Madhavrao Scindia, had a major confrontation with CM Giridhar Gamang, over the latter's inaction during the supercyclone. Scindia had returned to Delhi with his resignation, saying that he would not like to work with Gamang, who had refused to even move out of his room from upstairs to see off Scindia. Sonia ji further requested me that I should go to Odisha to oversee the havoc created by the supercyclone. She asked me to fly out the next morning itself, since there was no government worth its name to alleviate the sufferings of the people. I could have explained my personal predicament to her but did not because I thought she would think that I was making an excuse about my father's illness for declining to go. Besides, I thought, it was only a matter of two–three days. I agreed, and my father, accompanied by my cousin Dr Tariq Azad left for Jammu next morning without me.

When I reached the airport at Bhubaneswar, there was no trace of any senior Congressmen, barring a Youth Congress leader and MLA, Lalatendu Bidyadhar Mohapatra, popularly known as Lulu, to receive me. An influential, financially well-off Youth Congress leader, Lulu was a much-sought-after politician in the state. He was the undisputed leader of the youth and students from across the state. He had come with some 400–500 Youth Congress leaders and students to receive me. I was relieved by his presence; otherwise, I would have got nowhere.

Lulu said that we would have to make our way to the city from the airport on foot since the roads were paved with huge fallen trees. There were no police personnel, civic authorities or even district-level officers to clear the roads. We, therefore, trudged our way to the city, crossing the hurdle of fallen trees. It took us nearly two hours to complete the journey. I made my way to the guest house. There was neither power supply nor were the telephone lines functional. The entire guest house was manned by just one chowkidar.

The otherwise bustling city of Bhubaneswar looked like a ghost town. Shops were flooded with water and were closed; people were locked up in their homes. The immediate task was to clear the roads, beginning from the one that led from the airport to the city. Being the son of a forest contractor, I had seen how felled trees were cut and transported. I was aware of the implements that were used for the purpose, such as the one-way and the two-way saws, axes, etc. With Lulu and his brigade's help, hardware shops were made to open by bringing their owners from their respective houses. We purchased the required material of saws, axes and other equipment. Then I demonstrated to the boys ways to cut the wood logs. It took us nearly two days of virtually 24x7 work before we managed to clear the airport road.

We then concentrated on other roads, including the ones that led to the sea. I was traumatized to see thousands of human corpses floating by the seashore. Late estimates put the figure of dead to anywhere between 8,000 and 25,000.

Meanwhile, a few telephone lines were restored. I spoke to PM Vajpayee and requested him to conduct an aerial survey of the state and arrange for supply of relief materials. He promptly came and announced relief package. Relief materials were promptly despatched by the Centre, and we managed to distribute as much as we could. The only minister available during the distribution time was Jagannath Patnaik, minister of revenue, fisheries and animal resources development. He was of great help to me. Hemananda Biswal was another cooperative and helpful senior minister.

Though I had originally planned to be in Odisha for two–three days, the work was so enormous and the condition was so pathetic, particularly seeing thousands of dead bodies floating in the sea, that I had no option but to extend my stay. I had reached there with only two sets of kurta-pyjamas, which got dirty on the first day itself. Hence, I would wash my clothes every night and use them the following morning without ironing them.

Having witnessed the pain and agony faced by the people of the state, I had forgotten that the doctors had told me that my father would survive for just another 20–21 days. Unfortunately, I could not even call back home, owing to the enormity of the crisis and the complete devastation caused to the communication system, which was yet to be fully restored. It was on the nineteenth day of my stay in Odisha, when phone lines had been restored to a great extent, that my wife called me from Jammu. She berated me for my 'shamelessness' in ignoring my father, who was in the last days of his life. She told me that he was on the deathbed, and that I should return without delay. I directed Lulu and Jagannath Patnaik to continue with the relief and rehabilitation work in my absence.

I took a flight to Delhi and then to Jammu. I saw my father was in bed. I walked up, held his head in my palms and looked into his face. He was not in a position to talk or even move, and even though it seemed like he wanted to speak, he could not. Tears welled in my eyes and fell on his cheeks and mingled with his tears. He gazed at me. Soon, he was dead. It seemed that he had been alive just to have a final glimpse of me.

I had chosen duty over tending to my father in his last days. I don't know if I should regret it or be proud of it. However, I never informed Sonia ji about my personal issue; she remains unaware of the same till this day. This had been my habit right from the beginning, and remained till my last day in the Congress—if I had done something good for a person or for the party, I would never tell him or her that I did it. In my best days in politics, be it during the tenures of PMs Indira ji, Rajiv, Rao and Dr Singh or, for that matter, during Sonia ji's time, on my recommendations, hundreds of leaders were given tickets for Assembly and Parliament constituencies and dozens of people were made ministers at the state and national levels, but I never divulged to them that they were made so on my recommendation. Even few of my close former colleagues do not know till date that they got the position in Parliament or government on my recommendation.

Assam

The Congress party's determination to destroy itself was even more evident in Assam. We had our government led by Tarun Gogoi. He had become the CM in May 2001 and went on to serve in that post until May 2016.

For 14 years of his tenure, a young and dynamic politician, Dr Himanta Biswa Sarma, was his right-hand man and a minister who held several important portfolios, including health and education. He was among the best-performing health ministers in the country, and I interacted with him on several occasions when I was the Union minister for health and family welfare. I had also an opportunity to attend a number of health-related camps and functions organized by him in Assam.

He came across as smart and politically astute, with a huge following of his own. He also commanded the support of many MLAs. After Gogoi became CM for the first time in 2001, he promised Himanta that he would step down if the party got a second term and recommend him for chief ministership.

After the party won a second term in 2006, Gogoi went back on his word and assured Himanta, again, that he would most certainly suggest his name for chief ministership if the party returned to power. However, yet again, Gogoi refused to keep his promise when he was sworn-in for the third time in 2011. Himanta was justifiably upset.

Sometime during Gogoi's third term, Himanta decided to part ways with Gogoi. He had the support of a majority of legislators in the Assembly. He dashed off a letter to Governor J.B. Patnaik, claiming that he had backing of majority of MLAs and that he, along with his group, were withdrawing support to the Gogoi regime. He quit the Cabinet.

Parliament was not in session, and I had gone to Srinagar. Sonia ji asked me to visit Assam as an observer along with the general secretary in charge of the state to ascertain the situation. I told her that it was better to first verify the claims and counterclaims in Delhi because if I went to Assam straightaway and found Himanta's claim to be true, there would be no option but to ask Gogoi to step down right away. She agreed.

I called Himanta and his group to Delhi; he came with 45 plus MLAs to my residence, and I spoke to each one of them. A few days later, I asked Gogoi to come to Delhi or send his MLAs. He sent seven MLAs who were supporting him. I also deliberated with the rest of the 10 MLAs who had said they would abide by the party high command's decision on supporting either of the two leaders. In all these meetings, the general secretary concerned was present.

I reported the situation to Sonia ji, who remarked that it was obvious that Himanta had a clear majority and should be the new CM. She asked me to go to Assam the following day along with the general secretary in-charge and oversee the formal election of Himanta as the new leader. The evening before we were to proceed to Assam, Rahul, who had not been in the loop of deliberations so far, telephoned me with a request to cancel the visit to Assam. Instead, he asked me to visit his home the next morning along with the general secretary in charge of Assam.

When we arrived at Rahul's residence the next morning, we saw Tarun Gogoi and his son, Gaurav Gogoi, sitting with him. Rahul told us bluntly that there would be no change in leadership. We pointed out to him that Himanta had the majority of MLAs and would rebel and quit the party. 'Let him go,' Rahul said. The meeting was over. I am not sure if Rahul said this to assert himself or because he was ignorant that his decision would have far-reaching consequences, not only in the state of Assam but the entire Northeast. Himanta had been the party in-charge of the entire Northeast from time to time and particularly during elections in these states, where he was very popular. After leaving the Congress, he used this influence against the party and ensured the party's complete rout from the entire Northeast. So, the exit of one capable person sounded the death knell for the party in the entire region.

After our interaction with Rahul, I met Sonia ji and apprised her of the new twist in the tale. Despite understanding the disastrous consequences that lay ahead, it is rather unfortunate that she did not assert herself as the party president. Instead, she asked me to request Himanta to not rock the boat. She added that he would surely heed my appeal, since he had tremendous regard and respect for me. I spoke to Himanta, who was good enough to accept my request. However, he refused to take back his resignation. It goes to Himanta's credit that he allowed the Congress government to continue and did not pull the rug for another year.

However, the die was cast. Later on, Himanta quit the Congress and joined the BJP in August 2015. The BJP immediately appointed him as the convener of its election management committee for the upcoming state elections. He oversaw the BJP's victory in the elections in 2016 and became a Cabinet minister, holding more than a dozen portfolios and the number-two position in government. After the BJP won a second term in 2021, he was made the CM of the state. Meanwhile, the Congress party continues to pay for the mistakes committed by its leadership.

The Debacle Continues

The Congress has, unfortunately, learnt nothing from its past mistakes, which is why it continues to lose in state after state. The spate of defeats in Punjab, Uttarakhand, Goa, Manipur and UP in early 2022 is a testament to this. There is really no point in blaming X, Y or Z Opposition leader or party for these losses or for claiming that this leader spurned the party's offer to align or that leader whipped up caste and communal passions, which cost the Congress dearly. The party lost because of its own faults—due to its inaction, indecisions, wrong decisions and lack of hard work and initiative.

Punjab

Take the case of Punjab, the only poll-bound state that had a Congress government. I was taught, perhaps back in middle school, that one must not change horses mid-stream. If we change, then we shall be swept away by the waves. Yet, the party's central leadership did exactly what ought not to have been done. They changed the incumbent CM, Captain Amarinder Singh, just four months before the election, in fact, even as the campaigning was already on! Ideally, this leadership change should have been done at least two–three years earlier. It would have given the new CM time to settle down and perform, so that he could have appeared before the people with some concrete achievements.

This blunder was further compounded by the manner in which the change of leadership was undertaken. The Congress legislature party met to discuss leadership change without even informing the leader of the legislature party—Amarinder, who was also the CM! It was absolutely ridiculous and very insulting. The CLP meeting was Delhi sponsored; it should have been state sponsored. The result was that an insulted Amarinder walked out of the party. Moreover, even while he was the CM, a host of local Congress leaders launched a barrage of attacks on him, making the voters wonder whether the Congress was fighting the Opposition or its own leader. The leadership, instead of stopping this nonsense, was encouraging it.

If the central leadership wanted Amarinder to quit, it should have deputed a senior and experienced leader who commanded respect and had friendly relations with him, like Bhupinder Singh Hooda and few others who know him well, to persuade him. The matter could have been handled diplomatically and resolved without causing hurt to the incumbent CM and the party.

This was not the only mistake the leadership made in Punjab. Once Amarinder was out, the Congress leadership gave the responsibility to someone who was not up to the task. The leadership replaced the PCC president with a new face, who proceeded to attack his own CM, calling him and his family members corrupt. The new state president even warned the public in the midst of election campaigns against trusting the CM's promises because he would not return to power!

There is an old saying, 'God helps those who help themselves.' In Punjab, the Congress was determined to destroy itself; why would God have come forward to help the Congress?

The end result was only to be expected. The voters contemptuously rejected the Congress, and its warring leaders also lost their seats. Clearly, the Congress had handed over Punjab to the AAP on a platter. Perhaps many leaders of the Congress do not realize the impact this can have on their prospects in the neighbouring state of Haryana and the UT of J&K. Had the elections in another neighbouring state, such as Uttarakhand, been held after the AAP victory in Punjab, perhaps the Congress would have been replaced by AAP MLAs.

Uttarakhand

Similarly, the Congress's conduct in Uttarakhand is another classic example of how elections should not be fought and how to ensure your own party's defeat. There was no reason why the BJP should have returned to power there. There was public discontentment against the party, and a clear indication of that was the BJP's own realization of that fact. It changed two CMs in five years and the third one had hardly any time to consolidate his position. The mere change of the CM is itself an acknowledgment of the party's failure to provide good governance. Thus, the Congress should have been the natural replacement, and yet, the party lost comprehensively.

The party's acceptable chief ministerial face was Harish Rawat, an experienced hand. He had been a CM, Union minister, PCC president and earlier an active IYC leader. He had a mass following in Uttarakhand. He should have been asked to lead the state party at least a year before the elections. But the central leadership tied him down elsewhere, first in charge of Assam and later in Punjab. It was only when the time for filing nomination papers approached that he was asked to go to Uttarakhand and lead the poll campaign. Moreover, when Rawat reached Uttarakhand, he realized that he himself had no constituency to contest from. He convinced a sitting MLA to vacate his constituency in his favour—such was the level of the Congress party's mismanagement and lack of preparedness for elections.

Rawat had barely a few days to campaign and make a difference. He had to concentrate on his own new constituency and could not campaign elsewhere in the state. The result was that Rawat lost, and so did the Congress party. A state that should have been won easily slipped out of the party's hands because of mismanagement.

Manipur and Goa

As for Manipur and Goa, I believe that the Congress had prepared the ground for its loss five years earlier. In the 2017 Assembly Elections to both the states, the Congress had emerged as the single-largest party. It should have used it to its advantage and promptly pressed the claim to government formation. The governors of both these states were duty-bound first to invite the single-largest party to form the government. Also, the party ought to have, without delay, reached out to smaller parties and formed an alliance with them to get the numbers in the House. But the leaders who had been deputed to those states to oversee the government formation failed to respond to the situation timely. I do not know if the failure was on the part of the state leadership or observers or central leadership—whatever might have been the reason, the Congress missed the chance of government formation.

The net result, in any case, was that the BJP, which had fewer MLAs than the Congress party, struck alliances, approached the governor before the Congress and formed the government in both these states. The BJP, after that, used the position it had acquired to strengthen itself at the organizational and government level, and that ruined the Congress party's chances of a comeback in 2022.

Karnataka

I would like to contrast the party's failure in Goa and Manipur in 2017 to the case of Karnataka. A day before the 2018 assembly results were declared, the general belief was that the results would throw up a hung House. Ashok Gehlot and I were appointed as observers by the Congress president to oversee government formation. Of course, for Gehlot, Karnataka as a state and its leaders were totally alien. On the other hand, I had been general secretary in charge of Karnataka thrice earlier, had won all the elections successfully and knew its leaders, MLAs and the entire state like the back of my hand. I was even friendly with the leaders of like-minded parties, particularly Deve Gowda, chief of the Janata Dal (Secular) (JD[S]).

I reached Bengaluru along with Gehlot and headed straight to the residence of CM Siddaramaiah. I told Siddaramaiah that he should ask his people to put a television in his sitting room. I wanted eight–nine senior party leaders to watch TV together at his residence the next morning, in case we had to take any decision while the results were on, as I wanted all the senior leaders physically present at one place for instant consultation.

The next day, while the counting was on, I, along with all other senior leaders, realized midway that the BJP was emerging as the single-largest party, leaving the Congress behind. I immediately consulted the colleagues present in the room, which included the CM, PCC president and other senior leaders, and told them that since the Congress was losing, we should go for an alliance with the JD(S). My colleagues suggested that we should wait till final results were announced, but I insisted that it would be too late by then as the BJP could approach the governor to stake claim. Finally, they agreed to my proposal.

I telephoned Deve Gowda and told him that the Congress and his party should go for an alliance. Reluctantly, he told me that the BJP had already offered his party the deputy chief ministership if his party agreed to an alliance with them and this proposal was under consideration. Without losing time, I offered his party the chief ministership, to which he agreed. Notwithstanding this decision, I immediately addressed the media, saying that though the BJP may be leading, the Congress and the JD(S) together had more MLAs as far as the ongoing counting of votes was concerned, and both parties had decided to form the government together.

Before the final results were announced, I, along with the CM, Gehlot and other leaders of the Congress and the JD(S), met the governor with a letter that stated that since the coalition had more numbers than the BJP, they should be called to form the government.

Unfortunately, Governor Vajubhai Vala went against the normal practice of calling the majority coalition to form the government. Instead, he invited the BJP leader to form the government. But because of that timely decision of approaching the governor before the BJP did, we won the game in the Supreme Court and the coalition won the trust vote. The credit goes to Kapil Sibal and his team, who succeeded in procuring the order that the CM should have a floor test within 24 hours to prove the majority, instead of the three weeks the governor had allowed. The moral of the story is: Time is of great essence and timely decisions always pay off. But unfortunately, the

Congress government lasted barely a year due to mishandling of the state by the state leaders and the central leadership. The BJP formed the government. Who should one blame?

Uttar Pradesh

In the 2022 elections to India's most populous state, UP, let me make it clear that the Congress never had a chance, let alone of winning but also getting a decent number of seats.

This was rather unfortunate, considering that the party won 21 Lok Sabha seats from UP in the 2009 Lok Sabha Elections. If only the Congress had built on that and each one of its MPs had worked hard to get even five assembly seats from their respective constituencies (which means 105 MLAs), the Congress would have been a coalition partner in the government. That would have provided the party an opportunity to consolidate its position, and it could have, over time, won 100 plus assembly seats in the state. Sadly, Congress leaders tend to ignore the organization when it comes to power, while other national and regional parties, when in power, use that opportunity to strengthen their organization.

Having studied the elections in the state since my IYC days, I realized that even though the party had setbacks earlier, it bounced back on the strength of charismatic leaders such as Indira ji and Rajiv. They were the party's 'bank guarantees' in tough times, and we could always depend on them in times of need. But today, the party doesn't have a leader of comparable charisma. No doubt, Priyanka Gandhi Vadra worked hard during the campaign. But her appearances were more optical in nature. To reap a good crop, one needs fertile land. When the land is barren, nothing works. In this barren electoral land, Mayawati, for whatever reasons, appeared disinterested in the contest. In public opinions, most of her vote bank had shifted to other parties. The SP took away the entire Muslim and the Yadav votes, and the Congress was left with nothing.

Consistently Inconsistent

Of late, a trend has emerged in the Congress party—youngsters with good looks and oratorical skills are favoured over veterans. Promoting youth is welcome and necessary. After all, most veterans have come through that route, but the difference is that they worked hard for the organization. Despite holding top positions, they had no opportunity to stay or dine in five-star hotels or travel by air.

Sadly, a dashing persona and skills in English language cannot be the only criteria for selection. Voters are intelligent enough to understand who stands by them. They are not impressed by dashing looks, smart attire, English-medium education or the colour of the leader's skin.

The Congress has had leaders who suddenly don a dress or something else as a symbolic gesture to impress a certain section of the voters. If they think that influences the public, they are sadly mistaken. Leaders of my erstwhile party and other parties reach out by sharing food with poor families while sitting on a mat, especially in the run-up to elections. Symbolic gestures are mere optics and mean nothing. Such inconsistent consistency does not work. Mahatma Gandhi wore certain attire and stuck to it, even when he attended the Round Table Conferences in England, which was also attended by members dressed in smart western clothes. That is sincerity; that is consistency.

However, even this fad is not consistently followed. In some states, younger leaders are pushed forward despite opposition from seniors, but in others, the veterans are chosen over deserving youngsters. The failure to balance the expectations of the younger leaders with the experience of the seniors has resulted in discontent among the younger generation, elders as well as the veterans.

The bottom line is: A good leader is one who is able to seize the imagination of the people. He/she should be able to convince them that he is one of them, understands their needs and aspirations and is willing to address them. He/she should feel the pulse of the people.

As a former Congressman, I note with deep disappointment and sadness, the continuing downfall of the Grand Old Party at both the national and state levels. There are leadership tussles in Rajasthan,

Chhattisgarh and Karnataka. A sense of drift and directionless has set in. The party has also surrendered to the BJP the states that they had won—Karnataka and Madhya Pradesh, for example—because they failed to meet the aspirations of influential leaders and did not fulfil the promises made to them.

The root cause for the Congress's downfall is that it destroys its own potential leaders at the national and state levels by projecting parallel, incapable leadership against them, thus, destroying the party from the top to bottom in this process. Over a period of time, sycophancy has taken centre stage in the party. Sadly, no one wants to listen to the bitter truth.

18

GOODBYE, AND A NEW HELLO

The end of my tenure in the Rajya Sabha in February 2021 gave me the opportunity to look back at my four-and-a-half-decade-long political life, during which I had served the Congress party and its governments in various capacities. It was indeed a rewarding experience, both personally and professionally. I derived satisfaction from the fact that I did my best to strengthen the party, delivering results in various states that I held charge of as general secretary through the decades. Besides, I worked with sincerity and dedication for the larger interest and welfare of the people of my wonderful country, both as a Union minister and the CM of my home state.

During my momentous political journey, I had the occasion to meet and interact with a large number of global leaders, either on a one-on-one basis or as part of delegations, both in India and during my visits to foreign shores. I have headed more than a hundred delegations as the minister of various portfolios—parliamentary affairs, law and justice, company affairs, food and civil supplies, home, civil aviation and tourism, health and family welfare—and also as LoP of the Rajya Sabha. I also had the opportunity to accompany visiting presidents and PMs on trips within and outside the country. It was a great learning experience for me, as I gained fresh insights on several matters of national and international importance from the leaders I interacted with and also got to know them at close quarters.

In the latter half of the 1980s, when Russian forces had invaded Afghanistan, I led a Congress delegation to Kabul as general secretary at the behest of PM Rajiv Gandhi. During this visit, I met then president of Afghanistan, Mohammad Najibullah. The idea of the trip was twofold—first, to underline the strong ties that India and Afghanistan shared and second, to deliver a personal message of friendship from our PM to the Afghan president.

Najibullah was handsome, well-built, warm, affectionate and pro-India. He spoke English, Hindustani and Urdu fluently. I discussed several issues with him. He was, of course, battling with the internal problems his country faced as a result of challenges from several Afghan rebel groups. He often mentioned Gulbuddin Hekmatyar, a prominent Mujahideen leader who had taken up arms against the president and the Russians, as a major source of trouble. My second meeting with Najibullah in Kabul was just before the funeral of Khan Abdul Ghaffar Khan in 1988.

I spent a great deal of time interacting with His Majesty King Hussein bin Talal, the king of Jordan, during his ten-day official-cum-holiday trip to India in 1986. He was accompanied by his wife, Queen Noor, the PM of Jordan and the country's army chief. The royal couple had a young daughter with them, then a little over a year old. Surprisingly, the queen carried her daughter on her back throughout, like most Indian women in villages do. During our entire tour, the queen did not even once allow her help to carry her daughter. I believe therein lies a great lesson for most of our families.

I was the minister-in-waiting with the king, and my wife was to officially accompany Queen Noor during their stay in India. In Delhi, I attended all official functions held in honour of the visiting dignitaries. Once the king had completed the official leg of his visit in the first two–three days, he embarked on his holiday. My wife and I were supposed to accompany them till they were in India.

Our first visit was to Jaipur, where we stayed at the Rambagh Palace hotel. We visited several historical places. We would eat together, chat and take pictures. Our next place of visit was Goa, where we were received at the airport by the lieutenant governor. Arrangements for everyone were made at the Taj hotel on the seaside. We had a good time for two–three days, but, unfortunately, one morning, King Hussein received a threatening phone call through the hotel telephone line. His PM, army chief and I discussed the matter amongst ourselves first and then went together to inform King Hussein. After some discussion, we decided to not inform the police or the media, so as to avoid unnecessary adverse publicity. Finally, it was decided that the king would cut short his holiday by two days and fly back to Jordan.

By this time, however, the king and I had become quite informal, so we would discuss personal matters too. Before going back, he asked me many questions about Rajiv—his capabilities and popularity as the PM, and his secular views. I praised Rajiv, which was well-deserved. King Hussein then mentioned that Rajiv did not have a safe car, and that was not good for his security as the head of the government. He further told me that on his return to Jordan, he would be sending two bulletproof Mercedes cars for Rajiv. With these words, he wished Rajiv well and thanked me and Shameem for accompanying them all through their trip in India. Before saying goodbye, he invited us to visit Jordan.

On my return to Delhi, I informed Rajiv about my conversation with King Hussein and told him that he would be donating cars to the PM. A few months later, Rajiv informed me in Parliament that the cars had arrived outside Parliament. He was keen to do a test drive. He sat on the driver's seat and made me sit next to him. We drove around Lutyens' Delhi several times. It was the first time that I sat in a bulletproof Mercedes car replete with automatic doors, heavy auto glasses and excellent pickup.

A few years later, as the minister of civil aviation and tourism, I led an official delegation to Jordan. I informed the king's office of my visit through the embassy. On reaching the capital, Amman, I was informed by our embassy officers that there was a message from the palace—King Hussein was out of the country on a visit to the US. However, he had instructed the government that my delegation and I should be looked after well. The king had also directed that one Mi-8-type army helicopter be kept at our disposal to visit various historical places in Jordan. We were all well looked after and well fed throughout our trip. It is not surprising that this was one of the best overseas trips I have ever had.

A few months after the infamous Tiananmen Square massacre in April 1989, the all-powerful general secretary of the Chinese Communist Party (CCP), Jiang Zemin, who later became the president of China, extended an invitation to PM Rajiv to visit China. At that point in time, China was a pariah for the world community. Beijing was eager to demonstrate to the world that it was not really isolated, at least in Asia, and that it still enjoyed warm relations with India, a leading player in the region.

But given the global mood, the PM had sensibly avoided going. Besides, he was due for a visit to Russia and was busy with preparations for that. He had, however, visited China in December 1988, heralding a new chapter in the otherwise frosty ties between New Delhi and Beijing. Eager to keep up that momentum, the PM decided to send a small Congress delegation to China with me, then the general secretary of the party and also in charge of foreign affairs cell of the Congress, as the leader.

Our MEA had made the necessary arrangements and prepared a detailed brief for me so that I adhered to the official government line. (In China and Russia during those days, the organization was given a higher protocol than what ministers got.) On arrival, Shameem and I were given a warm welcome, generally accorded to visiting heads of government. Elaborate security was in place. Huge convoys of 15 cars or so waited on the tarmac to receive us. When we were taken on a tour to the Great Wall of China, all roads leading to the site were blocked, while security personnel were lined up on both sides of the road en route.

Since China was eager to demonstrate to the world that India was on their side, they made our meeting more high profile by ensuring the wide presence of the international media to cover visit. During my one-on-one meeting with Jiang Zemin, we discussed routine matters such as the Panchsheel Agreement and improvement in bilateral ties after Rajiv's visit a year earlier. However, that meeting was just for optics; Beijing's real purpose was to use my visit (as a representative of the PM of India) as an instrument to shore up its own credibility in the eyes of the world.

It was again during Rajiv's premiership that I met the president of North Korea, Kim Il-sung. I visited North Korea on the invitation of the government in the capacity of the general secretary of the Congress party. Kim Il-sung was a perfect gentleman and host.

The one meeting that I cherish to this day is with the iconic South African anti-apartheid leader Nelson Mandela in 1994. The apartheid regime had come to an end in South Africa, and Mandela had become the president. India had commenced its flights to South Africa on my initiative as the minister of civil aviation and tourism. To mark the occasion, I visited South Africa. Mandela received me in his study at his residence. We discussed a host of issues over a private dinner hosted by him in my honour. He was especially delighted to hear about my efforts to promote Gandhi's message of truth and non-violence from my student days. He was a great admirer of the Father of the Nation, and much of our discussion centred on that great figure.

But perhaps my most surprising and 'memorable' meeting was with the legendary but mercurial Libyan ruler Muammar Gaddafi. It was sometime in October 2005; I was the urban development and parliamentary affairs minister under PM Manmohan Singh. Out of the blue, the Libyan ambassador to India met me—the first for an ambassador from that country—and handed over an invitation on behalf of Gaddafi to visit Libya. I was stunned and sought the advice of the PM and the MEA. After I got the green signal from MEA and PM, I confirmed my visit.

Arrangements for my visit and stay were made through our embassy in the Libyan capital, Tripoli. Our embassy staff received me at the airport. My meeting with the Libyan leader the next day was straight out of a spy novel. Nobody had any clue as to where I was to meet him. His staff arrived and we drove off in vehicles to a destination unknown to any of the embassy people. We travelled through isolated roads and bustling colonies. I was told later that Gaddafi was super secretive about his whereabouts due to security reasons. I finally arrived at a vast plain area, where a massive tent had been erected. It was a tent only in name; it was more like a palace. I noticed that it was well decorated, and there must have been 10–12 well-equipped rooms and sitting rooms in the tent.

Finally, I was face to face with Gaddafi, who was tall and well-built with broad shoulders. He greeted me warmly in English. I wondered why he had chosen to invite me. After exchanging pleasantries for a few minutes, I posed the question to him. He smiled and said that he had been following my political career for years, along with that of many Kashmiri leaders, and was impressed with my consistency in statements and commitment towards the Congress party. The fact that I was a Muslim and, more importantly, hailed from J&K had added to his interest.

In addition, he had a complaint too. He said that despite him having a great amount of admiration for India, Indira Gandhi and Rajiv Gandhi in particular, and backing India's position on Kashmir at international fora, New Delhi had kept itself aloof from him. No Indian leader of prominence had visited his country in recent years, though at least 40–50 heads of states and governments of other countries had come to Libya to interact with him. He raved and ranted about the countries inimical to him and said the West was biased against him. He added that he was not against any country but was simply interested in the growth and development of his country. Yet, some countries, particularly the world's lone super power, were against him and his administration.

He treated me to a number of delicacies that night and said that high dinner was being hosted for me on his behalf in the city. He expressed his inability to attend for security reasons. Instead, he would depute a close relative who looked almost exactly like him! When I reached the dinner arranged in one of the hotels in the city, for a moment I said to myself, 'Oh my God! Gaddafi is here.' But when he opened his mouth, the man was a different person. I was told that he was Gaddafi's cousin and looked just like him. However, he was a little shorter than Gaddafi.

I also had a great equation with Yasser Arafat, the charismatic leader of the Palestine Liberation Organization (PLO). He was very close to both Indira ji and Rajiv. Both our leaders would ensure that I was present whenever Arafat was invited for dinner/lunch during his visit to India. Over a period of time, we got to know each other very well. We would often discuss Kashmir's politics. He was a wonderful person and very hospitable. During lunch/dinner, I would be seated next to him, and he would take lot of meat from his plate and put it on my plate.

There have been many other leaders from the political and corporate world that I met, not necessarily one-on-one. I met Bangladesh PM Sheikh Hasina on a number of occasions in Dhaka at her residence. I met Bill Gates in 2012 in my office, when I was the Union minister for health and family welfare. Gates, then one of world's richest men, has been deeply involved in philanthropic work in the areas of health, education and environment. I also had the opportunity to meet the then United Nations Secretary General Ban Ki-moon and the then director general of WHO, Dr Margaret Chan, in my health ministry office.

Finding the Gandhi in Me

My decades-long political career has been eventful and packed with many activities and achievements. However, my most enriching moments have been those where I have been involved in promoting Gandhi's teachings, especially those of truth and non-violence. I maintained my association with Gandhian work despite being neck-deep in political work. I never allowed the Gandhi in me to die.

As the president of the Gandhi Global Family (GGF), a UN-recognized peace NGO, I have been actively involved in promoting Gandhi's teachings and philosophy across the country. The genesis of this NGO lies in the trust run by Nirmala didi of Acharya Vinoba Bhave's ashram. After her death, the trust came to be managed by her associates. So, some of us like-minded people, including S.P. Verma, Ashok Kapoor, Ram Mohan Rai and Veena Behan, decided to float the GGF. Today, the organization comprises academics, retired army personnel, social activists and others, and is non-profit and non-political in nature. We do not ask for donations from anyone. We only ask people to help in organizing events by taking care of the various expenses that they can afford.

My colleagues and the GGF national office bearers have been doing commendable work. During the successive waves of COVID-19, we did a lot of work through webinars and established contacts with district- and state-level students participating from across the country. These three–four-hour-long webinars covered various subjects apart from Gandhi, like 'Know My State', 'Know my Economy', etc. Students from Classes 8 to 12 enthusiastically participated in these events. It was heartening to see how well the students had prepared. We issued certificates and trophies to the winners of the contests.

Besides these webinars, we have also conducted several functions over the years, with great success. About a decade ago, I organized an event to commemorate Gandhi Jayanti in Jammu's Parade Ground, which saw the participation of about 50,000 people. Similarly, Congress MP Rajgopal from Andhra Pradesh organized a function of the GGF in Vijayawada, in which about 40,000 people participated. It was strictly a non-party event. A similar function was held in Odisha, which saw a large participation of university students, followed by yet another function in Assam. As president of the organization, I can take pride in the fact that we at the GGF have worked tirelessly to propagate the Mahatma's teachings across India.

The Beginning after the End

The completion of my Rajya Sabha term meant that I was able to devote more time to my Gandhian pursuits. But this also meant that for the first time in my political career, I had no political work. Right from my IYC days till I was LoP, I used to have multiple responsibilities. When I was state president of the IYC, I was also in the parent organization. And while I was general secretary of the IYC at the national level, I had triple responsibilities: I was also president of the all-India Muslim youth conference, which was affiliated with the Congress, and district president of Congress of Doda district, the largest district of the state that time. Subsequently, I was a minister and also general secretary of the party in-charge of several states. Thereafter, I held the positions of LoP and general secretary of the party.

However, all this was set to change. The letter that the G23 leaders wrote to Congress President Sonia ji in August 2020 marked the beginning of the end. Unfortunately, instead of taking this letter as a wake-up call and strengthening the organization and holding party elections on the lines we had suggested, both Rahul and Sonia ji took offence and viewed it as a challenge to their authority. Instead of heeding our advice, they dubbed us as being pro-BJP. I still wonder—if we were pro-BJP, why would we suggest strengthening the organization? Rather, we would simply let things continue as they are and make the dream of a Congress-mukt Bharat (Congress-free India)—which the current leadership seems to have embarked upon—come true.

The immediate effect of this letter was that I was dropped from the general secretary position in the party. I was also dropped from the national star campaign after 40 years—I had been in the national campaign committee since 1980 and had the privilege of campaigning for the party across the country for panchayat, state and national elections and even for the president of the country. This was despite the fact that I have always liked party work more than government or parliamentary duties. But writing a letter to strengthen the same organization cost me heavily.

The last thing that I had was the Rajya Sabha seat, whose term ended in February 2021. I could have asked Sonia ji or Rahul for a renomination, but I didn't since my state assembly had been dissolved. I wasn't expecting it either. They had taken away the post of general secretary and my position in the star campaign committee after four decades, so how could I expect that I would be renominated from another state like several of my other G23 colleagues? So, from February that year till August 2022, I had no party or legislative work to do. I was sitting at home, meeting people coming from different parts of the country. But I could not do anything for them since none of my recommendations were entertained at any level within the party.

I realized that the situation in the Congress party had reached a point of no return. It was then I decided, albeit with an extremely leaden heart, to call time on my half-a-century old association with the party. On 26 August, in a letter addressed to then Congress President Sonia ji, I resigned from all positions including the primary membership of the party. From the complete demolition of the party's consultative mechanism by Rahul to the rise of a new coterie of inexperienced sycophants to run the affairs of the party; from the remote-control model that destroyed the institutional integrity of this great organization to the manner in which proxies were being propped up to take over the leadership of the party, it was a no-holds-barred account of how the Grand Old Party had lost both the will and the ability to fight for what is right for India.

Once the political storm triggered by my resignation subsided, I was left with two options: either to sit at home, rot and degenerate or do something worthwhile. Being a postgraduate science student, I knew of and remembered Lamarck's theory of use and disuse of an organ. According to this theory, the organs that are used more develop more, while those that are used less degenerate over a period of time or remain weak. I realized that if I didn't use my brain and vocal cords, they would degenerate. In the US, Americans don't retire as long as they are mentally capable and physically fit. I believed that I was both.

When I realized that my ambition of seeing the Congress party back in power was not in line with the present-day leadership of the Congress, I felt I should build my own nest, which I could nurture myself. This is how I came to the conclusion that, instead of letting the Congress and right-minded people die their own death in the most border-sensitive state of J&K, I must rejuvenate and encourage old and young, men and women to strengthen the time-tested secular foundations of the state. This was a fact that even Gandhi had acknowledged in 1947.

This was a unique opportunity for me to fulfil Gandhi's dream. And thus, Democratic Progressive Azad Party (DPAP), the newest political party in J&K, was born on 26 September. It stands for democracy, peace, and independence, as enumerated by its three colours: mustard, which indicates creativity and unity in diversity; white, which stands for peace, and blue, which stands for freedom to speak, open space, imagination and limits from the depths of the ocean to heights of the sky.

The initial response of the people was overwhelming and beyond my expectations. I was particularly happy that the response was the same from all religious communities and regions of the state. And this is what we need in J&K. All through my life, through school and college days I have been preaching brotherhood, love and affection for each other irrespective of religion and caste. As the CM and as a Union Cabinet minister, I have been preaching that our hearts and minds are free from religious fear and caste dogma. We are all creations of one God and, as human beings, different from other creations of God. We have different religions and caste, but our blood is the same.

However, I do realize that the road ahead for DPAP is full of challenges, the most important being the restoration of full statehood, right to land, and employment to native domiciles in the aftermath of the abrogation of Article 370 and 35A and the subsequent bifurcation of the state. I don't think the abrogation was required at all. When the issue of this Article was taken up by the BJP's earlier avatar, Jana Sangh, over 70 years ago, the Article was completely different from what it was in 2019. At the time, J&K had its own wazir-e-azam (PM) and an elected sadr-e-riyasat or president who was elected by the Legislative Assembly for a term of five years and recognized by the president of India. He enjoyed enormous powers, some of which even rivalled those vested with the Union government.

Over the decades, however, these provisions were modified through the legislations passed by the J&K assembly. There was hardly anything left in that original Article 370 except for the provision that any bill passed by Parliament would not automatically apply to the state unless adopted by the state assembly. But that too, over a period of time, had changed drastically, and almost 98 per cent bills passed by Parliament were adopted by the J&K assembly. The remaining not adopted had not caused any clash with the central government or the Constitution.

Article 370 was more of a sentimental issue for a majority of the people. After all, in politics and in real life, particularly in India, sentiments are of great importance. So, even if 370 had been watered down over a period of time, the local people had formed a sentimental attachment to it over the decades. In substance, neither the country and the BJP nor the J&K state has gained anything by abrogating Article 370.

Similarly, there was no need to change Article 35A, which stated that outsiders could not buy land and get local employment. This too was the practice from the Maharaja's time since 1925, implemented with the larger interest of the state in mind. The Maharaja, being a visionary, had rightly put these laws in place, realizing that J&K, whose landscape is dotted with hills and dense forests, has hardly any land for its growing population. There is very limited space for roads, buildings, infrastructure and virtually nothing for agriculture or horticulture. Should outsiders come and buy land, the local population will have no land for agriculture, horticulture or even for creating infrastructure. People do not realize that it is because of the scarcity of land that land prices in both Jammu and Srinagar are as high as in any metro city.

Most importantly, downgrading the state to a UT was totally uncalled for; in fact, it was never on the agenda of the BJP at any point in time. Jammu and Kashmir was one of the oldest states of the country. It was a state during the Mughal era, British era and the Maharaja's time. As a matter of fact, it is the Dogra rulers who expanded the boundaries of J&K state much beyond what the state was in previous decades.

The next immediate challenge is to ensure peace and progress in the region. Right from the beginning, J&K has been attacked and ruled by outsiders and insiders for centuries together. We have been looted by the Afghans; even our womenfolk were not spared. Subsequently, the writ of militants reigned for several decades. This is a state in which people of all hues need a healing touch and have to be brought together on one platform, from both Jammu and Kashmir regions, irrespective of religion and caste. There is an urgent need to ensure that peace and tranquillity prevails in the state, that people progress and that the state is made a safe and attractive destination for pilgrimage and leisure.

Our state is very poor and has very few resources to mobilize. In other states, funds are generated primarily from excise duty. In Kashmir and some areas of Jammu, there is hardly any sale of alcohol. There is no major industry, except for some minor mines that hardly earn any revenue for the government. We have to depend mostly on central funding like in the past. So, support from the Union government goes a long way in creating the required infrastructure, such as roads, buildings, hospitals, etc.

However, one area which has not been tapped to even 10 per cent of its potential is tourism, both pilgrimage and leisure. Leisure tourism in both regions, in particular, has huge potential that needs to be exploited. This will help in the overall growth and development of the regions. It will also help address the issue of massive unemployment among the educated youth—arguably one of the biggest challenges for any government in J&K. I am pained to see the plight of lakhs of educated boys and girls, who are jobless despite being highly qualified. I strongly feel that through initiatives in the tourism sector, I will be able to find some solution to this problem and create jobs in millions for both skilled and unskilled workers as well as for the educated class.

It is my fervent hope that my home state can match the rapid strides that our country has taken in various areas. However, I can only pray that the virus of communalism and casteism that has continued to spread with great speed throughout the nation does not singe J&K.

In the end, I would like to quote an Urdu couplet by noted poet and lyricist Shakeel Badayuni that sums up my thoughts for my beloved state:

Mera azm itna buland hai ke paraye sholo ka dar nahi
Mujhe khauf aatish-e-gul se hai kahin ye chaman ko jala na de

(My conviction is so great that I am not fearful of others' sparks,
My fear is of the fire in the flower that might set the garden aflame.)

Index